DIPLOMAT
UNDER
STRESS

DIPLOMAT
UNDER
STRESS

Visconti-Venosta and the Crisis of July, 1870

S. WILLIAM HALPERIN

THE UNIVERSITY OF CHICAGO PRESS

Library of Congress Catalog Card Number: 63-13065

The University of Chicago Press, Chicago & London
The University of Toronto Press, Toronto 5, Canada

© 1963 by The University of Chicago. All rights reserved
Published 1963. Composed and printed by The University
of Chicago Press, Chicago, Illinois, U.S.A.

To my son John

PREFACE

Great crises are a source of perennial interest to the historian. The prelude to the outbreak of the Franco-Prussian War is no exception. The first half of July, 1870, has often been recounted, and it seems quite safe to predict that it will continue to attract a good deal of attention. The many treatments that have appeared vary inevitably in scope and emphasis. One facet that has been rather slighted is the Italian, and the present study is intended to rectify this. The foreign office archives in Rome, Paris, London, and Vienna have provided the bulk of the material. The corresponding repository in Brussels has furnished some useful items; the one in Madrid has been searched but to no avail, so far as Italian diplomacy is concerned. Meager are the relevant bits in the files of the Prussian foreign ministry, and they are available in Robert H. Lord's classic volume. On the other hand, the press, the records of parliamentary proceedings, and sundry additional sources have contributed not a little.

In the foreground stands Emilio Visconti-Venosta. His career, a very long one even by Continental standards, began in his native Lombardy when he was nineteen. Scion of a noble family and an ardent patriot, he participated in the bloody "Five Days" of Milan in 1848. Banished by the Austrians, he returned to the city clandestinely and supported the Mazzinian program. Soon, however, he gravitated toward the liberal monarchists captained by Cavour. Early in 1859 he took up residence in Piedmont and became a trusted agent of the Sardinian government. During the war against Austria he served as Cavour's representative at the headquarters of Garibaldi in Varese. Afterward, in 1860, he assisted Luigi Carlo

Farini in Emilia. He accompanied Gioacchino Pepoli to Paris for the negotiations with Napoleon III that resulted in the annexation of central Italy. This marked the successful completion of his first major assignment in the field of diplomacy.

Almost simultaneously, his parliamentary career began. He was elected deputy for the Lombard constituency of Tirano. By now a confirmed moderate in politics, he naturally aligned himself with the Destra, the party of the Right. He had scarcely accustomed himself to his role in the chamber of deputies when he took his next step upward: at Farini's invitation, he accepted the general secretaryship of the ministry of foreign affairs. Then, in 1863, another of his patrons who had just become premier, Marco Minghetti, offered him the foreign ministry. Visconti-Venosta was only thirty-four—an astoundingly early age for the holder of the second most important post in the cabinet.

Like Cavour, he made amity with France and Great Britain the keystone of his policy. He prized freedom of action but warned his country against going it alone. "Always independent, never isolated"—in these words he once summed up his conception of Italy's role among the nations. Dedicating himself to the completion of Cavour's unfinished business, the Roman question, he was instrumental in negotiating with France the famous September Convention of 1864. Immediately afterward, however, the Minghetti cabinet fell. Visconti-Venosta went to Constantinople to head the Italian legation there, retaining all the while his seat in the chamber of deputies. In December, 1869, when a cabinet was formed by his friend and colleague, Giovanni Lanza, he resumed the foreign ministry and kept it without a break until 1878.

Somewhat isolated for a while, he was appointed to the senate in 1886. A decade later he took over the foreign ministry for the third time, serving under three premiers: Marquis Antonio di Rudinì, General Luigi Pelloux, and Giuseppe Saracco. True to his lifelong Francophilism, he helped to initiate the Franco-Italian rapprochement that was to make such steady progress before the coming of the First World War. He quit the foreign office in 1901 but returned to the diplomatic domain in 1906 when he served as his country's representative at the conference of Algeciras. Thereafter, until his death in 1914, he had the ear of successive governments, advising them on important questions of the day.

Many memorable moments punctuated the distinguished career of Visconti-Venosta. None, however, surpassed in drama and significance the first half of July, 1870.

Professors Lynn M. Case, René Albrecht-Carrié, Lawrence D. Steefel, and William C. Askew read the manuscript and made many useful suggestions. I should like to take this opportunity to thank them. I am also indebted to my wife, who helped me in innumerable ways. Finally, I wish to express my gratitude to the Social Science Research Committee of the University of Chicago for its generous financial assistance.

CONTENTS

CHAPTER ONE

THE CRISIS   1

CHAPTER TWO

FRENCH REQUESTS AND THE ROMAN QUESTION   19

CHAPTER THREE

THE AOSTA CANDIDATURE   38

CHAPTER FOUR

THE ROYAL GAME   59

CHAPTER FIVE

UNEASY INTERLUDE   79

CHAPTER SIX

DUEL WITH THE LEFT   100

CHAPTER SEVEN

THE FALSE PEACE   121

CHAPTER EIGHT

THE DENOUEMENT   134

CHAPTER NINE

WHICH WAY ITALY?   148

CHAPTER TEN

THE LEAGUE OF NEUTRALS   170

INDEX

193

CHAPTER ONE

THE CRISIS

On July 3, 1870, the French government learned from its ambassador in Madrid that a relative of King William of Prussia, Prince Leopold of Hohenzollern-Sigmaringen, was about to become the ruler of Spain. Twelve days later the two houses of the French parliament, having been requested to do so by the ministers of Napoleon III, voted a virtual declaration of war against Prussia. Throughout the crisis, one of the shortest and most momentous of modern history, there was a prodigious amount of diplomatic activity. Spain, as the country whose vacant throne had precipitated the trouble, was necessarily in the foreground until the last few days. But the principals were of course France and Prussia—or, to be more exact, Napoleon III and Bismarck. For these two the question of who was to rule in Spain was merely a side issue; a showdown between them had been brewing ever since 1866, when Bismarck and his generals wrought a revolution in international politics by expelling Austria from Germany and making themselves the masters of Central Europe. The balance of power had been disturbed to France's disadvantage, and she was determined to redress it. The Prussians for their part saw in France the lone remaining obstacle to a union of North and South Germany under their auspices. The inevitable struggle was finally touched off by the Hohenzollern candidature for the Spanish throne. The other great powers—Russia, Great Britain, Austria, and Italy—yielded the center of the stage to the main protagonists, but they were far from idle. Although their roles varied

widely, they all had something to say and do as the crisis un-
folded.

An account of what happened at the sundry levels and in
the different theaters of diplomatic activity is so difficult to
piece together that certain parts of the story still remain something of a puzzle. From the welter of evidence, however, a
number of facts do emerge with crystalline sharpness. One of
these is that nobody wanted peace more sincerely than Emilio
Visconti-Venosta, the Italian foreign minister. To be sure, his
exertions, like those of his British friends, proved heartbreak-
ingly futile; and at home some of his adversaries, while allowing for the difficulties that confronted him almost every inch
of the way, charged afterward that he might have been more
effective, that he was slow, timid, and hesitant. As a matter of
fact, there is much truth in this charge. Not only instantaneous
and forceful action but even emphatic gestures were quite
alien to Visconti-Venosta's nature. Owing to a sluggishness and
deliberateness that verged on irresolution, he preferred in most
cases to take his time, to defer decisions, sure that nothing vital
would be compromised thereby. Indeed, he was inclined to
assume that delays, far from doing harm, might actually help
to remove or attenuate difficulties of a certain order. Extremely cautious, on occasion excessively so, he had a keen aware-
ness of his own limitations and an absolute horror of overdoing.
On the other hand, his modesty and reticence served to conceal
his many splendid qualities. As a diplomat, he was all finesse
and delicacy, balance and discretion. Calm, coolly reflective
and clear-sighted, he was an excellent judge of men and situations, and tended to take the long view. Although far too
realistic to neglect or underestimate public opinion, he personally was indifferent to popular acclaim, abhorring those facile
answers that delighted the uninformed or unthinking. Firm and
tenacious in defense of certain causes despite his proneness to
indecision, he was also a master of the art of saying little or
promising nothing while giving the opposite impression.[1]

---

[1] See the excellent characterization of Visconti-Venosta in Federico
Chabod, *Storia della politica estera italiana dal 1870 al 1896*. Volume I:
Le premesse (Bari, 1951), pp. 117, 133, 215, 555, 563, 564–65, 567.

Above all, he seldom made mistakes of commission. Prince Bernhard von Bülow, Germany's chancellor from 1900 to 1909 and for many years an acquaintance of the Italian statesman, described him as "one of the most calculating and careful politicians I ever came across. I do not believe that he ever did a stupid thing in any sphere during the whole of his life."[2]

Two central premises underlay Visconti-Venosta's eagerness to dispel all threats to the peace of Europe. The first was that Italy could not afford to become involved in a war, regardless of why or how it started. The second was that, if a war did break out between France and Prussia, it might spread, engulfing Italy despite her wish to remain a mere looker-on. It was of course an open secret that Italy's economy was in a bad state. The war of 1866 had exhausted her slender resources.[3] She needed a long interval of tranquillity; without it she would be unable to put her chaotic finances in order or resolve some of her other internal problems. From this point of view, the late 1860's were especially critical.[4] Expenditures, including those for the army and navy, could not be maintained at their current levels and would have to be cut. Giovanni Lanza, who headed a cabinet of notables drawn from the Destra, the moderate party of the Right, had promised parliament that the government would retrench, and he intended to keep his word.[5]

Abiding by this pledge, the government presented a program of drastic economies in March, 1870. Its position was that the foremost task of the nation was to balance the budget by postponing or reducing non-urgent expenditures and by levying heavier taxes.[6] Lanza and his colleagues assumed that the

---

[2] *Memoirs of Prince von Bülow* (4 vols.; Boston, 1931–32), IV, 339.

[3] Piero Pieri, *Le forze armate nella età della destra* (Milan, 1962), p. 80.

[4] Carlo di Nola, "La situazione europea e la politica italiana dal 1867 al 1870," *Nuova rivista storica*, XXXIX (1955), 400.

[5] *Le carte di Giovanni Lanza* (11 vols.; Turin, 1935–43), V, Nos. 1536 and 1601, pp. 8, 75–76. On the proposed cut in military expenditures, see Luigi Izzo, *La finanza pubblica nel primo decennio dell'unità italiana* (Milan, 1962), p. 75.

[6] Nola, p. 260.

peace of Europe was safe for the time being; but, if they should be proved wrong, they would resist entanglement of any kind. To be sure, this meant forgoing rewards[7] as well as avoiding risks; but the Lanza cabinet took it for granted that diplomacy would eventually enable Italy to get what she wanted.[8]

Such non-financial considerations strengthened the case for a slash in military expenditures. Lanza was also influenced by the fact that, ever since 1866 when Italy lost the decisive battles while Prussia was winning them in their joint war against Austria, the armed forces had forfeited much of their popularity.[9] In addition, Lanza took stock in the views of General Giuseppe Govone, perhaps the most intelligent and certainly one of the most respected of Italy's commanding officers. Govone had accepted the post of minister of war under Lanza despite the certainty that he would be criticized for this by many of his fellow officers. As a patriot, he subordinated his own preference for a large army to what he considered to be the most urgent needs of the moment.[10] In any case, he believed that a financially shaky country could not build a dependable military force and that a balanced budget could be defended as the indispensable prerequisite of future prowess on the battlefield.[11]

Quintino Sella, the minister of finance and by far the most forceful member of the government, was absolutely rabid on the subject of retrenchment. With Lanza leading and Sella pushing—provided no unexpected obstacles intervened—the country could expect to move full steam ahead toward the financial goals that had been set for the next year or two. In a milder but nonetheless steadfast fashion, Visconti-Venosta subscribed to this program, and he was prepared to do his utmost as foreign minister to prevent it from being wrecked or jeopardized by the incalculable strains that belligerency would im-

---

[7] The list of those sought by King Victor Emmanuel II will be discussed in chap. iv.

[8] See Pieri, p. 80; Nola, pp. 260–61.

[9] *Le carte di Giovanni Lanza*, IV, No. 1525, p. 319.

[10] Pieri, pp. 81–82. [11] *Ibid.*, p. 82.

pose. The frailty of the national economy and the need to shield and bolster it for as long as possible were therefore very much in his mind throughout the July crisis. But economic vulnerability was by no means the sole consideration. For one thing, the army was unprepared and in no condition to be rushed at short notice to distant battlefields. For another, the bulk of the nation recoiled from the idea of war and clamored for a policy of strict neutrality.

Visconti-Venosta likewise knew that Italy could expect no gains commensurate with the sacrifices she would have to make if she threw in her lot with France, a course favored on certain conditions by a number of influential people including King Victor Emmanuel II. Only the revolutionary fringe of the Sinistra, the militantly liberal party of the Left, considered the contingency of eventual intervention on the side of Prussia. To be sure, Visconti-Venosta himself was unequivocally and unabashedly Francophile in his sympathies, but he leaned over backward in an effort to prevent this predilection for the ally of 1859 from influencing his judgment of what was good and right for his country in 1870. Although favorable in principle to a close political liaison with France, he could see little sense in fighting alongside her, especially in view of Napoleon's persistent refusal during the past few years to grant Italy's most cherished aspiration.

In the summer of 1870, a satisfactory solution of the Roman question was the paramount goal of Italian foreign policy. Destra and Sinistra, although at loggerheads about virtually everything else, were at one on this. Only the certain prospect of getting Rome with a minimum of risk stood any chance of inducing the country to jettison neutrality and accept the status of an active belligerent. Even this was problematical in view of the strength of the pacifist sentiment, the widespread if Platonic sympathy for the aims of German nationalism, and the Francophobia of a large part of the Sinistra rank and file. Besides, the most one could reasonably expect from France was reactivation of the moribund September Convention of 1864. Italy of course would have welcomed such a step; the September Convention obligated France to evacuate Rome, and the removal of her troops, rushed back to the Eternal City in 1867 in time to thwart the Garibaldians at Mentana, was the prerequisite of *Roma capitale*. But Napoleon, fearful of the repercussions at home, could not make up his mind to recall the garrison; and precisely because the September Convention obligated Italy, for her part, to leave Rome severely alone, its mere reactivation would have been insufficient to induce most Italians to resign themselves to military intervention on the side of France. It is quite true that Visconti-Venosta frowned on the use of force against the papacy even if the way were cleared by the tacit connivance of the French. He much preferred negotiations and an understanding with the Holy See.[12] Actually, a negotiated Italo-papal settlement was inconceivable so long as Napoleon continued to protect the remnants of the temporal power. But that harassed sovereign could not do otherwise; his hands were tied by the dependence of his regime on the support or sufferance of the powerful Catholic party. And so long as the impasse continued, the overwhelming reasons in favor of neutrality had little to countervail them in Visconti-Venosta's eyes.

His second premise, that it might prove impossible to localize a Franco-Prussian war, was based on his assessment of Austria's intentions. In 1867 Napoleon had secretly turned first to Austria, then to Italy, in an effort to promote an anti-Prussian alliance. Prussia's victory in the war with Austria had dismayed the French emperor and filled his subjects with jealousy and fear. He and they had reacted to the battle of Sadowa, which had forced Austria to sue for peace, as if it were a defeat for France. They had seen the balance of power upset, the traditional predominance of their country threatened. Stymied in his attempts to secure territorial "compensations," Napoleon had decided to seek redress by making France the spearhead of an invincible alignment. His overtures to Vienna and Florence had stemmed from this decision.

Austria's ruling circles were manifestly loath to resign themselves to the verdict of 1866, but they had hesitated to accept an alliance aimed exclusively at Prussia. They would fight if

[12] Chabod, p. 213.

France were at war with both Russia and Prussia,[13] if eastern Europe too were drawn into the maelstrom through military action by Tsar Alexander II. In the end, no treaty of any kind had been concluded because of the attitude of Victor Emmanuel, who refused to sign unless Napoleon bowed to his demands on the Roman question. Although Austria thus remained formally uncommitted, Visconti-Venosta feared that she might still intervene in a purely bilateral struggle between France and Prussia. His main reason for thinking so was the bitterly anti-Prussian attitude of the Austrian chancellor, Count Friedrich von Beust.

An old and unrelenting foe of Bismarck, Beust had been appointed to the post he now held because his views and aims fitted so well into the settled plan of Emperor Francis Joseph to avenge Sadowa. It is therefore hardly surprising that Beust should have relished Napoleon's original proposal, which called for an offensive and defensive alliance against Prussia alone. But the Francophobia of powerful elements in ethnically conscious German Austria and the Russophobia of the Magyar co-rulers of the Hapsburg empire, who had little interest in Germany and none at all in seeing Austria regain her pre-eminence there, had forced Beust to shift his ground. The Hungarian premier, Count Gyula Andrássy, feared the Slavs, not the Prussians; consequently, he favored strict neutrality in the event of a Franco-Prussian war.[14]

Realizing that for the moment at least the Magyar and Germanic population of the empire could not be persuaded to accept an anti-Prussian partnership with France, Beust had suggested to Napoleon an alliance based on the common opposition of Austria and France to Russian designs in the Near East. Should a conflict of interests in the Balkans lead to war, Great Britain would probably aid the allies. Prussia would then have to abandon her ally, Russia, or participate in a struggle that could not command the support of German national feeling.[15]

[13] Nola, p. 386.   [14] *Ibid.,* p. 421.

[15] Lawrence D. Steefel, *Bismarck, the Hohenzollern Candidacy, and the Origins of the Franco-German War of 1870* (Cambridge, Mass., 1962), pp. 7–8.

But the important point was that the *casus foederis* was to arise for Austria only if Russia intervened. This did not suit the French, just as their position on Rome displeased the Italians.

However, the crux of the matter, as Visconti-Venosta saw it, was that once a Franco-Prussian war was in progress, Beust might get around the proposed restriction by exploiting the desire of court circles to reverse the verdict of 1866. The Austrian minister of war, Baron Franz Kuhn von Kühnenfeld, believed that Prussia could not win,[16] a view which Francis Joseph as well as Beust undoubtedly shared. Austrian intervention would automatically bring Russia in, and from such a war Italy could hardly expect to remain aloof. Because, in Visconti-Venosta's opinion, everything thus depended on Austria, he watched her with special vigilance. Indeed, he sought the closest possible contact with her in the hope of exerting a restraining influence. He also sought the closest possible contact with Great Britain, but for a different reason: pathologically sensitive to Russian moves in the Balkans, the British were strongly for peace everywhere else in Europe. They could therefore be trusted to co-operate wholeheartedly and consistently in efforts to prevent a Franco-Prussian clash.[17] A second and powerful reason for working closely with them was the help they could give in any attempt to keep such a clash, if it came, from developing into a general war. Here, in embryo, was the league of neutrals that England, at Italy's urgent request, was to promote in August, 1870.

2

July 5 marked the beginning of the crisis for Visconti-Venosta. On that day he received a disturbing telegram from Costantino Nigra, the Italian minister to France. Nigra had gone to the Quai d'Orsay to inquire about the French reaction to newspaper reports that Prince Leopold had been offered the

[16] Nola, p. 423.

[17] Italy's reliance on Great Britain from the very start of the crisis is clearly analyzed in Solvyns to d'Anethan, July 11, 1870, No. 76, Belgium, Archives du ministère des affaires étrangères, Correspondance politique, Légations: Italie, IV, 1868–1870.

Spanish crown by Marshal Juan Prim, head of the provisional government in Madrid, and that the offer had been accepted. France's foreign minister, the Duke of Gramont, had of course seen the reports. Far more important, he was in possession of a confirmatory statement from the French ambassador to Spain. This served as his point of departure. He told Nigra that the news of the Hohenzollern candidature had created a very unfavorable impression in France. However, his government would abstain from interfering in the internal affairs of Spain. It blamed the Prussians; they could have prevented the candidature, and they still had time to put an end to it. At all events, this was something France would not tolerate.[18]

Gramont's concluding remark indicated that Leopold and the Prussians would either have to retreat from the Spanish venture or face the prospect of war. The next day, after a meeting of the council of ministers at which the emperor presided, Gramont proclaimed his government's stand. The carefully prepared declaration he read before the corps législatif minced no words. It informed the world that France would fight rather than allow the Hohenzollerns to instal themselves in Spain. Long simmering resentment, suddenly exacerbated by the latest news, was reflected in the closing sentences of Gramont's declaration:[19]

But we do not think that respect for the rights of a neighboring people [the Spaniards] compels us to suffer that a foreign power, by placing one of its princes on the throne of Charles V, should disturb to our disadvantage the present balance of power in Europe and endanger the interests and honor of France.

This eventuality, we firmly hope, will not be realized.

To prevent it, we count at once on the wisdom of the German people and the friendship of the Spanish people.

If it should be otherwise, strong in your support, gentlemen, and

[18] Nigra to Visconti-Venosta, July 5, 1870, No. 2344, Italy, Ministero degli affari esteri, Archivio storico (hereafter cited as MAE, AS), Dispacci telegrafici arrivati, busta 28: dal 12 gennaio 1869 al 16 luglio 1870 (hereafter cited as DTA).

[19] *Annales du sénat et du corps législatif* (Paris, 1870), V: du 21 juin au 12 juillet 1870, p. 448.

in that of the nation, we shall know how to discharge our duty without hesitation and without weakness.

Visconti-Venosta saw the text of the declaration late in the morning of July 7. From Nigra he had already had intimations of what it would contain.[20] Thanks to the same source, he knew that Gramont's remarks had been repeatedly applauded by the corps législatif and that they had made a tremendous impression in Paris.[21] Now that he himself had had a chance to read the pronouncement, he realized that a Franco-Prussian clash might be imminent. Just then Marquis Francisco de Montemar, the Spanish minister to Italy, was announced. Montemar had received from his government a circular note which he was to communicate to Visconti-Venosta. The document, with its recital of arguments and explanations, furnished formal notice of the fact that all the members of the Prim cabinet together with the regent, Marshal Francisco Serrano, had agreed to the candidature of Prince Leopold and were planning to submit his name to the Cortes. Montemar emphasized that his government had had but one thought when it united in support of Leopold: to give satisfaction to the monarchical sentiment and sovereign will of the nation it represented.[22]

Here was an opportunity, especially favorable because unsought, of urging upon the Spaniards the wisdom of reconsidering their decision. To be sure, Gramont's sword-brandishing performance before the corps législatif had offended their pride, and this would make retreat more difficult. But it was equally true that however much they might resent the attitude of France, they could hardly afford to ignore it. Their fear provided a powerful lever, and vigorous use of it by Italy would have reinforced the effect of the French ultimatum. Visconti-Venosta saw this clearly enough, but his inveterate caution stood in the way. Instead of employing the strongest language that the amenities of diplomatic intercourse would

[20] Nigra to Visconti-Venosta, July 6, 1870, No. 2352, MAE, AS, DTA.

[21] Nigra to Visconti-Venosta, July 6, 1870, No. 2350, *ibid.*

[22] Visconti-Venosta to Cerruti, July 7, 1870, No. 25, MAE, AS, Divisione politica, 1867–1888, registri copia-lettere in partenza, Spagna, busta 1212: 13 febbraio 1867–31 luglio 1873.

permit, he tamely began by observing that respect for the sovereign will of every nation was one of the principles of Italian foreign policy; the Italian government would therefore defer to the desires of the Spanish people in connection with the choice of a new monarch. After this bit of politesse, Visconti-Venosta did not go on to discuss what was really on his mind: the need to remove the Hohenzollern candidature somehow before France and Prussia were at each other's throats. Rather, he assured Montemar that if complications should arise as a result of Leopold's election to the Spanish throne, Italy would co-operate with other countries to smooth things over and contribute in this fashion to the preservation of peace.[23]

Visconti-Venosta was to wait more than twenty-four hours before adopting a different tactic with the Spaniards, and even then he did so only at the insistence of the French. The strategy he proposed to follow was evident from his concluding remarks to Montemar. Although Gramont's declaration showed that a Franco-Prussian clash might be imminent, as usual Visconti-Venosta betrayed no hurry. First he would sound other governments and explore the possibility of a collective *démarche* on behalf of a peaceful solution. The instructions he sent to his envoys in London and Vienna specified that they were to avoid formal proposals of any kind. Only when an opportunity offered were they to inform the governments to which they were accredited that Italy wished to unite her good offices with those of other powers in order to prevent a conflict between France and Prussia.[24] Carlo Cadorna, a veteran of Italian politics, was the minister to Great Britain; Count Francesco Curtopassi, the chargé d'affaires in Vienna, headed the legation there pending the appointment of a successor to Count Gioacchino Pepoli, who had quit his post some months before. In order to make sure that Cadorna and Curtopassi would have

23 *Ibid.* See also the account in Solvyns to d'Anethan, July 11, 1870, No. 77, Belgium, Archives du ministère des affaires étrangères, Correspondance politique, Légations: Italie, IV, 1868–1870.

24 Visconti-Venosta to the Italian legations in London and Vienna, July 7, 1870, No. 1170, MAE, AS, Telegrammi spediti, busta 20: dal 2 settembre 1869 al 10 ottobre 1872 (hereafter cited as TS).

a proper sense of the seriousness of the situation, Visconti-Venosta did remind them of Gramont's declaration. He also called their attention to the reports flowing into his office which depicted the Franco-Prussian dispute in the blackest colors.[25] But speed, in his *modus operandi*, did not seem of the essence.

Meanwhile, through the columns of the *Opinione*, the Florentine daily that was generally and quite correctly regarded as the semiofficial organ of the government,[26] Visconti-Venosta gave the country a clear indication of how the cabinet viewed the crisis. The main concern of the Italian people, the *Opinione* explained from the very outset, was the possible effect of the flare-up on the relations of the various powers: after all, there had once been a war over the Spanish succession.[27] As for the merits of the controversy between France on the one side and Spain and Prussia on the other, there could be no denying that Prince Leopold had reached the age of discretion. If he chose to become involved in this affair, it must be assumed that he had first considered all the possible consequences. The state of public opinion in the Second Empire, especially the well-known fact that Prussia was regarded there as an enemy and Sadowa as a calamitous defeat for France, must have made it rather easy for Leopold to foresee that his candidature would be ill-received by the government of Napoleon III. True, the

[25] Visconti-Venosta to Cadorna, July 7, 1870, No. 49, MAE, AS, Divisione politica, 1867–1888, registri copia-lettere in partenza, Inghilterra, busta 1167: 22 maggio 1869–29 luglio 1872; Visconti-Venosta to Curtopassi, July 7, 1870, No. 21, MAE, AS, Divisione politica, 1867–1888, registri copia-lettere in partenza, Austria, busta 1108: 25 agosto 1869–15 febbraio 1875. See also, for an allusion to the *démarche* of July 7, Visconti-Venosta to Minghetti, undated but marked "end of August 1870," No. 19, MAE, AS, Archivi di gabinetto (1861–1887), busta 219: guerra franco-prussiana e trattative segrete 8 luglio–14 settembre 1870, fascicolo 4.

[26] Chabod, pp. 115, 398; Friedrich Engel-Janosi, "The Roman Question in the Diplomatic Negotiations of 1869–70," *Review of Politics*, III (1941), p. 343. On the close relations between Giacomo Dina, the editor of the *Opinione*, and the Lanza cabinet, see *Le carte di Giovanni Lanza*, IV, Nos. 1526 and 1530, pp. 319–20, 324; V, Nos. 1538, 1539, 1551, 1596, 1639, 1640, and 1641, pp. 11, 12, 24–25, 69, 128–30.

[27] *L'Opinione*, July 6, 1870.

emperor had allowed Leopold's brother, Prince Charles of Hohenzollern-Sigmaringen, to instal himself on the throne of Rumania. But the Danubian Principalities were important to Austria rather than to France. A Hohenzollern prince in Madrid, a Prussian colonel on the throne of Spain, was a vastly different matter. Spain could not be compared to Rumania, and the Pyrenees, as a French king once remarked, no longer existed. In a war with Prussia, France would have to guard her southern border, for below it there would be an army of 100,000 men commanded by a sovereign of German blood.[28]

As for Italy, the *Opinione* was emphatic in saying that she must steer clear of direct involvement. Happily, the Italian people were geographically far removed from the Iberian peninsula, and they had renounced the ambition of providing a king for Spain. The choice of Leopold could not greatly affect them one way or the other. But the *Opinione* did foresee a rather strenuous time for the king-designate. Very soon he would be caught in the same toils that had entrapped every other pretender. After all, he was the choice, not of the Spanish people, but only of one faction that sought through him to escape from an embarrassing situation. No doubt foreign interference would rally to his side all patriotic Spaniards; but unity achieved at the price of a European conflagration would prove far too dear.[29]

Could war be averted? The *Opinione* was inclined to say yes, despite Gramont's declaration. With the return of a measure of calm, good sense and diplomacy would probably prevail. All the governments of Europe wanted peace, and the selection of Leopold could not alter this fact. It was likewise true that the Spaniards had knocked on every door. Their quest for a Portuguese candidate, whose advent would have led to Iberian union, had proved fruitless. Two Italian princes, the Dukes of Aosta and Genoa, had turned them down. No Austrian prince was available. Napoleon had shut a few other doors by vetoing the candidature of certain Spanish aspirants and by excluding a republican solution. It was therefore unfair

[28] *Ibid.*   [29] *Ibid.*

to stigmatize the choice of a Hohenzollern as an intrigue against France. Prim could say that he had selected Leopold solely because there was nobody else and that he would gladly abandon him if some satisfactory alternative could be proposed.[30] At all events, the French would have to learn to adapt themselves to the new realities of international politics. They must realize that relations between states were no longer determined by family ties or the whims of individual rulers. Identity or similarity of interests and institutions—this, the *Opinione* insisted, was the sole and irreplaceable basis of the present international order. In suggesting that France's fears, if not unfounded, were at least exaggerated, Visconti-Venosta's mouthpiece touched upon one of his favorite theses: that wars waged for dynastic reasons had ceased to make sense. To forestall such folly, the powers must enable Spain to resolve her difficulties; they must help her to place her political institutions on a stable and permanent basis. Italy must lend a hand: to that extent, she could not escape involvement. The French, despite their obvious irritation, were fundamentally too prudent and realistic to obstruct a settlement of that kind.[31]

Thus, through the medium of a trusted newspaper, Visconti-Venosta adumbrated views which he was loath to express in diplomatic communications and private conversations or which he preferred to put forward only at some later, more opportune moment.

3

The outcome of the overture to Vienna and London would not be known for at least a day or longer. While waiting to hear, Visconti-Venosta sought information which could help him to estimate where joint mediation by Austria, England, and Italy might be initiated with the best chance of success. There were of course four possibilities: Paris, Sigmaringen, Berlin, and Madrid. The first of these he preferred to keep in reserve for the time being, on the theory that a premature move there might turn out to be especially harmful. To the second, the abode of Leopold's father, Prince Karl Anton, and

[30] *Ibid.*, July 8, 1870.   [31] *Ibid.*

the rest of the family, Visconti-Venosta never gave any serious consideration. He assumed, and he was quite correct, that effective pressure could be exerted on Leopold only through the Prussian government or King William. For this reason, from the very outset Berlin figured in his calculations. Information just received encouraged him to look hopefully toward the Prussian capital. Nigra reported that Baron Werther, the Prussian ambassador to France, was leaving for Ems, where King William was taking the cure. The excursion, which had been arranged long in advance, would give Werther a chance to tell the sovereign just how agitated the French were. It was expected that William would be asked to refuse his consent to Leopold's candidature. According to Nigra, French official circles believed that the king would heed this request and put an end to the crisis.[32] No doubt, in the short interval since Nigra had passed along this information, the Prussians had had a chance to digest Gramont's declaration, and it was hardly likely to put them in an obliging mood. But Visconti-Venosta did not allow this to deter him. After due reflection, he authorized the head of the legation in Berlin, Count Edoardo de Launay, to inform the Prussian government of Italy's wholehearted interest in a multilateral attempt to mediate the dispute with France. He supposed, in the light of the king's probable attitude, that diplomatic intervention by the powers might well begin with an approach to Prussia. This was his principal reason for telegraphing Launay on the seventh; the envoy would need a little time in which to prepare the terrain. However, Visconti-Venosta took the precaution of asking for confirmation of the sanguine report from Paris. Launay was first to ascertain what he could and transmit his findings by telegraph.[33]

As for Madrid, it too seemed an auspicious theater. To be sure, a message from Marcello Cerruti, the Italian minister to Spain, suggested that the Prim cabinet, backed to the hilt by Serrano, was planning to move full speed ahead with the

[32] Nigra to Visconti-Venosta, July 6, 1870, No. 2352, MAE, AS, DTA.

[33] Visconti-Venosta to Launay, July 7, 1870, No. 1172, MAE, AS, TS.

Hohenzollern candidature.[34] This, however, was before word
of Gramont's declaration had arrived in Madrid. Now, on the
seventh, Visconti-Venosta asked Cerruti to let him know exactly how the Spaniards were reacting to that pronouncement. He
was also anxious to find out whether Prim and Serrano were
planning any new moves as a consequence of it.[35] A telegram
from Cerruti crossed with his. It stated only that the minatory
attitude assumed by Gramont was causing widespread consternation in Madrid.[36]

In the meantime, Visconti-Venosta received odds and ends
of information that rounded out what he already knew or suspected. From Marquis Caracciolo, the Italian minister to Russia, he learned that France had not been idle in St. Petersburg.
Through her ambassador there, she had let it be known how
much she objected to a Prussian king for Spain.[37] Of much
greater immediate interest to Visconti-Venosta was a remark
by Lord Lyons, the British ambassador in Paris, which Nigra
had hastened to transmit. Lyons disclosed that his government
was about to make friendly representations in both Berlin and
Madrid in an effort to secure the withdrawal of the Hohenzollern candidature.[38]

This good news was counterbalanced by a disturbing communication from Launay. Writing on the seventh, several hours
before the arrival of Visconti-Venosta's telegram of the same
date, Launay confided that on the basis of information in his
possession, he could state rather positively that Leopold had
accepted the Spanish offer with the knowledge of both King
William and Bismarck. Although the sovereign and his minister
had adroitly concealed their game from the eyes of Europe's
diplomatists, at least he, Launay, had not been taken in.[39] After

[34] Cerruti to Visconti-Venosta, July 6, 1870, No. 2347, MAE, AS, DTA.

[35] Visconti-Venosta to Cerruti, July 7, 1870, No. 1174, MAE, AS, TS.

[36] Cerruti to Visconti-Venosta, July 7, 1870, No. 2353, MAE, AS, DTA.

[37] Caracciolo to Visconti-Venosta, July 8, 1870, No. 2356, *ibid.* This
telegram was received at 5:00 A.M.

[38] Nigra to Visconti-Venosta, July 7, 1870, No. 2354, *ibid.*

[39] Launay to Visconti-Venosta, July 7, 1870, No. 2355, *ibid.*

this characteristic display of vanity—Launay was probably
the most conceited as well as the most opinionated member of
the Italian foreign service—the envoy noted that the Prussian
secretary of state for foreign affairs, Karl von Thile, had not
changed his line despite Gramont's blast of the sixth.[40] Since
Thile was known to be Bismarck's faithful mouthpiece—the
great Prussian statesman, supposedly ailing, was still at Varzin,
his country estate in Pomerania whither he had withdrawn
about a month before—the views expressed by this otherwise
unimpressive subordinate had the gilt-edged importance of
statements emanating from the absent chief himself. But all
questions laid before Thile by foreign diplomats that had not
been anticipated, and to which answers could not have been
rehearsed, had to be referred to Varzin. The inevitable delays
did not please embassy and legation heads in Berlin; but, needless to say, the arrangement suited Bismarck perfectly.

Although cognizant of the mounting tension, Thile blandly
maintained just as he had before that Leopold was free to do
as he pleased and that the Spaniards should be allowed to decide their own dynastic questions without interference from
anyone. Repeating what Thile and other Prussian spokesmen
had told him, Launay painted a very dark picture. Gramont's
challenge had suddenly worsened the situation. Official circles
in Berlin did not go so far as to assume that war would break
out within the next few hours. But they made no secret of their
conviction that it might come rather soon if Gramont and his
colleagues continued to inflame French public opinion. At all
events, even if the present trouble should blow over, the danger of future complications would remain.[41]

Thus, according to Launay's informants, the long-range outlook was distinctly unfavorable. Visconti-Venosta shared this
pessimism. How much chance, he wondered, would there be
of averting a clash when Paris learned that despite so many
Prussian protestations to the contrary, King William and Bismarck had been privy all along to the clandestine transaction
between Prim and Leopold? The anger of the French, already
intense, was likely to boil over. The foreign minister's brooding

40 *Ibid.*   41 *Ibid.*

uneasiness was heightened by Nigra's full report of the conversation with Gramont on July 5. The dispatch, which supple-
mented the telegraphic summary Nigra had sent the same day,
reached the Italian foreign office not long after the arrival of
Launay's telegram. It disclosed in some detail the background
of Gramont's declaration before the corps législatif and made
that utterance seem all the more ominous. Unburdening himself to Nigra, Gramont had assailed the Hohenzollern candidature as an anti-French move by Prussia. When Nigra asked
what inferences might be drawn from the attitude of the French
government, Gramont had brusquely answered that "under no
circumstances will France tolerate this thing; in other words,
she will not if need be confine herself to protests alone." Convinced that Gramont was not bluffing, Nigra said as much in
his report. He warned that if the candidature was not withdrawn, it could lead straight to war. In support of this forecast,
he cited the vigor with which the organs of public opinion in
France were speaking out against the "sudden" Hohenzollern
aspiration to capture the Spanish throne.[42]

An interesting sidelight on the conversation was Gramont's
silence about a secret to which both he and Nigra were privy:
the negotiations for an alliance between France and the two
powers she had been courting. Although a Franco-Prussian war
now seemed an imminent possibility, Gramont had not yet
received from the emperor any precise instructions on when
and how to revive the question of a Franco-Italian alliance.
But the omission was soon to be rectified.

[42] Nigra to Visconti-Venosta, July 5, 1870, No. 1175, MAE, AS, Serie
politica (1867–1888), Francia, busta 1307: 1869–1870.

CHAPTER TWO

FRENCH REQUESTS
AND THE ROMAN QUESTION

It was a little after midday on July 8. Visconti-Venosta had left Florence briefly on business unconnected with the Franco-Prussian crisis. Now, back in his office, his thoughts reverted to Madrid. How, he wondered, would the Cortes vote when Leopold's name was laid before it? Would Gramont's declaration deter it from following the dangerous lead given by the government and Serrano? Or would it, out of resentment against the bullying attitude of the French, throw caution to the winds and sanction the enthronement of a Prussian prince? Anxious to find out what he could, Visconti-Venosta sent off a query to Cerruti,[1] then had to dismiss the matter temporarily because Baron Malaret, the French minister to Italy, was waiting in the anteroom to see him. Visconti-Venosta did not relish the prospect of a conversation with Malaret; he had a strong premonition that it might prove rather unpleasant. After all, the nature of Malaret's business was not difficult to surmise.

Very late the night before, the French envoy had received an urgent telegram from Gramont. The message evidenced Napoleon's determination to bring to a head his prolonged, fitfully conducted quest for allies. Ever since the beginning of the Hohenzollern crisis, the emperor had professed to believe that Italy as well as Austria would not fail him in a showdown with Prussia. He exuded complete confidence on this score at the meeting of his council of ministers on the morning of July 6,

---

[1] Visconti-Venosta to Cerruti, July 8, 1870, No. 1175, MAE, AS, TS.

just before Gramont addressed the corps législatif. Sure of Victor Emmanuel's loyalty and assuming that the king would continue as before to dictate Italian foreign policy, Napoleon in his own mind had already resolved to remove the Roman roadblock by reactivating the September Convention and recalling the garrison as soon as war should become certain. Now, with Gramont's declaration out of the way, the emperor authorized a series of moves in pursuit of what was to prove a cruel but only gradually dissolving mirage. The foreign minister was told to prepare the Italians for the supporting role they were expected to play. On the night of the seventh, Gramont carried out the charge.

Explaining that he could not at this time go into the details of the grave situation created by the Hohenzollern candidature, Gramont proceeded to stress the extent to which the imperial government was relying on the friendship of Italy. To begin with, her diplomatic help was needed in Madrid; Malaret's first assignment was to make this clear. Visconti-Venosta must urge the Spanish leaders, especially Serrano who was considered more amenable and better disposed than Prim, to discard Leopold. Malaret's second assignment was to obtain from the Italian government a formal promise of military aid in the event that Prussia's continued support for the Hohenzollern candidature should compel France to fight.[2] This was the primary purpose of the démarche. Nevertheless, Gramont said nothing about the Roman question, although it accounted for Italy's previous refusal to commit herself to an alliance with France and Austria. For one thing, Napoleon was not yet ready to announce the evacuation of Rome. For another, Gramont questioned the wisdom of such a move and hoped to dissuade his master from making it. If the duke thought there was some other way to entice the Italians, he neglected to divulge it.

Malaret attempted to contact Visconti-Venosta on the morning of the eighth but discovered he was away and would not be

[2] Telegram from Gramont to Malaret, July 7, 1870, France, Archives du ministère des affaires étrangères (hereafter cited as AMAE), Italie, janvier–juillet 1870, tome 378. This document has been published as No. 8292 in Les origines diplomatiques de la guerre de 1870–1871 (hereafter cited as OD [29 vols.; Paris, 1910–1932]), XXVIII, 85.

back until later in the day. An appointment was arranged for 1:00 P.M.,[3] and exactly at that time Malaret was ushered in. The Hohenzollern candidature, he began, had confronted France and all Europe with a serious crisis. Visconti-Venosta was therefore being requested to endeavor by diplomatic action in Madrid to foil the scheme which Prim personally had cooked up and which France, concerned for her security and dignity, could not abide. Then, in the same direct fashion, Malaret said he wanted to know how far his government would be able to count on Italy's help if war should become inevitable.[4] He put the question in the manner of one requesting not a fresh commitment but merely the elucidation of an already existing obligation; yet he himself was anything but sanguine about the kind of response this second query would elicit.

Until now Visconti-Venosta had frowned on the idea of unilateral action in Madrid or anywhere else, believing as he did that joint mediation was bound to prove the most efficacious procedure. He still preferred to wait for the answers he was expecting from London and Vienna, but under the circumstances he could hardly refuse to comply with the French request. Besides, he knew that Great Britain, whose judgment he respected, had already decided to do what France was asking of Italy; and anything that gave promise of furthering the object he had in view was to be welcomed.

Consequently, Visconti-Venosta readily agreed to urge retreat upon the Spaniards. Nor did he find it any harder to brush aside a disturbing thought that had flashed into his mind. In January, 1869, the second son of Victor Emmanuel, Amadeus, Duke of Aosta, had been invited by Prim to be a candidate for the Spanish throne. But the prince had refused, much to Prim's disappointment. The marshal had put Aosta near the

[3] Telegram from Malaret to Gramont, July 8, 1870, AMAE, Italie, janvier–juillet 1870, tome 378 (*OD*, XXVIII, No. 8313, p. 113).

[4] Malaret to Gramont, July 9, 1870, No. 50, AMAE, Italie, janvier–juillet 1870, tome 378 (*OD*, XXVIII, No. 8363, p. 172). See also Costantino Nigra, *Poesie originali e tradotte, aggiuntovi un capitolo dei suoi ricordi diplomatici. A cura di Alessandro d'Ancona* (Florence, 1914), p. 107.

top of his list of candidates, just below the Portuguese princes whose accession would have resulted in Iberian union, the dearest hope of all Spanish patriots. Almost a year later Prim had failed in his second Italian try, with Victor Emmanuel's youthful nephew, the Duke of Genoa, substituted for Aosta. This time, just when the transaction seemed on the verge of success, it had been ruined by the fiery opposition of the candidate's mother and by the misgivings of the Italian cabinet, which did not relish involvement in Spain's dynastic troubles.[5] Of course, a good deal had happened since then, but it occurred to Visconti-Venosta that perhaps this part of the record should not be disregarded. After all, the fact that two princes of the House of Savoy were among those previously considered for the Spanish throne and the possibility that encouragement from Victor Emmanuel might lead to their being considered anew if the Hohenzollern candidature should be scotched could conceivably create some embarrassment for Italy if she intervened now on the side of Leopold's adversaries. It was exactly like Visconti-Venosta to overlook nothing, even though, with a speed that was amazing for him, he had already made up his mind.

He told Malaret that the resources of Italian diplomacy would be pitted against the Hohenzollern candidature. Not only the Italian minister in Madrid but also his colleague in Berlin would be instructed to work with might and main to end the crisis by helping to remove its cause.[6] The actions and counsels of the Italian government, he solemnly declared, were wholly dedicated to the cause of peace.[7] Needless to say, it was Malaret's second request that perturbed him. He realized of

[5] For a discussion of the Italian candidatures, see Steefel, pp. 29, 32–33, 41, 45–46; on the attitude of the mother of the Duke of Genoa, see Conde de Romanones, *Amedeo de Saboya, el rey efímero: España y los orígenes de la guerra franco-prusiana de 1870* (Madrid, 1935), p. 16. The collapse of the Genoa candidature is dealt with at length in Malaret to La Tour d'Auvergne, December 30, 1869, No. 107, AMAE, Italie, septembre–décembre 1869, tome 377; Malaret to Daru, January 5, 1870, No. 1, *ibid.*, janvier–juillet 1870, tome 378.

[6] Telegram from Malaret to Gramont, July 8, 1870, *ibid.*, Italie, janvier–juillet 1870, tome 378 (*OD*, XXVIII, No. 8320, p. 117).

[7] Visconti-Venosta to Nigra, July 8, 1870, No. 1177, MAE, AS, TS.

course that the demand for a military pledge was inspired by Napoleon's assumption that, as a result of the secret negotiations with Francis Joseph and Victor Emmanuel over the past few years, France could for all practical purposes rely on the active aid of both those sovereigns despite the fact that no instrument of alliance had been executed. Now, with Malaret waiting for an answer, he decided to put a damper on French expectations but not to go so far as to extinguish them altogether; that would have accorded ill with his style and his competence. Indicating a passive role for Italy, he did not altogether rule out the adoption of an active one. Choosing his words carefully, he said not once but several times that, if a war broke out between France and Prussia, France could rest assured that she would not find Italy among her enemies.[8] As for the definitive attitude of the Italian government, it could take shape only after the situation had become somewhat clearer.[9] In the meanwhile, it was impossible to promise more.[10] Actually, Visconti-Venosta had promised nothing. An alliance with Prussia against France was out of the question; to imply, by making it the subject of a pledge, that this was not necessarily so, was the kind of diplomatic sleight of hand at which he excelled. Pushed into a corner by Malaret, he took refuge in tactics that came naturally to him: evasion and procrastination. His intent was of course to take the steam out of the French diplomatic offensive. It remained to be seen whether his language would have the desired effect, but he was too realistic to nurse any illusions.

2

This ended the official part of the conversation. In the informal exchange that followed, Visconti-Venosta talked to Malaret about another matter that was very much on his mind.

[8] *Ibid.*; telegram from Malaret to Gramont, July 8, 1870, AMAE, Italie, janvier–juillet 1870, tome 378 (*OD*, XXVIII, No. 8320, p. 117); Malaret to Gramont, July 9, 1870, No. 50, *ibid.* (*OD*, XXVIII, No. 8363, p. 173); Nigra, p. 108.

[9] Visconti-Venosta to Nigra, July 8, 1870, No. 1177, MAE, AS, TS.

[10] Telegram from Malaret to Gramont, July 8, 1870, AMAE, Italie, janvier–juillet 1870, tome 378 (*OD*, XXVIII, No. 8320, p. 117).

According to certain Paris newspapers, a delegation consisting of clerical members of the corps législatif had recently called on Émile Ollivier, the French minister of justice and *de facto* head of the imperial cabinet.[11] Their action was prompted by published reports that the French government intended to alter its Roman policy and that with this in view it was planning to recall its troops from papal soil. The deputies were naturally worried, and they demanded an explanation from Ollivier, whose reputation as a liberal and an Italophile made him suspect in their eyes. They could not have picked a better moment from their point of view. Of late Ollivier's position had become extremely shaky, and he was in no mood or condition to cross swords with the powerful clerical contingent in the corps législatif. Although the various newspaper accounts of what he told the delegation did not tally exactly, they nonetheless seemed to establish that he did say three things: (1) The situation in Italy was currently so unstable that the government there could not enforce the terms of the September Convention—in other words, the Italian authorities would find themselves incapable of preventing an armed invasion of papal territory by bands of freebooters if the protective shield of French troops were removed; (2) for the time being at least, the political interests of France precluded the recall of her garrison; (3) at all events, even if such a move were considered, it would not be carried out without prior consultation of the corps législatif—a pledge that was tantamount to indefinite postponement of any change in the Roman status quo.[12]

Visconti-Venosta first learned of Ollivier's statement from the capsule summary relayed by Stefani, the great Italian news

[11] Although the press did not make this clear, the visit had occurred in April, 1870. It was not publicized until the end of June and the beginning of July.

[12] The Paris newspapers that played up Ollivier's remarks were the violently ultramontane *Univers,* organ of Louis Veuillot; the clerical *Monde;* the legitimist *Union;* and the influential Orleanist daily, *Le Journal des débats.* See Ollivier's own version of what he said in his *L'Empire libéral* (18 vols.; Paris, 1895–1912), XV, 442. For the résumé that was bandied about in Florence, see Solvyns to d'Anethan, July 12, 1870, No. 82, Belgium, Archives du ministère des affaires étrangères, Correspondance politique, Légations: Italie, IV, 1868–1870.

agency.[13] Then, as fuller but somewhat varying versions became available, his displeasure grew. The thing was bad enough in itself, but it would be incalculably magnified by the reaction of Italian public opinion, which needed very little to be provoked into hateful outbursts against the French in their dual character as perpetrators of Garibaldi's defeat at Mentana and occupiers of the kingdom's predestined capital. Ollivier's reported slur on Italy's capacity to enforce law and order against restive foes of the unpopular September Convention would be deeply resented as still another expression of France's patronizing and depreciatory attitude; and the fact that it came from a man hitherto regarded, and quite justifiably, as a supporter of the official Italian position on Rome, would make the reaction all the more vitriolic.

Visconti-Venosta had not the slightest doubt that the flare-up of Italian feeling would increase his own difficulties in parliament, where a large and vocal opposition repeatedly taxed him with slavish subservience to France bordering on treachery.[14] He, for his part, was especially irritated by the assurance apparently given the clerical deputies that the corps législatif would be consulted prior to any action concerning the French garrison. Apart from the possibly endless delay which this portended, he decried it as quite inconsistent with the juridical character of the September Convention. A treaty, once it had been duly ratified by the signatory countries, was thenceforward the exclusive concern of the cabinets involved. At least, that was his view. In any case, he disliked to see the whims of legislative majorities injected into the conduct of diplomacy.

But before attempting to elicit from the French government a retraction or repudiation of Ollivier's remarks, Visconti-Venosta sought to protect himself by first making sure that the statement as recapitulated in the various press versions (the actual text had so far not been published) and upon which he

[13] Visconti-Venosta to Nigra, July 5, 1870, No. 53, MAE, AS, Divisione politica, 1867–1888, registri copia-lettere in partenza, Francia, busta 1144: 20 luglio 1869–14 febbraio 1871.

[14] Certain press organs of the opposition echoed the charge. See the example cited in P. M. Arcari, *La Francia nell'opinione pubblica italiana dal '59 al '70* (Milan, 1938), p. 134.

planned to base his representations was for all practical purposes correct. He naturally turned to Nigra and asked him to ascertain as exactly as possible what the minister of justice was supposed to have said about the French occupation of Rome.[15] But Nigra, already in a highly agitated state as a result of the sudden eruption of the Franco-Prussian crisis, had not waited for instructions from his chief. Instead, he had hurried to arrange for an interview with Gramont as soon as the story of the meeting between Ollivier and the clerical delegation began to make the rounds of the French press. In the course of the interview Nigra called the foreign minister's attention to the accounts that had appeared in such newspapers as the *Univers*, the *Union*, and the *Journal des débats*, and in a manner which indicated that he was not to be put off, he demanded to know whether the remarks attributed to Ollivier had actually been uttered. Gramont, who had taken the precaution of checking with Ollivier, affected an air of absolute innocence. Unhesitatingly and categorically he asserted that neither the statement reported in the press nor any other of similar import had been made by Ollivier. For good measure he added that the story which the newspapers had been disseminating was incorrect in every detail. Orders had already been given for the publication of a rectified version of the incident.[16] However, no such communiqué ever appeared.

Gramont's reputation for veracity was not of the highest; Ollivier's was scarcely any better. And both men, with delicate diplomatic negotiations under way and more in the offing, were under tremendous pressure to sweep the affair under the rug and keep it there. Consequently, when Nigra wired home a brief résumé of the conversation (his telegram crossed with Visconti-Venosta's request for information), he carefully refrained from corroborating the foreign minister's denial. Instead, he merely forwarded without comment the gist of Gramont's remarks.[17] Visconti-Venosta received Nigra's message

15 Visconti-Venosta to Nigra, July 5, 1870, No. 1165, MAE, AS, TS.

16 Nigra to Visconti-Venosta, July 5, 1870, No. 1176, MAE, AS, Serie politica (1867–1888), Francia, busta 1307: 1869–1870.

17 Nigra to Visconti-Venosta, July 5, 1870, No. 2345, MAE, AS, DTA.

during the evening of July 5. He too was not impressed; he wanted something more than mere protestations of innocence. The following day he saw the account put out by Havas, the great French news agency which had a high and well-deserved reputation for accuracy. He was now even less inclined than before to accept Gramont's statement. With unwonted sharpness he asked Nigra to inform the French government that he could not be satisfied with vague declarations about the inexactitude of a story as widely publicized as this one.[18]

Nigra was a staunch Francophile and an advocate of closer relations between Italy and France. Dismayed by the prospect which now seemed to unfold, he sought to make amends for his failure to back up Gramont's denial. For the time being at least, he belatedly assured Visconti-Venosta, it was possible to confirm what Gramont had told him. But virtually in the same breath he contradicted himself; for after promising to seek additional explanations, he confessed that, so far as he knew, the Havas account correctly stated the attitude of the imperial government on the Roman question.[19] This version tallied with the three-point consensus of the journalists who had pieced the story together for the French press.

The newspaper accounts and the emotions they aroused on both sides of the Alps were at this moment of greater concern to Visconti-Venosta than the real as distinguished from the reported intentions of Napoleon and his ministers in regard to Rome. The Havas story, as much for the reputability of the agency which distributed it as for its provocative content, had been featured by a large section of the European press, and it was altogether likely that the matter might be aired in the corps législatif. The virtual certainty that in any such debate violent language would be employed preyed on Visconti-Venosta's mind. French outbursts on the subject of the Roman question were bound to elicit answers in kind in the Italian parliament, and the net result would be a new crescendo of anti-French feeling and fierce attacks on the foreign policy of the government. Anxious to prevent such unpleasantness,

---

[18] Visconti-Venosta to Nigra, July 6, 1870, No. 1168, MAE, AS, TS.

[19] Nigra to Visconti-Venosta, July 6, 1870, No. 2349, MAE, AS, DTA.

which could prove costly to the Lanza cabinet, Visconti-Venosta did something that for him was most unusual: he took a stiff line with the French. He warned that they had no right to subject the implementation of the September Convention either to unwarranted estimates of the Italian government's command of the situation at home or to a vote in the corps législatif. If nonetheless the French government should claim such a right and announce its position before the corps législatif, the Italian government would be forced to retaliate by protesting against the failure of Napoleon to carry out the obligations he had assumed under the terms of the September Convention. More than that, the Italian government would suspend the execution of its own obligations as fixed by the treaty. Finally—and this was by far the most menacing portion of Visconti-Venosta's message to Gramont—it would stop recognizing the right of France to intervene in the affairs of Rome.[20]

Nigra duly conveyed this warning.[21] It was while he was doing so that Malaret presented France's request for diplomatic and military help. Still without any satisfactory reply from Gramont, it was natural that Visconti-Venosta should have utilized the informal part of his conversation with Malaret to bring the matter up. He alluded to his distress at the unfortunate effect which the remarks attributed to Ollivier had had on Italian public opinion.[22] By calling attention to the resentment of his countrymen, Visconti-Venosta served notice that even tolerable relations between France and Italy, not to speak of a rapprochement or an accord, could hardly be hoped for so long as imperial troops remained on papal soil in defiance of the September Convention. As one of the authors of that treaty —it had been negotiated during his brief first tenure of the foreign ministry—he sincerely wished to see it reactivated, for France's sake as well as Italy's. Unless France fulfilled her part of the original bargain, unless she ended her illegal occupation

---

[20] Visconti-Venosta to Nigra, July 7, 1870, No. 1171, MAE, AS, TS.

[21] Nigra to Visconti-Venosta, July 8, 1870, No. 2357, MAE, AS, DTA.

[22] Visconti-Venosta to Nigra, July 8, 1870, No. 2, MAE, AS, Archivi di gabinetto (1861–1887), busta 219: guerra franco-prussiana e trattative segrete 8 luglio–14 settembre 1870, fascicolo 4.

of Rome, the two countries would drift farther and farther apart, with deplorable consequences for both.

Malaret, who knew the peninsula well, was the last person to disagree with this judgment. In his long report of the conversation, he contended that if the French government really wished to obtain from Italy something more satisfactory than Platonic or covert good will, it must at once set about to heal the wounds it had inflicted on that country's self-esteem. Above all, it must seek to establish for Italy's benefit a direct and material stake in the outcome of the war in which she would be asked to participate. In alluding to the lacerations of Italy's pride, Malaret explained that he was of course thinking of the presence of French soldiers on Italian soil. To be sure, a very large number of Italians of moderate outlook appreciated the political and moral considerations that had compelled France to reoccupy Rome in 1867 and to stay on thereafter. But they refused to concede that in 1870 a case could be made for a continuation of the occupation. In their estimation, the fine reputation of the men who made up the Lanza cabinet offered a sufficient guaranty that treaty stipulations would be faithfully carried out; and as a matter of fact, Italy was now doing everything that the September Convention required her to do. When viewed against such a backdrop, the policy pursued by the French government seemed open to question. Malaret, who undoubtedly shared this opinion, here injected the name of Urbano Rattazzi. France, the envoy observed, justified her nonfulfilment of the treaty by adducing the possibility that Rattazzi, a former premier whose underhanded maneuvers to possess himself of Rome had set the stage for the encounter at Mentana, might be returned to power. But inasmuch as there was no chance of doing away with Rattazzi, the French position amounted to a plea of exception, which neither the Italian government nor the nation's self-esteem could tolerate indefinitely. Even the calmest Italians argued thus, and according to Malaret their reasoning could not be refuted.[23] That he too favored the evacuation of Rome he made no effort to conceal.

[23] Malaret to Gramont, July 9, 1870, No. 50, AMAE, Italie, janvier–juillet 1870, tome 378 (OD, XXVIII, No. 8363, pp. 174–75).

It was a matter of paying a certain price or getting nothing at all.

Malaret's analysis disclosed nothing new. In March, 1870, the Italian government had conveyed the same message to Paris. Insisting that tranquillity now reigned throughout the peninsula, it had branded the continued occupation of Rome as completely indefensible. The behavior of the French, it had argued, could not be reconciled with their frequent invocation of the September Convention. Italy's position in this matter was so unassailable that it should not have to be reaffirmed. The renewal of the convention must be deferred no longer.[24] Now, after his conversation with Visconti-Venosta, Malaret was in effect reminding his superiors that the attitude of Florence had not changed.

His appraisal of Italy's internal situation was unsparingly factual. He had long understood why she could not pursue a forceful or ambitious foreign policy, and Visconti-Venosta's remarks prompted him to dwell on this. "It is my impression," he reported to Gramont, "that in case of war, Italy will begin by proclaiming her neutrality, and will attempt to maintain it as long as possible."[25] Although both the majority of the ministers and the rank and file of the Right were more sympathetic to France than to Prussia, they agreed with the rest of the nation that Italy needed repose. Unless they could be persuaded that intervention would prove more beneficial than neutrality, they too would insist on a policy of non-belligerency.[26]

Needless to say, the chances of demonstrating that it was in Italy's interest to go to war were inordinately slender. To underscore the point, Malaret painted a stark picture. Italy, he noted, had reduced the size of her land forces. Her navy had been virtually dismantled. She was in financial straits and could scarcely find enough money for her minimal peacetime

[24] *Le carte di Giovanni Lanza*, V, No. 1586, pp. 56–57.

[25] Telegram from Malaret to Gramont, July 8, 1870, AMAE, Italie, janvier–juillet 1870, tome 378 (*OD*, XXVIII, No. 8320, p. 117).

[26] Malaret to Gramont, July 9, 1870, No. 50, *ibid.* (*OD*, XXVIII, No. 8363, p. 174).

requirements. Little wonder that she should wish to avoid war-like complications. Malaret had no need to add that this desire was as profound as it was widespread. And as if prepared to write the Italians off in advance, he intimated that their help would be of small value.[27]

Reversing his train of thought, Malaret suggested to Gramont that, if France should nevertheless persist in seeking Italy's assistance, a boundary rectification could be the means of obtaining it. Recalling that during and after the war of 1866 against Austria the Italians had displayed an avid appetite for the Trentino, he concluded that only the prospect of such gains would overcome their reluctance to fight.[28]

Here it was Malaret's turn to be unrealistic: the southern Tyrol, although coveted by Italy, would never have sufficed as a *quid pro quo*. Napoleon himself had found this out in the course of the secret negotiations for a tripartite alliance. He had urged the Austrians to cede the Trentino to Italy and they had conditionally agreed. But Rome, which they in turn had vainly urged him to evacuate, was the key to success. Unfortunately for Napoleon, it was also of prime concern to the conservative and clerical elements in France on whom his rule depended. Now, confronted by the prospect of a life-and-death struggle with Prussia and anxious above all to make victory doubly certain, he chose the lesser of two evils. Had Malaret known that Napoleon was finally prepared to do something about the Roman roadblock, he undoubtedly would have sounded a different note.

The members of the diplomatic corps in Paris shared Malaret's ignorance of the emperor's intentions. Frequent visitors to the Quai d'Orsay, they were led to expect not a solution but an aggravation of the Roman imbroglio. Lyons, one of the best informed among them, pictured official circles as concerned lest Italy should exploit a Franco-Prussian war to press for the recall of the garrison. Indeed, the British ambassador reported, it was even feared at the Tuileries that, if the Italians should decide that the moment was propitious, they might

27 *Ibid.* (*OD*, XXVIII, No. 8363, p. 174).
28 *Ibid.* (*OD*, XXVIII, No. 8363, p. 176).

attempt to cut the Gordian knot by rushing in to seize the Eternal City. This being so, the French government could not help finding itself impaled on the horns of a most embarrassing dilemma. If any troops were to be kept in Rome, they would have to be numerically strong enough to repel a possible Italian invasion. But any appreciable augmentation of the garrison would mean the loss of a French force "which might be serviceable on the great theatre of hostilities." It was equally plain, however, that if the garrison were withdrawn and the pope left at the mercy of the Italians, Catholic opinion in France would be alienated and the rest of Europe would interpret Napoleon's move as a sign of weakness. To be sure, Lyons conceded, neither Gramont nor Nigra had so far mentioned the subject to him, but he prophesied that the question was very likely to arise "if the present unhappy state of affairs should not improve."[29]

3

Malaret's reaction to the statement of Italy's position had been reasonable enough, but this did not deceive Visconti-Venosta. He knew both Napoleon and Gramont too well to assume even for a moment that they would prove equally understanding or forbearing. Actually, neither the emperor nor his foreign minister had any intention of allowing the matter to rest there.[30] Still counting on Victor Emmanuel, Napoleon remained sanguine of success and was mainly anxious to complete the necessary formalities. Visconti-Venosta was sure the imperial government would waste no time. He also suspected that it would bring pressure to bear via Vienna. This suggested the first counterstep. Immediately after his conversation with Malaret, he conferred with Baron Kübeck, the Austrian minister to Italy. He alluded to France's request for diplomatic assistance, then dwelt at length on her demand for armed help.

[29] Lyons to Granville, July 8, 1870, No. 709, Great Britain, Public Record Office (hereafter cited as PRO), FO 27/1805.

[30] For a belated statement of the French government's reaction to Malaret's report of his conversation with Visconti-Venosta, see Gramont to Malaret, July 12, 1870, No. 19, AMAE, Italie, janvier–juillet 1870, tome 378 (OD, XXVIII, No. 8445, pp. 268–69).

He repeated what he had told Malaret, adding that in any case no decision could be reached until the Italian cabinet had had a chance to deliberate and to ascertain the wishes of Victor Emmanuel. In the meantime, because he was anxious to see Austria and Italy follow the same course, he would welcome an interchange of views with Beust.[31]

Although Visconti-Venosta's principal concern in talking to Kübeck was to set the stage for an Austro-Italian accord to prevent or, failing that, to localize a Franco-Prussian war, he also utilized the conversation to complain that the prolonged occupation of Rome made a mockery of the September Convention, embarrassed the Italian government, and embittered Italian public opinion.[32] As he listened, Kübeck made certain inferences of his own. He deduced from Visconti-Venosta's remarks that the Lanza cabinet, while remaining outwardly deferential to the wishes of France, would in fact yield nothing except on the basis of *do ut des*. It would seek suitable compensation for any deviation from the passive role prescribed by the political interests and internal conditions of the country. At the same time Kübeck noted that the policy of non-intervention not only suited the cautious temperament of Visconti-Venosta but was also marked out for him by the entire Italian press. Throughout the length and breadth of the peninsula newspapers were at one in counseling the country to stay out of other people's quarrels. This was plain even from a casual reading, but Kübeck thought he could likewise detect in the spate of editorials on the subject an unavowed but firm assumption that non-intervention was more likely than not to hasten the French evacuation of Rome.[33]

Visconti-Venosta was careful to point out to Kübeck that the

---

[31] Kübeck to Beust, July 9, 1870, No. 51, Austria-Hungary, Haus-, Hof-, und Staatsarchiv, Politisches Archiv (hereafter cited as HHSA, PA), Italien, Berichte 1870, Karton XI/77.

[32] Telegram from Kübeck to Beust, July 8, 1870, No. 4841/547, *ibid.* This document is reproduced in Hermann Oncken, *Die Rheinpolitik Kaiser Napoleons III von 1863 bis 1870* (3 vols.; Berlin and Leipzig, 1926), III, No. 856, p. 409.

[33] Kübeck to Beust, July 9, 1870, No. 51, HHSA, PA, Italien, Berichte 1870, Karton XI/77.

ultimate fate of the city had not been touched upon either by Malaret or himself. He did not have to add that any discussion of the matter would be premature so long as only one of the parties to the September Convention was fulfilling its obligations. It was to France's cavalier treatment of the pact that the foreign minister naturally and insistently returned. For some time, he observed, Italy had abstained from making a formal complaint. She had appreciated the rather awkward situation that would arise for Napoleon if the issue were to be seized upon by the corps législatif and made the object of a passionately partisan debate. Her restraint had been motivated by a desire for good relations with France. However, it was becoming impossible to ignore the mood of the Italian people. Discontent was widespread, and this placed the government in an untenable position.[34] Visconti-Venosta thus gave the impression that the ministry might be overthrown. Since his hope in doing so was to encourage Austrian co-operation with Italy in all future dealings with France, it was a comfort to him to know that Kübeck had lost no time in telegraphing a summary of their conversation.[35]

4

During the remaining hours of July 8, the foreign minister was busy with other sequents of the French *démarche*. He telegraphed Nigra an account of the conversation with Malaret, asked him for an estimate of the directive from Gramont which Malaret had passed along, and solicited his advice on the entire range of Franco-Italian relations.[36] In accordance with the promise given Malaret, Visconti-Venosta instructed Cerruti to impress upon the Spaniards the expediency of discarding Leopold. Cerruti was to point out that the Italian government would continue to respect the will of the Spanish people. However, he was also to emphasize that the well-being of Spain,

[34] *Ibid.*

[35] The telegram (see n. 32) was sent immediately after the two men separated.

[36] Visconti-Venosta to Nigra, July 8, 1870, No. 1177, MAE, AS, TS.

like that of Italy herself, depended on avoiding a war which the state of public opinion in France rendered altogether possible. But while offering this admonition, Cerruti was to exhibit an appropriate reserve. Nothing he might say or do was to suggest too patently that he was taking the initiative.[37] As Visconti-Venosta put it in a supplementary dispatch, one could not be too circumspect in a matter of such delicacy.[38]

But more than anything else, Italy's vulnerability to French pressure preyed on his mind. It was therefore with a particular sense of urgency that he sought to make sure of England's cooperation. The French government, he telegraphed Cadorna, wanted Italy's assistance in preserving the peace of Europe. Would England conclude with Italy an arrangement for joint action to resolve the crisis? Cadorna was to see Lord Granville, who had just succeeded the late Lord Clarendon as foreign secretary, then report the views and intentions of the British government.[39] A partnership with London, surely as eager as Florence to localize a Franco-Prussian war if it could not be prevented, was the necessary complement of an understanding with Austria. Together, they would form the keystone of Italian security.

Just how soon such bulwarking might be needed became frighteningly clear that evening. A telegram from Nigra reported that there was still no reply from Prussia and that within the next twenty-four hours an order would go out for the mobilization of the French army.[40] Visconti-Venosta's reaction was that only a speedy withdrawal by Leopold could keep the crisis from getting out of hand. But a telegram from Launay which arrived not long after Nigra's afforded little ground for supposing that the prince would be so obliging. It was also plain, according to Launay, that King William had no intention

37 Visconti-Venosta to Cerruti, July 8, 1870, No. 1176, ibid.

38 Visconti-Venosta to Cerruti, July 8, 1870, No. 1, MAE, AS, Archivi di gabinetto (1861–1887), busta 219: guerra franco-prussiana e trattative segrete 8 luglio–14 settembre 1870, fascicolo 4.

39 Visconti-Venosta to Cadorna, July 8, 1870, No. 1178, MAE, AS, TS.

40 Nigra to Visconti-Venosta, July 8, 1870, No. 2358, MAE, AS, DTA.

of contributing to a peaceful settlement. As for Bismarck, he continued to take an evasive line, arguing as before that the Hohenzollern candidature was not Prussia's concern, that she had nothing whatever to discuss with either the Spaniards or Leopold (the latter was of age and a free agent), and that she was in no way responsible for the present situation. Similarly, Juan Antonio Rascón, the Spanish minister in Berlin, was assuring everyone that Prussia, true to her oft-reiterated professions of disinterestedness, had decided to wash her hands of the whole affair. In view of Prussia's attitude, Launay advised Visconti-Venosta to concentrate on Madrid. Pressure should be exerted there with the object of influencing if possible the vote in the Cortes. This could be crucial. If the pro-Hohenzollern majority turned out to be small, William might yet be induced to talk to Leopold. Of course, if he counseled his errant but obedient kinsman to renounce the Spanish throne, the squabble between France and Prussia would automatically be over. The British court, thanks to family ties between Queen Victoria and the Hohenzollerns, was in the best position to sway the Prussian sovereign. In the meanwhile, it was imperative that the French should show some self-control.[41]

With this last observation Visconti-Venosta could not have agreed more. That he had been shaken by Nigra's telegram was evident from the language of Alberto Blanc, the general secretary of the Italian foreign ministry. On the night of the eighth, Blanc told Count Georg von Wesdehlen, the Prussian chargé d'affaires (the Prussian minister to Italy, Count Brassier de Saint Simon, was absent on leave), that the attitude of France was causing very grave anxiety. Not content with pressing Prussia to countermand Leopold's acceptance of the Spanish crown, she was about to mobilize her armed forces.[42] Another indication of Visconti-Venosta's state of mind was pro-

[41] Launay to Visconti-Venosta, July 8, 1870, No. 2360, *ibid.*

[42] Telegram from Wesdehlen to Bismarck, July 9, 1870, Robert H. Lord, *The Origins of the War of 1870: New Documents from the German Archives* (Cambridge, Mass., 1924), No. 66, pp. 162–63.

vided by the *Opinione*. The French, it complained, were prepared to fight unless they had their way. They must somehow be induced to allow time for a diplomatic solution. As for Prussia, it was to be hoped that she would decline to become involved in a war whose only rationale, from her point of view, was the installation of a Prussian princeling on a foreign throne.[43]

[43] *L'Opinione*, July 9, 1870.

CHAPTER THREE

THE AOSTA CANDIDATURE

During the predawn hours of July 9, the tensely awaited forecast of how the voting in the Cortes was likely to go reached the Italian foreign office. Cerruti, who had made a hurried but reasonably thorough study, estimated that Gramont's declaration before the corps législatif had hurt the prospects of the Hohenzollern candidature, diminishing somewhat the number of its parliamentary supporters. Nonetheless, and despite the threatening language of Baron Mercier de Lostende, the French ambassador, Prim was telling his subordinates that he intended to go ahead with the plans as announced. The Cortes was scheduled to assemble on July 20, and the election itself was fixed for August 1. With final action near, Prim continued to count on a comfortable majority. To be sure, his adversaries, who called themselves the friends of peace, were busily rallying deputies to their side, but the opposition still seemed much too weak to prevent the choice of Prince Leopold.[1]

Visconti-Venosta was not surprised. The prediction that Prim would persist despite mounting French pressure and that the Hohenzollern candidature would win out in the Spanish parliament dovetailed altogether too well with other black items that had recently been transmitted to Florence: Launay's guess that King William would refuse to help and Nigra's report of an impending mobilization of the French army. The morning of the ninth was further marred by the arrival of depressing intelligence from Paris. In a review of the situation, Nigra cited

[1] Cerruti to Visconti-Venosta, July 8, 1870, No. 2362, MAE, AS, DTA. This telegram was received in Florence at 1:55 A.M. on the ninth.

38

data collected by the local prefecture of police which indicated overwhelming popular support for the government in the event of a war with Prussia.[2] As everyone knew, Napoleon's vulnerability to the whims of public opinion was matched by his need to restore the fading prestige of his regime. He could depend on both Ollivier and Gramont, who were loyal servants of the dynasty. These men, as Nigra observed to the Prussian chargé d'affaires in Paris, Count Eberhard von Solms, seemed bent on exploiting the Spanish affair for ulterior political purposes.[3]

Disheartening information also came from Berlin. In a lengthy dispatch Launay detailed the unco-operative attitude of the Prussian government.[4] It seemed plainer than ever that, short of a miraculous turnabout, no help in resolving the impasse was to be expected from either King William or Bismarck. Thus all three parties to the quarrel—Spain, France, and Prussia—appeared loath to do anything that might facilitate the work of mediation. But despite the tenor of Cerruti's last report, Visconti-Venosta was inclined to think that, if a peace-saving gesture was to materialize before the situation became irretrievable, it would have to be extracted from the Spaniards. Prim, although a formidable antagonist when driven into a corner, was also reputed to be a bluffer. Besides, his country was weak and divided, and he himself had powerful enemies who were waiting for a chance to destroy him. To be sure, it would be dangerous for him to abandon a candidature to which he had so thoroughly committed himself. Apart from the blow to his prestige, he would have to reckon with the chagrin that most Spaniards would feel at the collapse of still another attempt to solve the nation's paramount problem. On the other hand, the tremendous harm that France was in a position to inflict, together with the displeasure and pressure of at least some of the other powers, could sap Prim's seeming

2 Nigra to Visconti-Venosta, July 6, 1870, No. 1179, MAE, AS, Serie politica (1867–1888), Francia, busta 1307: 1869–1870.

3 Solms to Bismarck, July 7, 1870, Lord, No. 41, pp. 147–48.

4 Launay to Visconti-Venosta, July 5, 1870, No. 578, MAE, AS, Serie politica (1867–1888), Prussia, busta 1328: 1867–1870.

resolve to resist, and it was not at all unlikely that he would end up by capitulating.

In the hope of hastening the process, Visconti-Venosta talked with unwonted bluntness to Montemar. The Spanish envoy came to see him shortly before noon on the ninth, and the conversation turned immediately to the question of the Hohenzollern candidature. After a rather perfunctory reiteration of the Italian government's respect for the will of the Spanish people, Visconti-Venosta cited the hazards of the situation. Spain, he said, was on the verge of a decision that could make war inevitable. At such a moment she must weigh all the possible consequences. If, by her continued support of Leopold's candidature, she should bring on a conflict, she would assume an enormous responsibility. She would also expose herself to great peril, for larger interests were bound to come into play, and to these she might find herself sacrificed.[5]

Montemar made no reply. Shortly after he had hurried away, Sir Augustus Paget, the British minister to Italy, was ushered into the foreign office. Visconti-Venosta welcomed the opportunity to talk with Paget, whose co-operation and good judgment he had come to value. Besides, there was something rather special that he wanted to convey to the British government. First he recounted his remarks to Montemar, then discussed Malaret's visit. He alluded to the French request for support in Madrid and underlined the affirmative character of his response. It was distressingly plain, he went on, that France would make war on Prussia if the Cortes ratified the Hohenzollern candidature. Since everything seemed to depend on what the members of that body would do, the knot of the question must be considered to be in Madrid.[6] Berlin, however, should not be neglected; there, Visconti-Venosta pointed out,

[5] Visconti-Venosta to Cerruti, July 9, 1870, No. 4, MAE, AS, Archivi di gabinetto (1861–1887), busta 219: guerra franco-prussiana e trattative segrete 8 luglio–14 settembre 1870, fascicolo 4.

[6] Paget to Granville, July 9, 1870, *British and Foreign State Papers 1869–1870* (London, 1876), LX, 824–25, 826.

"the advice of Her Majesty's Government was more likely to be listened to . . . than that of any other Government."[7]

He was particularly anxious to impress upon Paget the nature of the line which he represented the Italian government as taking with the Spaniards. It was insisting that it had no desire to interfere with their acknowledged right to do as they pleased about the choice of a sovereign. But inasmuch as neither the Spanish nation nor the Cortes had as yet been consulted, Italy was using this interval to point out how important it was, from the point of view of Spain's own interests, to make sure that the advent of a new king would not be the cause of a European conflagration. More than that, Italy was already telling Madrid that she would always be ready to combine with other powers for the purpose of assisting the Spaniards "in the solution of the embarrassment in which they might be placed in regard to the future constitutional organization of their country should they forego the candidature of Prince Hohenzollern."[8] In other words, Italy would be prepared to associate herself with an international effort to find Spain another candidate if Leopold were discarded. This was obviously a significant commitment.

Actually, Visconti-Venosta had not yet said anything of the kind to the Spaniards, but he did expect to do so. First, however, he wanted Paget's reaction. During the past few hours he had been turning over in his mind the idea of reviving the candidature of the Duke of Aosta, who had ranked so high in Prim's hierarchy of preferences. He did not know whether Amadeus would be any more receptive now than he had been before, and he had not discussed the matter with any of his cabinet colleagues or with the king. Consequently, it was perfectly possible that the whole thing would come to nought. But Visconti-Venosta had a suspicion that in view of the seriousness of the crisis and the dangers that might befall Italy in the event of a Franco-Prussian war, both the duke and the

[7] Paget to Granville, July 9, 1870, No. 4, PRO, FO 45/164.

[8] Paget to Granville, July 9, 1870, *British and Foreign State Papers 1869–1870,* LX, 825–26.

majority of the ministers, who until now had dreaded to see the House of Savoy become entangled in the Spanish imbroglio, would prove more amenable. As for Victor Emmanuel, he had all along favored the seating of an Italian prince on the Spanish throne—the candidature of both the Duke of Aosta and the Duke of Genoa had received his warmest blessings—and there was no reason to suppose that he felt differently now. If Prim and Serrano were given to understand that such a solution, which they had previously welcomed, was in the offing and that a retreat, far from exposing them to further humiliation, would be accompanied by a brilliant success in their quest for a new king, they might not hesitate to rid themselves of Prince Leopold.

2

By an interesting coincidence, the idea of reviving the Aosta candidature also occurred to Great Britain's able and indefatigable minister in Madrid, Austen Henry Layard. As soon as he learned that Leopold had been offered the crown, Layard, who was genuinely attached to Spain and worried about her future, began to rack his brains for an honorable way out of the crisis. On July 6, after a lengthy conversation with Prim, he wrote Granville that if circumstances had not intervened to make a speedy decision imperative, the marshal would have welcomed encouragement to try again for a prince of the House of Savoy, and that negotiations to this end might have been reopened with the king of Italy. As a matter of fact, the name of the Duke of Aosta had recently reappeared in the Spanish press, and for a multitude of reasons the nation would have preferred him to a prince of German origin.[9]

When Granville was apprised of Gramont's declaration before the corps législatif, he sent Layard the following telegram:[10]

The step taken by the Provisional Government of offering the sovereignty of Spain to the Hereditary Prince of Hohenzollern appears

[9] Layard to Her Majesty's Principal Secretary of State, Foreign Office, July 6, 1870, No. 202, confidential, PRO, FO 72/1234.

[10] Granville to Layard, July 6, 1870, unnumbered, PRO, FO 72/1231.

to be viewed with great disfavour in France. It is not for England to recommend any particular sovereign for Spain, or in any way to interfere with the choice of the Spanish people; but wishing as they do, well to Spain, Her Majesty's Government cannot but feel anxious as to the consequences of the selection now made, which has called forth a very decided declaration this day to the French Chambers as to the view which the French Government would take of the election if persevered in.

This communication reached Layard during the morning of the seventh. Later in the day he received a second telegram from the foreign minister. It was brief but most explicit:[11]

Use every pressure, which will not offend the Spanish Government, but which, in your judgment, will promote the abandonment of the Hohenzollern project. You will say nothing that would provoke them to adhere to it.

Layard was delighted to comply. He was convinced that the advent of Leopold would plunge the country into civil war. In his opinion, the only way to prevent a fratricidal struggle or a republic or both was to lay before the Cortes the name of another candidate who would be acceptable to the Spanish people and to all the great powers. This would have to be done without delay. As for the identity of such a substitute, the attitude of Prim indicated unmistakably that the Duke of Aosta would be the happiest choice, although of course that reluctant prince would first have to be induced to change his mind about the crown which he had turned down so peremptorily eighteen months before. Layard planned to go into the matter with both Prim and Práxedes M. Sagasta, the Spanish foreign minister. But before making arrangements to see them, he decided to pay a call on Mercier de Lostende. He wished to ascertain whether his French colleague had already taken steps about which he should know when he addressed himself to the task that Granville wanted done. The two men conferred on July 9. Choosing his words carefully, Layard put the following question to Mercier: would the French government help the Span-

[11] This telegram is reproduced in No. 3, Granville to Layard, July 7, 1870, *ibid.*

iards find some other prince for the throne if Leopold were jettisoned? Mercier read Layard's mind, for he answered that France would not object to the accession of an Italian prince. He even mentioned the Duke of Aosta, adding that Napoleon, when consulted about the candidature of the Duke of Genoa, had exhibited a sympathetic attitude toward the House of Savoy. However, Mercier suggested that any counsel of this sort should come from Great Britain, which was on exceptionally good terms with the Spaniards. If the Gladstone cabinet were to volunteer its good offices and offer to seek Aosta's consent, Prim and his associates might yet be induced to abandon Leopold.[12]

Of course Layard agreed.[13] He did not discover then nor did he find out later whether Mercier had mentioned the subject to the French government.[14] But he was encouraged by a confidential communication from Cerruti, who said there was reason to believe that Aosta "would . . . be more inclined to accept the Spanish Crown at this time than he had been when the offer was first made to him."[15] Why Cerruti, who had not yet received anything on this from Visconti-Venosta, should already have thought so is not clear. At all events, Layard felt justified in going ahead because he had learned that Prim was definitely considering a return to the Aosta candidature.[16]

Shortly past midday on the ninth, Layard alerted his superiors by dispatching the following telegram to Granville:[17]

If the Spanish Government were to promise to find the means to prevent the election of Hohenzollern, would Her Majesty's Government, on the other hand, be inclined to promise the Spanish Government their assistance in obtaining the assent of the Duke of Aosta, if an offer were made to him of the Crown? There appear to be two

[12] Layard to Granville, July 10, 1870, No. 9, confidential, PRO, FO 72/1234.

[13] *Ibid.*

[14] See Layard to Granville, July 14, 1870, No. 22, secret, PRO, FO 72/1235.

[15] *Ibid.*   [16] *Ibid.*

[17] The text of this telegram is reproduced in No. 6, Layard to Granville, July 9, 1870, PRO, FO 72/1234.

ways out of the present difficulty: either to get the King of Prussia, as the head of the family, to refuse his assent to the acceptance of the Crown by his relative, a solution at which the Regent [Serrano] has hinted, or to prevent the Prince having the requisite majority in the Cortes; this the Spanish Government could manage. The French Ambassador has told Prim that the election of Hohenzollern would inevitably lead to war. I am to see Prim late today, after a Council of Ministers.

Before closeting himself with the marshal, Layard reviewed the situation with Sagasta. He painted a disconsolate picture. The situation, Sagasta agreed, was far from cheering: ". . . unless Her Majesty's Government would suggest a way for Spain to get out of the difficulty with honour, and any suggestion coming from Her Majesty's Government would receive the utmost consideration—he did not see what else there was to be done but to present the Prince to the Cortes and to be prepared for the consequences."[18] Sagasta did not mention Aosta, but it was plain that he was thinking of the duke when he alluded to the possibility of an honorable escape.

Taking leave of the foreign minister, Layard awaited the rendezvous with Prim. Just before they met, he managed to have a short conversation with Moret y Prendergast, the minister of the colonies. Significantly enough, Moret at once asked Layard whether,

if a way could be found by which the candidature of the Prince of Hohenzollern could be put aside, the English Government would be disposed to help the Spanish Government to find another candidate for the throne, as this was an absolute necessity—for instance, would they endeavour to obtain the consent of the Duke of Aosta to accept the Crown?

Layard replied that he had no authority whatsoever to express an opinion on this matter. But, speaking quite unofficially, he wondered whether the Spanish government would consent to give up the Hohenzollern candidature if the British government undertook to approach the Duke of Aosta. Moret's reaction was all that could have been desired. Without any hesita-

18 Layard to Granville, July 10, 1870, No. 9, confidential, *ibid.*

tion whatsoever he promised to make the replacement of Leopold by Amadeus a cabinet question.[19]

Layard was enormously heartened. Moret's attitude showed that among the leading politicians of Madrid, the first defiant resolve to push ahead with the Hohenzollern candidature regardless of the consequences had been succeeded by a desperate anxiety to extricate the Spanish government as gracefully as possible from the week-old crisis. Layard was struck anew with the completeness of the change when he finally saw Prim. Although the latter was still seething with rage over Gramont's declaration before the corps législatif, he readily dropped that subject and proceeded, in response to some prodding by Layard, to insist that he was not a whit less enthusiastic about Aosta than he had been before. To prove this, he related some of the lengths to which he had gone in his previous efforts to woo the duke. The possible alternatives having been defined, Layard put the following question to Prim: "Can anything be done to enable the Spanish Government to retreat with honour and dignity?" The marshal answered that he had already set the stage for such a withdrawal by informing Salustiano de Olózaga, the Spanish ambassador in Paris, that the cabinet of Madrid was prepared to seek "any lane" out of the controversy with France provided the honor and safety of Spain remained inviolate. He assured Layard that he was ready to expedite matters by giving serious consideration to any proposal that the British government might care to make.[20]

Having got what he wanted, Layard hurried to place the issue squarely before his government. The telegram which he sent to Granville that evening minced no words, but it also made out Prim's position to be less tractable than it actually was. Knowing the reluctance with which the British cabinet ordinarily moved in such matters, Layard darkened the picture in order to accelerate the tempo of decision in London. He wrote:[21]

I find Prim very determined. He says that the speech of the Duc de Gramont has greatly exasperated the Spanish people and army,

[19] *Ibid.*   [20] *Ibid.*

[21] Reproduced in No. 10, Layard to Granville, July 11, 1870, *ibid.*

and has rendered a retreat on the part of the Government impossible. He and his colleagues, and even the Regent, are prepared to sacrifice anything but their honour and the safety of their country. To throw over their candidate would be dishonourable; to resign would be to cause civil war and probably the proclamation of the Republic. The only way out of the difficulty would be for England to prevail upon the King of Prussia to withhold his consent to the acceptance of the Crown by the Prince of Hohenzollern, who could then, on the plea of State necessity and duty to the King, withdraw his consent. Prim would not even then answer for the consequences, but he and his colleagues would do their best to maintain order in the country. If the Prince is put to the vote, he feels certain that, after the Duc de Gramont's speech, he will have a considerable majority in the Cortes. He and the Regent are willing to give their best consideration to any arrangement that you may propose, and to adopt it if possible.—The Duke of Aosta would be acceptable now, if the Prince of Hohenzollern could retire in a manner not offensive to the dignity of the country. Prim has instructed Olózaga to say that even now the Spanish Government would be willing to retreat if they could find an honourable way of doing so.

Thus, at the very moment that Paget heard Visconti-Venosta affirm the willingness of the Italian government to co-operate in any international effort to extricate the Spaniards from the embarrassment which the abandonment of Leopold would cause them, Layard had already begun to prepare the ground for a British *démarche* in support of a renewal of the Aosta candidature. It was clear to Paget, when Visconti-Venosta had finished, that the House of Savoy was destined to re-enter the seemingly interminable drama of the Spanish succession. "Perhaps," the British envoy now observed, "Italy might be disposed to provide a future Sovereign for Spain."[22] Visconti-Venosta, who had been waiting for this cue, responded with unwonted expansiveness. It was necessary, he said, to put one's self in the position of the Spanish leaders. They "had knocked at almost every door in Europe for a Sovereign and had met with nothing but refusals and rebuffs." Consequently, the governments that were counseling abandonment of the Hohen-

[22] Paget to Granville, July 10, 1870, No. 5, secret and confidential, PRO, FO 45/64.

zollern candidature must do more than offer advice. They must assist the Spaniards "in placing the future of their country upon a monarchical basis, which was evidently the one desired by the Spanish people." The primary goal was of course "the avoidance of war"; nothing should be left undone to attain that objective. Coming to the crux of the matter, Visconti-Venosta remarked that there was reason to believe that the Spanish government "might be more disposed to give up the Prince of Hohenzollern, if another Prince could be offered as a substitute."[23] In answer to Paget's query, he examined the question of Italy's possible role:[24]

His Excellency alluded to the invincible repugnance which had been manifested by the Duke of Aosta to accepting the Crown at the time it had been offered, and said he had not the smallest reason for supposing that this repugnance had since then diminished, as he . . . had had no communication with His Royal Highness on the subject. He had highly approved His Royal Highness's refusal at the time, but His Excellency admitted . . . that if it became a question of saving Europe from the calamities of war, the case would present itself in a different light from that in which it had been possible to view it when the offer of the throne had been made to His Royal Highness. This, however, . . . was only his own personal view, for he had not exchanged one word with any one of his colleagues on the subject.

Here the conversation ended, but Paget decided to seek further details before broaching the matter to his own government. During the afternoon of the ninth, he sent a telegraphic message to London that touched upon other subjects exclusively: Visconti-Venosta's exchange with Malaret and Nigra's report that the French army was about to be mobilized.[25] When Paget returned to the Italian foreign office to resume the discussion, he mentioned the Duke of Genoa as well as Aosta. The response elicited by his searching questions satisfied him that formal overtures were now in order. It was his belief that

if the idea of the Duke of Aosta or the Duke of Genoa . . . were revived, and an appeal were made by the Spanish Government to

23 *Ibid.*   24 *Ibid.*
25 Reproduced in No. 2, Paget to Granville, July 9, 1870, *ibid.*

that of Italy to furnish one of the above Princes for the Throne of Spain, Visconti-Venosta would for his part, in his anxious desire for the maintenance of peace, be favourably disposed to entertain that appeal. . . .[26]

Paget naturally assumed that the British government would want to co-operate, but at the same time he advised a maximum of caution in order to increase the chances of success. Specifically, he suggested that before the Spanish government was encouraged to take any steps toward a renewal of the Italian candidature, the cabinet of Florence, as distinguished from its only member who had so far declared himself, should be requested to state in advance what answer it would give to Madrid.[27]

At 6:00 P.M., as soon as he was back in the British legation, Paget sent Granville a telegram in which he sketched the latest developments and requested permission to make a formal overture to the Italian government:[28]

An observation of Visconti's as to his desire of aiding Spain out of her embarrassment while urging her to abandon Prince Hohenzollern induced me to inquire if Italy would not perhaps be disposed to find her a King. His reply was very reserved, but I am inclined to think that if an appeal were made from the Spanish Government for either the Duke of Aosta or Genoa the Italian Government, in order to prevent war, might try to induce one of these Princes to accept. Shall I ask the question more clearly?

Thus, on the night of July 9, Granville found himself the recipient of earnest entreaties on precisely the same subject from his envoys in Madrid and Florence.

3

In the meanwhile, Visconti-Venosta prepared in his own fashion to pave the way for a revival of the Aosta candidature; unlike Paget, he at no time included the Duke of Genoa in his

[26] Paget to Granville, July 10, 1870, No. 5, secret and confidential, *ibid.*

[27] *Ibid.*

[28] Reproduced in No. 3, Paget to Granville, July 9, 1870, secret and confidential, *ibid.*

plans. He informed Nigra that a warning to Madrid about the grave consequences of its decisions had been accompanied by an assurance of help from Italy if the warning were heeded. Italy had made it clear that she was prepared, in conjunction with other peace-loving countries, to seek a way by which the Spaniards might safely and even advantageously disentangle themselves from their present difficulties.[29] In a message to Cerruti, Visconti-Venosta stressed the sincerity of Italy's desire to be of assistance. Cerruti was to insist with the Spaniards that they must have faith in the Italian government, which would like nothing better than to co-operate in the quest for a satisfactory solution.[30] To his envoy in London Visconti-Venosta strongly underscored the point that the powers should concert among themselves how they might help Spain to find a way out. If Great Britain believed that something could be done, Italy would be pleased to reach an understanding with her. Cadorna was to make this plain to Granville.[31]

As soon as he had taken these preparatory steps, Visconti-Venosta concentrated on the two hurdles that remained. One was the possible if not probable unwillingness of Aosta to reconsider his earlier decision. The other was the manifest reluctance of the majority of the Italian cabinet to see the country drawn into the Spanish maelstrom. To do something about the first, the aid of the king would of course have to be enlisted, although just how much Victor Emmanuel could accomplish was problematical in view of the son's well-known capacity to resist parental pressure on this as on other matters. The monarch's help would also be needed with the cabinet majority. Here the influence he wielded could prove decisive,

[29] Visconti-Venosta to Nigra, July 9, 1870, No. 1182, MAE, AS, TS. See also Nigra, p. 97.

[30] Visconti-Venosta to Cerruti, July 9, 1870, No. 1180, MAE, AS, TS; Visconti-Venosta to Cerruti, July 9, 1870, No. 4, MAE, AS, Archivi di gabinetto (1861–1887), busta 219: guerra franco-prussiana e trattative segrete 8 luglio–14 settembre 1870, fascicolo 4.

[31] Visconti-Venosta to Cadorna, July 9, 1870, No. 1181, MAE, AS, TS; Visconti-Venosta to Cadorna, July 9, 1870, No. 3, MAE, AS, Archivi di gabinetto (1861–1887), busta 219: guerra franco-prussiana e trattative segrete 8 luglio–14 settembre 1870, fascicolo 4.

yet it seemed likely that a vigorous battle would nonetheless ensue. The sole certainty in the situation—from the outset Visconti-Venosta counted heavily on it— was the king's burning desire to enhance the fortunes and prestige of the House of Savoy. He wanted to make his family the first or second in Europe; by annexing the crown of Spain he would go far toward achieving his aim.

At 6:30 p.m., an hour or so after his second conversation with Paget, Visconti-Venosta addressed the following telegram to Victor Emmanuel, who had left Florence at the beginning of the month and was enjoying the delights of hunting at Valsavaranche, his beloved retreat in the Piedmontese Alps:[32]

If the name of the Duke of Aosta is brought up in the course of the current negotiations, I should like to have Your Majesty's authorization to follow the path that would thus open before us. This would be the best solution. However, in order to obtain the right result, assuming that that is still possible, it will be necessary to proceed with the utmost prudence. The Duke of Aosta cannot present himself as the candidate imposed by French pressure. We must endeavor to make the idea come from the Spanish government, and the indispensable condition of success is absolute secrecy.

Inasmuch as Victor Emmanuel's forays into the mountainous forests surrounding Valsavaranche often rendered him incommunicado for hours at a time, a reply to this message might not arrive for a good while; and, until it came, the cabinet could not be sounded.

In the interim Visconti-Venosta busied himself with the manifold aspects of what seemed to be a rapidly deteriorating international situation. Citing the extraordinary gravity of the crisis, he ordered Caracciolo to remain at his post[33] (the marquis had been promised an early leave of absence). It was assumed in Florence that Prince Aleksandr Gorchakov, the Russian foreign minister, would want to join other governments in an attempt to avert a Franco-Prussian war or to prevent it from

---

[32] E. Mayor des Planches, "Re Vittorio Emanuele II alla vigilia della guerra del settanta (con documenti inediti)," *Nuova antologia*, CCV (1920), 344.

[33] Visconti-Venosta to Caracciolo, July 9, 1870, No. 1179, MAE, AS, TS.

spreading if mediation proved futile. At all events, the Italian government deemed it wise to keep a man of Caracciolo's experience in St. Petersburg until the situation had had time to crystallize. So he stayed on, although, as it turned out, he had very little to do. The south German states—Bavaria, Württemberg, and Baden—likewise attracted a share of Visconti-Venosta's attention. For a number of reasons their attitude could be of considerable influence in a crisis that pitted Prussia, the leader of the movement for German unification, against France, the traditional enemy of Germany but also the protector of German particularism. Recognizing the special factors at play here as well as the potential importance of the region, Visconti-Venosta turned to his envoys in Munich, Stuttgart, and Karlsruhe. What he wanted from them was information that would help him to assess with some degree of accuracy the trends of public sentiment in the three south German capitals.[34] Needless to say, however, the restiveness of the French continued to be at the center of his concern. In the hope of tranquilizing Paris even a little, he recapitulated to Malaret the admonitory line he was taking with the Spaniards. They were being warned of the tragic consequences that would befall them and the rest of Europe if they persisted in their ill-advised decision to bestow the kingship upon Leopold.[35]

Definitely the most encouraging sign at the moment was Prim's receptivity to the idea of reviving the Aosta candidature. Visconti-Venosta had learned about the marshal's attitude in time to take it into account in charting his next moves. Another bit of cheer came in a telegram from Cerruti, who had revised somewhat his previous estimate of what was likely to happen in the Spanish parliament. He was now inclined to think that the election of Leopold, although still highly probable, was no longer a foregone conclusion. It was all but impossible, he conceded, to visualize in advance the ensemble of factors that might affect the currents of public opinion and the behavior of

[34] Visconti-Venosta to the legations in Karlsruhe, Stuttgart, and Munich, July 9, 1870, No. 1183, *ibid.*

[35] See the telegram from Malaret to Gramont, July 9, 1870, AMAE, Italie, janvier–juillet 1870, tome 378 (*OD*, XXVIII, No. 8350, p. 146).

the Cortes.[36] He thus implied that the nation and the deputies as well as the government might deem it expedient if not imperative to give way before the concerted pressure from the outside. On the other hand, there were some who postulated the opposite or at least did not rule out the possibility that mounting pressures within the country would compel Prim to remain steadfast in his support of the Hohenzollern candidature. A telegram from Count Camillo de Barral, the Italian minister to Belgium, seemed to suggest that the marshal's hand might yet be forced by his own countrymen. Barral reported that his Spanish colleague, who was evidently thought to be a good barometer in such matters, was quite rabid on the subject of honoring the commitment to Leopold whether France liked it or not.[37]

If Prim should prove unable or unwilling to resist the angry insistence of Leopold's partisans, and if as a consequence he should have to be subjected to additional pressure from abroad, could the crisis be made to stand still long enough to permit further intercession in Madrid? The precipitancy of the French government, its hurry to begin military preparations, had brought the question of war and peace to the brink of decision. Visconti-Venosta hardly needed Nigra to tell him this, but the envoy, flitting incessantly between the Quai d'Orsay and the Italian legation, kept interlarding his reports with prophecies of imminent catastrophe. In one of his telegrams he declared that everything hinged on the attitude of King William, whose complaisance was no longer being taken for granted in Paris. The French ambassador to Prussia, Count Vincent Benedetti, was to see William at Ems. If the conversation, which was scheduled for some time on the ninth, should prove inconclusive, or if the king should definitely refuse to disavow Leopold's candidature, then within twenty-four hours the French government would publish the order to mobilize.[38]

On the heels of this communication came a second from

[36] Cerruti to Visconti-Venosta, July 9, 1870, No. 2363, MAE, AS, DTA.

[37] Barral to Visconti-Venosta, July 9, 1870, No. 2364, *ibid.*

[38] Nigra to Visconti-Venosta, July 9, 1870, No. 2365, *ibid.*

Nigra. After pondering Malaret's *démarche*, he had decided that Visconti-Venosta's answer was the only possible one that could be given at this particular stage of the crisis. The fact that papal territory was still under French military occupation barred Italy from saying any more. If Napoleon wished to settle the Roman question, on which the future of Franco-Italian relations depended, it was up to him to take the initiative and come forward with concrete proposals. But, instead, Gramont had merely duplicated Malaret's move by querying the Italian legation in Paris on the question of an alliance. Under the circumstances, Nigra saw no need for fresh instructions from Florence; in reply to this second inquiry, he intended to repeat what Visconti-Venosta had already told Malaret.[39] This, of course, met with Visconti-Venosta's approval, and so Napoleon's follow-up feeler proved no more fruitful than the first.

Despite his Francophile sympathies, Nigra made no attempt to excuse the French. Without circumlocution he admitted that they were bent on drawing the sword. However, he was also persuaded that they were not irrevocably committed to the use of force, that they might still be satisfied with a diplomatic victory provided it was sufficiently complete. Accordingly, he urged Visconti-Venosta to make a supreme effort in Berlin and Madrid. He assigned priority to the Prussian capital because, of all possible solutions, Leopold's voluntary withdrawal would be the best. But in any case, with military preparations already under way or impending, time was obviously of the essence.[40]

Thus, in the view of Nigra, the campaign to save the peace of Europe was necessarily a race against the clock. Visconti-Venosta was not the only one to whom the veteran envoy unburdened himself. He sought out Solms, who was still filling in for Werther. The Prussian chargé was a genuine partisan of peace. Distressed by the warlike spirit around him, he was the last person to play down the gravity of the situation. Nevertheless, Nigra bombarded him with warnings in the hope that he

[39] Unnumbered private telegram from Nigra to Visconti-Venosta, July 9, 1870, MAE, AS, Archivi di gabinetto (1861–1887), busta 219: guerra franco-prussiana e trattative segrete 8 luglio–14 settembre 1870, fascicolo 4.
[40] *Ibid.*

would use even stronger language when he reported to his superiors. It was barely possible that they still did not grasp the intensity of France's resolve to lose not a moment in declaring war if nothing was done about Leopold's ambitions.[41] In addition, to an unnamed intimate who relayed this to Solms, Nigra went out of his way to predict that in the event of a Franco-Prussian war, Italy would have no choice but to behave ungratefully toward Prussia and to align herself with France.[42] This was not merely intended for Prussian consumption; Nigra really believed it.

Although a man of stable outlook, the rapid flux and shifts that marked this crisis occasionally caught him off balance. His handling of Gramont's disavowal of the remarks attributed to Ollivier was one example. Now he exhibited a similar tendency to tack. No sooner had he urged Visconti-Venosta to concentrate on both the Prussians and the Spaniards, though more on the former than on the latter, than he came to a different and, as it turned out, far more astute conclusion. The Prussophobia that had reared its head in Paris from the very beginning of the crisis was quickly becoming so rampant that the truth commenced to dawn on Nigra: so far as the imperial government was concerned, satisfaction in regard to the Hohenzollern candidature would have to come from Prussia rather than from Spain. The full import of this did not become plain to him until later, but the glimmering he had was enough. He promptly implored his chief virtually to ignore the Spaniards and to give undivided attention to the Prussians. However, a pitifully small amount of time remained. It was now July 9. In forty-eight hours, if by then Leopold's acceptance of the Spanish crown had not been countermanded by King William, there would be war.[43]

Nigra's eagerness to see more pressure brought to bear on the Prussians was not interpreted in Florence as signifying that the removal of the Hohenzollern candidature by some other

41 Solms to Bismarck, July 10, 1870, Lord, No. 96, p. 181.

42 *Ibid.*

43 Nigra to Visconti-Venosta, July 9, 1870, No. 2366, MAE, AS, DTA.

procedure would not suffice. At all events, Visconti-Venosta wondered whether there would be enough time to do anything in Berlin. Influenced by Nigra's own appraisal of the situation, he calculated that even forty-eight hours might be an overly sanguine estimate. France was evidently hurrying toward full mobilization. If the reports emanating from Paris were true, she would refuse to allow either the Prussians or the Spaniards a sufficient interval in which to get free of the present entanglement. As for his own favorite solution, collective mediation by the powers, its chances too seemed to have been all but destroyed by France's precipitancy.

Visconti-Venosta remarked on this in a dispatch to Nigra.[44] His mood was doleful, but he intended all the same to make the maximum use of whatever breathing space might still be left. In particular, although France's unwillingness to accept satisfaction from anyone except the Prussians was not yet apparent to him, he agreed that it was now imperative to take a far stiffer line in Berlin. Launay was therefore not only instructed to join other foreign envoys, notably the British ambassador, in offering to mediate the Franco-Prussian quarrel; he was also authorized to go beyond the circumspect position hitherto assumed toward Prussia in regard to the merits of the controversy and to state quite baldly that the Spanish affair involved, not a German national interest, but only a purely dynastic aspiration of very secondary importance.[45] This amounted to saying that Prussia had no business making a *casus belli* of the Hohenzollern candidature. To be sure, Launay was to emphasize that in view of the relative insignificance of the matter at stake, Italy felt justified in volunteering such advice. He was also reminded by Visconti-Venosta of Italy's duty in any case to participate in all attempts at mediation, for later it must not be said that she had failed to do her utmost on behalf of peace. But these explanations could hardly obscure the fact that this was the first departure from Visconti-Veno-

[44] Visconti-Venosta to Nigra, July 9, 1870, No. 1183, MAE, AS, TS. As the reader will observe, this telegram and the one cited in n. 34 above have the same number.

[45] Visconti-Venosta to Launay, July 9, 1870, No. 1184, *ibid.*

sta's habitual reserve in dealing with the Prussians. Like the blunt admonition to Spain, it seemed to foreshadow a more forceful role for Italian diplomacy.

A similar inference could be drawn from the language of the *Opinione*. The paper duly noted Gramont's insistence that France preferred peace with honor to war, but it scored his contention that, pending the outcome of efforts to end the crisis, France would have to take certain military measures.[46] It was about Prussia, however, that the *Opinione* was particularly outspoken, and the tone as well as the content of its remarks was obviously inspired by Visconti-Venosta. The Prussian government, it complained, was taking the position that the Hohenzollern candidature did not concern it in the least, that Leopold was a free and independent agent who could do exactly as he pleased. This, the *Opinione* objected, was not the issue; rather, it was whether the Prussian government had enough influence to prevent the prince from carrying out a decision that almost certainly would lead to war. Was it possible that the Prussian people would willingly incur such a risk in order to help Leopold obtain a foreign throne? Where in such a venture would lie the interest of Prussia and Germany? Where would one find considerations of sufficient weight to justify the sacrifices and perils of a war with France? Was it over this Prussian princeling that the two great nations of Western Europe would finally come to blows? Admittedly, the violence of France's official language was so deeply resented throughout Germany that a diplomatic solution might no longer be within reach; but it was also possible that the French were fuming not so much over the candidature itself as over the secrecy in which it had been cloaked. The French government had been taken by surprise. This gave the opposition at home a pretext for some telling broadsides, and as a consequence Napoleon was forced to assume a more menacing pose than he might otherwise have done.[47]

Having scolded the two main disputants, but especially Prus-

[46] *L'Opinione*, July 10, 1870.
[47] *Ibid.*

sia, the *Opinione* reverted to a matter that preoccupied Visconti-Venosta: the responsibility of the powers that were hoping to settle the controversy by mediation. It was pointless, the paper urged, to consider ways and means of eliminating the Hohenzollern candidature unless there was also a readiness to explore other possible solutions to the Spanish dynastic problem. Nobody in Spain really wanted Leopold, and he in turn would never manage to lose his Germanness in the midst of subjects who were so passionately xenophobic. Should the Spanish government decide to give him up, it would have every right to ask the powers whether they were prepared to suggest the name of some other prince. The question was no longer a purely Spanish concern; Europe would have to extend a helping hand.[48] Needless to say, the *Opinione* did not mention the Duke of Aosta. But it strongly advised, if Leopold were excluded, that the Cortes be presented with a candidate who would be acceptable to all the powers.[49]

[48] *Ibid.*
[49] *Ibid.*, July 11, 1870.

CHAPTER FOUR

THE ROYAL GAME

The king was now to take a more active part in the proceedings. To understand his role in the summer of 1870, it is necessary to retrace one's steps and go back to the 1860's, specifically to the death of Cavour, the principal architect of Italian unity and the first prime minister of the Italian kingdom. His passing in June, 1861, left a political void that no one was quite able to fill. Into this vacuum stepped Victor Emmanuel. During the years of Cavour's stewardship, the king had learned to curb his autocratic inclinations and to conduct himself in the manner befitting a constitutional monarch. The disappearance of the great statesman altered the situation overnight and permitted the sovereign to give free rein to his penchant for personal rule. Under Cavour's successors, the parliamentary regime which Cavour had worked so hard to consolidate was vitiated by Victor Emmanuel's frequent encroachments upon the powers of the cabinet. Throughout the better part of a decade, the king either dominated the government or influenced it to a very marked degree. This was especially true in regard to diplomatic affairs. As one well-informed observer noted in speaking of this domain: "It is the king who does and directs everything."[1]

Questions of foreign policy, together with military matters, monopolized Victor Emmanuel's attention. Quite understandably, Venetia and the last remnants of the papal monarchy (the

[1] *Le carte di Giovanni Lanza*, IV, 266. See also Engel-Janosi, p. 323; Pietro Pirri, *Pio IX e Vittorio Emanuele II dal loro carteggio privato*. Vol. III: *La questione romana dalla convenzione di settembre alla caduta del potere temporale, 1864–1870* (Rome, 1961), Part 1, p. 224.

Patrimony of St. Peter with Rome at its center) loomed in the
foreground: after 1861 they alone remained outside the con-
fines of the new kingdom. The sovereign, like successive
premiers and cabinets, made the acquisition of these regions
his chief goal. However, he differed from most of his ministers
in one essential respect: whereas they, mindful of Italy's economic and military weakness, hoped to succeed by diplomacy
alone, Victor Emmanuel preferred the arbitrament of war. On
one occasion he remarked to the Prussian crown prince, the
future Frederick III, that fighting was his favorite occupation,
so much so in fact that he planned to make war "as often as
the opportunity presents itself."[2]

A golden opportunity presented itself in 1866, when he
joined Prussia in the war against Austria. Sadowa, followed by
the capitulation of Austria, opened the door to the acquisition
of Venetia. But Victor Emmanuel, although Italy had been
signally unsuccessful on both land and sea, wanted more than
the long-coveted province in the northeast. Shifting his gaze to
the Trentino, he demanded it too. Without it, he contended,
Italy's frontiers in this area would be militarily indefensible.
Napoleon, to whom as go-between this demand was addressed,
rejected it flatly on behalf of the Austrians; and he warned
Victor Emmanuel that if the Italians persisted in their clamor
for additional Hapsburg territory, they would not only forfeit
Venetia but also find France arrayed against them. Supported
by the cabinet and by a thoroughly aroused country, the king
refused to be cowed. The war was prosecuted with renewed
vigor. A force under the command of Garibaldi moved into the
Tyrol and approached the city of Trent. But just as victory for
the hero seemed near, Bismarck signed a truce with the
Austrians. This he did without bothering to consult his allies,
the Italians, who reacted bitterly to the news. An immediate
armistice made sense from Prussia's point of view but not from
Italy's. However, Bismarck's stab in the back coincided with
the catastrophic naval defeat at Lissa. In the circumstances, the
Italian government could hardly afford to spurn the call for a
truce. Yet even now it continued to demand the Trentino as

[2] Engel-Janosi, p. 324.

well as the direct cession of Venetia (France and Austria had agreed that Venetia would first be ceded to France for transmission to Italy).

In the dispute over the Trentino, Austria had both Napoleon and Bismarck on her side. With their approval she ordered the Italians out of the Tyrol and set a time limit of five days. The Italian cabinet, still supported by public opinion, preferred to go on fighting. The army leaders dissented. Advising immediate capitulation, they warned that there would be additional defeats if the fighting continued. Austria, they pointed out, was now free to move all her forces to the Italian front, and in the end even Venetia might be lost. Victor Emmanuel reluctantly agreed. His troops evacuated the Tyrol before the expiration of the ultimatum. The armistice with Austria followed. Victor Emmanuel renounced the Trentino, but only for the time being; he was determined to try again. In the meanwhile, he had obtained Venetia through the intermediary of France. Although Italians resented Napoleon's obtrusion and even decried it as a "humiliating affront,"[3] they greeted the annexation with ecstasy.

The liberation of Venetia satisfied one of the nation's principal aspirations. It also whetted the yearning for Rome. The Italian government, to be sure, had to respect existing international obligations and to exhibit the utmost prudence. But no such restraints fettered the revolutionary fringe of the Sinistra. Seething with impatience, these elements formed insurrectional committees and planned a rising in Rome which would open the way for a Garibaldian invasion. The program of these hotheads threatened to prevail over official policy.[4]

2

Like every sensitive Italian, Victor Emmanuel found the French occupation of Rome extremely wounding. At the same time, he visualized great benefits for Italy from a renewal of

[3] Nola, p. 403.

[4] Franco Valsecchi, "Le potenze europee e la questione romana nel periodo dell'unificazione italiana (1859–1870)," *Storia e politica,* I (1962), 188–89.

the military alliance with Napoleon which in 1859 had launched the peninsula on the road to unification. There were of course limits to the price he was willing to pay for the withdrawal of the French garrison, but if necessary he would make heavy sacrifices. This came to light in 1864, in the negotiations that led to the September Convention. At one point Napoleon insisted that without the transfer of the Italian capital from Turin to a city other than Rome, there could be no treaty. Victor Emmanuel, who was deeply attached to his ancestral seat, refused to move. He adjured Napoleon to relent, but to no avail. Finally and with much ill grace he yielded, stipulating only that Florence must become the new capital. Under the terms of the convention, Italy undertook "not to attack the present territory of the Holy Father and to prevent, by force if necessary, any attack on the said territory coming from without." France promised to withdraw her garrison gradually over a two-year period in order to give the pope sufficient time to organize an army of his own. In an appended protocol, it was provided that the treaty would go into effect as soon as Victor Emmanuel had moved his capital. (The transfer was completed in June, 1865.) In a subsequent exchange of notes, the two governments agreed that in the event of "exceptional contingencies," each would be entitled to resume its freedom of action. Napoleon thus reserved the right to return to Rome if the pope's safety or the integrity of his territory should be menaced.

Such a threat arose in the autumn of 1867, nine months after the withdrawal of the French corps. At the head of hastily recruited volunteers, Garibaldi crossed the papal frontier and prepared to move directly on the Eternal City. To meet this peril, which the conniving Italian government headed by Rattazzi had permitted to burgeon,[5] two French divisions were landed at Civitavecchia and rushed inland. The clash occurred at Mentana, northeast of Rome, on November 3. The Garibaldians wilted before the murderous fire of the new French *chassepots* and fled in confusion. Garibaldi himself was

[5] Rattazzi had allowed the Garibaldian forces to organize and had even secretly supplied them with arms (*ibid.*, p. 189).

arrested and returned to Caprera, his island retreat. The temporal power had been saved, but the September Convention lay in ruins, and Franco-Italian relations plummeted to their lowest point since the cession of Nice and Savoy in 1860. Thereafter a fierce Francophobia characterized some of the most articulate segments of Italian public opinion.[6]

The moment was especially painful for Napoleon. His entire Italian policy was based on the maintenance of a balance between the two conflicting roles he had assumed: on the one hand, protector of the papacy's temporal power; on the other, patron of the Italian national movement. Now the balance had been destroyed: with sword in hand, France had intervened against Italy and in favor of the Holy See. In their bitterness, many Italians ceased to think of Napoleon as the savior of 1859. Instead, they saw in him only the victor of Mentana, the murderer of heroic crusaders for *Roma capitale*. Yet, as the gulf between the Latin countries widened, Napoleon remained chained to his role as "gendarme" of the church.[7]

The conduct of the imperial government was assailed by the veteran statesman and Orleanist leader, Adolphe Thiers. Speaking in the corps législatif in the wake of Mentana, Thiers denounced the errors and contradictions of Napoleon's Italian policy. Eugène Rouher, the head of the imperial cabinet, retorted that French troops would remain in Rome just as long as the safety of the Holy Father required their presence. In the name of his government he declared that Italy would "never" take possession of Rome; France would "never" tolerate such an insult to her honor.[8] These words provoked a new surge of anger throughout the peninsula. The Destra and Sinistra joined in insisting that sooner or later Rome would have to become the capital of the kingdom.[9]

Victor Emmanuel of course lamented the reinstallation of France on papal soil, but he had no patience with the methods

6 Nola, p. 405.

7 Valsecchi, pp. 189–90.

8 *Annales du sénat et du corps législatif*. I: *Du 18 novembre au 11 décembre 1867* (Paris, 1867), p. 135.

9 Valsecchi, p. 190.

of Garibaldi, whose followers he contemptuously dismissed as rabble. To get the French out of Rome in order to set the stage for the annexation of the city was the object to which he now dedicated himself with characteristic single-mindedness. Napoleon for his part had already launched his secret campaign to forge a tripartite coalition directed against Prussia. Confident of success, he thought of Italy as indissolubly bound to France by ties of necessity as well as gratitude. Given the internal and international conditions under which Italy had to operate, how could she possibly pursue an independent course in foreign affairs? As for Austria, Napoleon regarded her as still the captive of her traditional competition with the Prussians in Germany. She would be impelled by an inescapable need to avenge the defeat of 1866.[10] This was the bedrock of the French government's calculations.

Late in December, 1867, Napoleon made his first overture to Italy. Through the medium of Rouher, he proposed a hard and fast alliance between the two countries. In conveying the proposal to Nigra, Rouher denied that his master wanted war with Prussia. On the contrary, the purpose of the alliance would be to assist in preserving the peace of Europe. When Nigra alluded to the Roman question, Rouher suggested the possibility of an understanding along the following lines: at some given time, Italy would garrison all of the papal territory except Rome itself, which would continue to be the pope's residence.[11]

Nigra, who was thoroughly familiar with the French political scene, knew that the emperor was in earnest when he proposed a Franco-Italian alliance but doubted his sincerity in offering such sweeping concessions in the Roman question. These concessions would obviously encourage an Italian move toward Rome, yet Rouher, amid thunderous applause, had recently promised the nation's representatives that France would "never" allow Italy to take the Eternal City. Nigra's skepticism proved justified. Napoleon quickly retracted the offer, stating

[10] *Ibid.*, p. 191.

[11] "Dai 'ricordi diplomatici' di Costantino Nigra," *Nuova antologia*, CCCLXXI (1934), 182.

that for the time being, he could not commit himself to a solution of the Roman question which would satisfy Italy's national aspirations. Rouher was authorized to draft a plan that showed how far the artful, erratic emperor had retreated. Nothing more was said about Italian garrisons on papal soil.[12]

However, inasmuch as the recall of the French corps from Rome represented Victor Emmanuel's immediate goal, there was a readiness in Florence to enter into serious negotiations even on this basis. Besides, in his attitude toward international affairs, the king was the product of his relations with the sister Latin country. He was profoundly attached to the idea of an alliance with the emperor, having become accustomed to think in terms of a French-dominated Europe. In this phase of Italian foreign policy, the alliance with Prussia in 1866 was merely an episode, without great or long-range significance. Victor Emmanuel's fundamentally pro-French outlook was scarcely affected by it.[13] Toward the Prussians, he nursed a rancor that dated precisely from their joint war against Austria. "I detest them," he said on one occasion, "even though we and they were allies in 1866. I will never forget how they behaved when they made peace at Nikolsburg without consulting me."[14] True, Austria, still the natural foe of Prussia, had also been the traditional enemy of Italy. But, after 1866, this old pattern seemed an anachronism.[15]

A unique opportunity presented itself to Victor Emmanuel late in 1868, when the Austrian government, as a participant in the negotiations for a triple alliance, actively supported the Italian position on the Roman question. (Beust was a Protestant, and this undoubtedly influenced his attitude.) Engaging in secret personal diplomacy to which only the premier and foreign minister, General Luigi Menabrea, and a few others (including Nigra, of course) were privy, the king attempted to exploit the situation to the full. Menabrea, a great favorite of his, was quite subservient, as were also most of the other

[12] *Ibid.*, pp. 183–85.   [15] See Chabod, p. 663.

[13] Chabod, p. 656.

[14] Oncken, III, No. 939, p. 497; Nola, p. 384.

cabinet members, with the result that the wilful monarch was able to do pretty much as he pleased. From the outset, he showed himself to be highly receptive to the Franco-Austrian overtures. He enjoyed the prospect of hitting back at the Prussians. He also wished, by a victorious campaign waged alongside France and Austria, to efface the memory of earlier defeats and demonstrate that his country deserved recognition as a military power of the first rank.

But pride and the desire for revenge did not prevent Victor Emmanuel from seeking to drive the hardest possible bargain. Austria was expected to foot a large part of the bill. Actually, she did not balk at ceding the Trentino, provided territorial compensation could be found for her elsewhere. But neither the king nor his ministers had any intention of selling their aid for the Trentino alone. They had a formidable list of demands which included Nice, Tunis, the Swiss canton of Ticino, and the region of the Isonzo along the northeastern frontier with Austria. France agreed to a boundary rectification around Nice and to an Italian establishment in Tunis. It was also understood that if the Swiss deviated ever so little from the line of neutrality, the Ticino would be taken away from them and given to Italy. The Austrians, although irritated because the Italians had said nothing about the Isonzo until the very last moment, were loath to jeopardize the success of the negotiations for the sake of this small strip of borderland. Everything seemed settled.[16]

Then, in the summer of 1869, the king and Menabrea caused a stalemate by insisting on the following conditions: immediate withdrawal of the French garrison from Rome; acceptance by France of the principle of non-intervention in Roman affairs; clarification of the aims of the proposed alliance; renunciation of action against the unification of Germany. Because of the attitude of the powerful Catholic party in France, Napoleon could not accept the first two conditions, whose net effect would have been to launch Italy on the road to Rome; and compliance with the fourth would have made the alliance worthless from France's point of view.

Anxious to avoid a complete rupture, Victor Emmanuel and

16 Nola, p. 387; Valsecchi, p. 192.

Menabrea took everything back except their demand for the evacuation of Rome, which was clearly not negotiable. Although Beust continued to support the Italian position, Napoleon would not budge. The king and Menabrea also stood firm.[17] To be sure, in a letter which Victor Emmanuel addressed to Napoleon in September, 1869, he emphasized anew that he subscribed to the idea of an alliance between France, Austria, and Italy, "whose union will present a powerful barrier against unjust claims and thus help to establish the peace of Europe on more solid foundations." He had not forgotten, he said, how much he owed to Napoleon's "constant benevolence," and it was therefore his wish that the treaty should be concluded as soon as possible. But—and here he came to the heart of the matter—he could not assume a formal engagement until the September Convention had been restored by the recall of the French garrison.[18]

The king's close friend and trusted emissary, Count Ottaviano Vimercati, saw Napoleon early in October. As his country's military attaché in Paris and as an original participant in the secret negotiations, Vimercati was on intimate terms with the occupant of the Tuileries and often the recipient of his confidences. On this occasion Napoleon remarked that he desired nothing better than to quit Rome as soon as possible. Unlike his ministers, he believed that the French people shared this desire. But it was true that first the corps législatif, with its massive majority of conservatives, clericals, and assorted moderates, would have to be readied for such a step. To this end he was planning to give a cabinet post to Ollivier, the leader of the liberal Imperialists and a power in parliamentary circles.[19] Ollivier reputedly favored an early withdrawal of the garrison but agreed that the government would have to proceed with caution. Shortly before he took office he advised Victor Emmanuel that internal political considerations necessi-

[17] "Dai 'ricordi diplomatici' di Costantino Nigra," p. 191; Pirri, p. 236.

[18] Victor Emmanuel II to Napoleon III, ca. September 25, 1869, Ollivier, XI, 611–12. The letter is also in Oncken, III, No. 733, pp. 240–41.

[19] See Vitzthum to Beust, October 5, 1869, Oncken, III, No. 739, pp. 247–49.

tated a delay but held out the hope that something might be done within the next several months.[20] This, in the king's view, left matters exactly where they had been. He would sign the treaty of alliance, and with alacrity, only when the garrison was gone.[21]

Napoleon's plight was illustrated by the pressure brought to bear by the Holy See. Fearful of being abandoned by the emperor, the papacy sought to forestall such treachery by demanding a clarification of France's intentions. The nuncio in Paris, Mgr. Flavio Chigi, was instructed to find out what he could. In March, 1869, he elicited from the government a statement strongly implying that it had no intention whatever of recalling the expeditionary corps from Civitavecchia.[22] A few months later, during a conversation with Napoleon, Chigi brought the matter up again. He called attention to the forthcoming opening of the ecumenical council in Rome and noted the importance which the Vatican, in view of this, attached to the continued presence of French troops. Napoleon assured the nuncio that he had not the slightest intention of recalling the troops. The present state of affairs in Italy definitely precluded such a step.[23]

Despite further statements by the French government to the effect that the garrison would not be withdrawn, the Vatican lost no opportunity of reminding Napoleon of the precarious situation in which the papal state found itself and of the absolute necessity of French military protection if a minimum of stability and tranquillity was to be preserved. The Quai d'Orsay did its best to dispel the Vatican's uneasiness. In June, 1869, Chigi was informed that Napoleon had reserved to himself alone the right of deciding whether the prerequisites for a return to the September Convention had been met by Italy.[24] A year later, on the eve of the July crisis, Gramont indicated

[20] Kübeck to Beust, December 18, 1869, *ibid.*, No. 758, p. 273.
[21] *Ibid.*
[22] Chigi to Antonelli, March 12, 1869, No. 1372, cited in Pirri, p. 241.
[23] Chigi to Antonelli, May 28, 1869, unnumbered, cited in *ibid.*, p. 242.
[24] Chigi to Antonelli, June 18, 1869, No. 1423, cited in *ibid.*

that there was no change in the French position. The imperial government, he told Chigi, had not even considered the idea of recalling the garrison.[25] This hardly squared with Napoleon's remarks to Vimercati, but the "sphinx" of the Tuileries was nothing if not devious.

The Italian government was subjected to heavy pressure against a rapprochement with France. It came mainly from extreme nationalist and anticlerical elements. The peninsula was rife with rumors that France and Italy were on the verge of signing an anti-Prussian alliance, and the reaction was immediate and violent. In a fury, Garibaldi sent the following message to Bismarck: "I am prepared to die on the seven hills rather than allow Italy to fight against Prussia, her ally in the struggle for the liberation of Venetia. Like a prefect, Napoleon orders Italy about. Our dignity requires that we should free ourselves from his baneful influence."[26] With talk of a Franco-Prussian conflict in the air, the left wing of the Sinistra assailed Italy's alleged intention of siding with the odious "man of December 2." Declaring themselves for Prussia, these revolutionaries hoped to see her fell the emperor and thus end the "control" which he exercised over their own country. The legendary prophet of Italian republicanism, Giuseppe Mazzini, stoked the agitation by threatening to lead an uprising against the Italian government if it dared to ally itself with France. He even asked Bismarck for the arms that would be needed to stage such an insurrection.[27]

3

The fall of Menabrea in November, 1869, and the advent of the Lanza cabinet the following month failed to deter Victor Emmanuel from continuing his personal diplomacy. No doubt Lanza, Visconti-Venosta, and especially Sella seemed less manageable than Menabrea, but the king made light of this and contemptuously referred to them as nonentities who would do as they were told. Although he never changed his mind about

[25] Chigi to Antonelli, June 3, 1870, No. 1520, cited in *ibid.*, p. 246.

[26] Valsecchi, p. 191.　　　　　　　[27] *Ibid.*

Lanza, he came to fear Sella and to think he saw in Visconti-Venosta a kindred soul. In the beginning, however, he proposed to treat the new foreign minister with the utmost disdain, even going so far as to insist on keeping him in the dark about the secret negotiations with France and Austria. Kübeck, one of the few on the Austrian side who was in the know, was actually asked by Victor Emmanuel to refrain from mentioning the negotiations to Visconti-Venosta. According to the king, Visconti-Venosta was not the right sort of person to handle such matters.[28] Kübeck soothingly replied that his instructions from Vienna forbade him to discuss the negotiations with anyone except the Italian sovereign.[29]

Reassured on this score, and manifestly in one of his rare talkative moods, Victor Emmanuel went on to recount to Kübeck what he had recently learned from Ollivier. He reiterated his readiness to sign the moment the French troops withdrew. Admitting that the Prussians had been helpful in 1866, he nevertheless declared that he could never forget how cruelly they had embarrassed him by hurrying to conclude an armistice with the Austrians. It was perfectly true that Napoleon had been something of a thorn in his side, asking that the advance against the Austrians should be prematurely halted. But at least he had known what to expect from that quarter, whereas his ally, the king of Prussia, had not even deigned to reply to his urgent telegraphic messages. Naturally, at the present moment, neither he nor Francis Joseph had any desire to go to war. However, if war should come, he would be ready.[30]

Abruptly, Victor Emmanuel introduced a different theme: the possibility of a successful rising against Napoleon. Apparently supposing that something of the sort might materialize before long, he broached to Kübeck the idea of an Austro-Italian alliance for the purpose of marching on the French capital and crushing the revolution before it could spread to other countries. In reporting the suggestion, Kübeck did not call attention to the king's obsessive dread of republicanism in Italy. Rather, he pointedly noted that in the character of Victor

[28] Kübeck to Beust, December 18, 1869, Oncken, III, No. 758, p. 273.
[29] *Ibid.*   [30] *Ibid.*

Emmanuel there was an element of vainglory as well as cunning and sincerity. Kübeck himself guessed that the king was intrigued by the thought of having not one but several irons in the fire. The restless sovereign evidently relished the opportunity for action that an early evacuation of Rome would open up; he had his eye on the Trentino; finally, he could already see himself exploiting a revolution in Paris to recover Nice and Savoy.[31]

How a monarch so disposed could be fitted into the framework of a partnership with France seemed to present some difficulty. Actually, however, Victor Emmanuel fully intended to resume the negotiations and even to push them. Although he apparently did expect the fall of the Second Empire in the not distant future—in subsequent discussions he reverted to the subject more than once—he was resolved in the meanwhile to extract what he could from Napoleon. To obtain what he wanted, he would continue to dangle the bait of a Franco-Italian alliance.

4

Kübeck had alluded to Victor Emmanuel's cunning. This was no misrepresentation. The king, despite his straightforward, soldierly manner, could be quite disingenuous. Thus, when the Lanza government had been in office only a short while, he told Visconti-Venosta about the negotiations with France and Austria, but made no mention of this to Kübeck. As a matter of fact, he even gave Kübeck to understand that the foreign minister had not been admitted into the secret. This particular bit of camouflage seemed utterly gratuitous, yet for some unaccountable reason Victor Emmanuel persisted in it. So Kübeck, who was to find out only belatedly that Visconti-Venosta was privy to the negotiations, continued in the meantime to maintain a profound silence about them in his dealings with the Italian government.

Shortly after the middle of June, 1870, Kübeck was instructed by Beust to remind Victor Emmanuel that the arrangements discussed by the three sovereigns had, in the eyes of the

31 *Ibid.*, p. 274.

Austrian government, "all the force of serious obligations."[32] However, not until July 3, a few hours before the king's departure for Valsavaranche, was Kübeck able to get an interview. After a few generalities—the sensational news from Madrid had not yet reached the Italian capital—Kübeck steered the conversation around to the tripartite negotiations. He alluded to the unsigned treaty and to his government's view of it as a morally binding instrument. Recalling Victor Emmanuel's previous assurances on the subject, Kübeck pointedly observed that Francis Joseph believed in the principle of reciprocity and would not attempt to stray a hair's breadth from any engagements contracted between himself and others. The king's response was beyond reproach. "Tell your emperor," he said, "that nothing has changed and that I still regard myself as bound to the two sovereigns." Some time ago, the French government had dropped a hint that the negotiations would be resumed and the treaty signed. As yet the hint had had no sequel, but he nonetheless continued to feel morally obligated.[33]

Having clarified his stand on the principal issue, Victor Emmanuel remarked that the overthrow of Napoleon, which might occur when it was least expected, would of course annul any existing tripartite understanding and force a consideration of other alignments.[34] Naturally enough, this troubled Kübeck, but he had no difficulty eliciting from the king a promise to remain faithful to Francis Joseph if the Second Empire should disappear. Seeing that Victor Emmanuel seemed in no hurry to end the interview, Kübeck volunteered the information that in accordance with His Majesty's wishes, he had refrained from saying anything to Visconti-Venosta about the secret negotiations despite his own excellent relations with the foreign minister. Betraying neither hesitation nor self-consciousness, the king commended him. "You have done very well," he said, "and I thank you. With all these continual changes of ministry, it

---

[32] Cited in Engel-Janosi, p. 338.

[33] Kübeck to Beust, July 4, 1870, Oncken, III, No. 839, p. 386.

[34] *Ibid.*

would be dangerous to divulge the secret, and Visconti-Venosta is too irresponsible to be trusted with such things."[35]

In his report to Beust, Kübeck did not question the risks for foreign policy that could grow out of ministerial instability in Italy, but he took strong exception to Victor Emmanuel's characterization of Visconti-Venosta. He correctly described the king as far less discreet than the foreign minister. Visconti-Venosta was "reserved" as well as "intelligent." If he had a fault, it was "a certain lack of initiative." Kübeck put his finger on the real reason for Victor Emmanuel's attitude when he wrote: "It is true that in his capacity as a constitutional minister, Visconti-Venosta would perhaps hesitate to assume engagements on behalf of the country without first consulting his colleagues or at least the President of the Council, who is an honest person but limited and maladroit."[36] That the presence in the cabinet of men like Visconti-Venosta, Sella, and Lanza might interfere with unfettered exercise of the royal will was corroborated by Victor Emmanuel himself. In his arrogant fashion he told Kübeck: "As soon as the moment arrives for the preparation of a great action abroad, I shall be . . . obliged to change the ministry."[37]

This prompted Kübeck to speculate about the identity of Lanza's probable successor. He guessed that the king would reinstate Menabrea, who could be relied upon to obey his master and patron. But to set Beust straight, Kübeck was at pains to emphasize that despite Victor Emmanuel's penchant for personal rule, even he in the last analysis remained dependent on the will of parliament. This was demonstrated in December, 1869, when His Majesty was compelled to do two things: part with a cabinet he liked and abandon a commitment he had irresponsibly assumed toward Spain in connection with the candidature of the Duke of Genoa.[38]

When the interview finally ended, Kübeck bade farewell to the king, who was expected to be away for the entire summer, and returned to the Austrian legation to ponder the significance

---

[35] *Ibid.*, p. 387.   [37] *Ibid.*

[36] *Ibid.*   [38] *Ibid.*

of what he had heard. Summing up his impressions, he accented the suspicion that Victor Emmanuel, despite explicit assurances of loyalty to France and Austria, might already be considering a turnabout in foreign policy. What struck Kübeck with special force was the sovereign's preoccupation with the possibility of a revolution in France and his premature concern with the question of new alignments.[39] Evidently Kübeck did not rule out the possibility of a bargain between Victor Emmanuel and Bismarck. As a matter of fact, the king sometimes gave the impression of being less resentful toward the Prussians than he really was. On one occasion he even told the Prussian minister to Italy that he would welcome a return to the alliance of 1866, with France instead of Austria as the common target.[40] Actually, he had no intention of doing anything of the kind, but this did not deter him from indulging in such talk now and then.

5

In accordance with his constitutional duty, Visconti-Venosta kept the king informed of all important developments. On July 7 he telegraphed to Valsavaranche a recapitulation of the international flare-up over the Hohenzollern candidature. He noted the menacing attitude of France, then tersely summed up: "The situation is grave."[41] The following day he dispatched three more telegrams. The first emphasized that France would doubtless go to war if King William did not get Leopold to retract his acceptance and if the Cortes went on to elect the prince as scheduled.[42] The second, after alluding to France's request for military aid in the event of a war with Prussia, included in the résumé of the Italian reply the statement that no answer could be given until the orders of His Majesty had been

[39] *Ibid.*, p. 388.

[40] See Engel-Janosi, p. 324. In July, 1870, the Spanish minister in Berlin actually believed that an offensive and defensive alliance existed between Italy and Prussia (Rascón to Sagasta, July 7, 1870, Romanones, pp. 192–93).

[41] Mayor des Planches, p. 341.

[42] *Ibid.*, p. 342.

received.[43] The third consisted of a single but portentous sentence: "Nigra has just telegraphed that tomorrow [July 9] an order to mobilize will be issued in France."[44]

Victor Emmanuel had his own sources of information and already knew how serious the situation was. After pondering the messages from Florence, he telegraphed Visconti-Venosta:[45]

I am surprised that this was not foreseen. If this is a scheme planned in advance by Bismarck, we shall have war. If there should be war, remember that we have on our hands some anterior promises for which I am more or less responsible. . . .

Please keep me informed. If there is a halt, I can remain here; otherwise I shall have to leave for Florence. Start preparing the ministry on the question of the anterior promises, and tell Lanza and Sella that the problem of money should not disturb them. I am still hopeful that everything will be settled.

The king's preoccupation with his "anterior promises" and his insistence that the cabinet should get ready to do something about them regardless of the drain on the country's finances revealed only too clearly what he was thinking: if war broke out, Napoleon would hurry the conclusion of a Franco-Italian alliance by recalling the garrison from papal soil. Once the troops were gone, a way would probably be found to replace the September Convention with a permanent settlement of the Roman question. But in any case, the promise of military help would be fulfilled by Italy.

The message from Valsavaranche reached the foreign office early in the afternoon of the ninth, and Visconti-Venosta's chief concern after reading it was to keep Victor Emmanuel where he was as long as possible. Although the Italian government's efforts on behalf of peace seemed well-nigh hopeless in the light of the latest intelligence from France and Prussia, there appeared to be a slight chance that they might yet accomplish something. Accordingly, they would have to be continued. But this was bound to prove difficult if not impossible if the king rushed back to Florence and pressed his views in person on the various members of the cabinet. Blessed with a clear vision of what ought to be done, Visconti-Venosta also knew his own irresoluteness well enough to fear that he might yield to Victor Emmanuel's importunity; and the same could be said of all the other ministers with the sole exception of Sella.

Visconti-Venosta's reply, which was sent at 3:00 p.m., was designed to immobilize the king, at least for the time being. The foreign minister sought to make light of the situation by asserting that Gramont's saber-rattling declaration had reduced the number of Leopold's partisans in Madrid. This being so, it was perfectly possible that the Cortes would decide to reject the Hohenzollern candidature outright or accept it by a small majority. In either case, the danger to peace would be removed. Meanwhile, the powers were exerting themselves to bring the Spaniards into line. There was therefore no immediate need for Victor Emmanuel to return.[46] Naturally, Visconti-Venosta said nothing about preparing the cabinet for the conclusion of an alliance with France; that was a task the king himself would have to undertake.

The advantages of having Victor Emmanuel far away from Florence were considerable, but in a flash they all seemed to vanish into thin air. For it was precisely at this juncture, when the king was supposedly giving more attention to the delights of the chase than to affairs of state, that Visconti-Venosta received a nasty shock. He learned that his royal master, relentlessly pursuing the goal of *Roma capitale* even from his summer retreat, was on the verge of giving effect to an independent course which threatened to bring war still closer than it actually was. Acting entirely on his own, and spurred by the possibilities springing from the sudden deterioration of the international situation, the sovereign had summoned Vimercati from Paris and had instructed him to resume the secret talks suspended because of the emperor's refusal to evacuate Rome. Vimercati was to review with Napoleon the conditions of a Franco-Italian alliance, including of course the recall of the French garrison.[47] The departure of the troops would, to be

[46] *Ibid.*, p. 343.

[47] Cf. *OD*, XXVIII, n. 3, pp. 383–84. The Vimercati papers in the archives of the Italian foreign ministry contain nothing on this. The pri-

sure, be a great gain in itself. In addition, it could be made the springboard for a truly "national" solution of the Roman question arrived at with or without the concurrence of the Holy See. As for Napoleon, how could he object to a renewal of the September Convention now that the showdown with Prussia appeared to be in the offing?

Remaining in close telegraphic contact with the king, Vimercati returned to Paris. On July 9, immediately after his arrival, he notified the Quai d'Orsay that he had a communication to deliver and asked to see the emperor.[48] The audience was fixed for nine the next morning.[49] All this, from Visconti-Venosta's point of view, was bad enough, but what made the situation appear even more ominous was the king's studied silence about his instructions to Vimercati. During the afternoon of the ninth, at approximately the time Vimercati was making his arrangements for a meeting with Napoleon, the worried foreign minister addressed a private telegram to Nigra, which the latter and no one else was to decipher. Visconti-Venosta wanted to know whether Vimercati had received any additional messages from Victor Emmanuel.[50] Nigra's answer, which reached Florence late that night, stated that the king had telegraphed Vimercati, but only to ask for information.[51] Nigra also supplied these items: Vimercati, who of course had not yet seen the emperor, could report nothing new to Victor Emmanuel. In his reply, however, Vimercati did express the belief that a Franco-Italian pact would be concluded at any moment. He said he was advising the king to pass this communication along to Visconti-Venosta, who still did not know the details of the

---

vate archives of Victor Emmanuel were removed from Italy by King Humbert II when he went into exile (Nola, p. 257).

[48] Ministry of foreign affairs to the emperor, July 9, 1870, OD, XXVIII, No. 8345, p. 143.

[49] Private secretary of the emperor to the ministry of foreign affairs, July 9, 1870, ibid., No. 8346, p. 143.

[50] Visconti-Venosta to Nigra, July 9, 1870, unnumbered, MAE, AS, Archivi di gabinetto (1861–1887), busta 219: guerra franco-prussiana e trattative segrete 8 luglio–14 settembre 1870, fascicolo 4.

[51] Nigra to Visconti-Venosta, July 9, 1870, unnumbered, ibid.

intrigue.[52] Thus, in the midst of a tense international situation, Visconti-Venosta had to contend with his own sovereign as well as with Paris, Berlin, and Madrid. This was not the least of his trials.[53]

[52] *Ibid.*

[53] On Victor Emmanuel's penchant for operating behind the backs of his ministers, see Isacco and Ernesto Artom, *Iniziative neutralistiche della diplomazia italiana nel 1870 e nel 1915: documenti inediti a cura di Angelo Artom* (Turin, 1954), p. 33.

CHAPTER FIVE

UNEASY INTERLUDE

When Curtopassi received Visconti-Venosta's telegram inviting multilateral mediation, he promptly requested an interview with Beust. However, the chancellor could not see him until the morning of July 9. At their meeting Beust evinced keen satisfaction with the message from Florence. He seemed gratified by Italy's readiness to unite with other powers in an attempt to prevent dangerous complications.[1] But his interest in peace was not altogether genuine. Doubtless he had neither the means to start a war nor the wish; but if an armed conflict between France and Prussia did break out, he would almost certainly try to exploit it. His implacable hatred of the Prussians, his determination to avenge the defeat of 1866 and restore Austria to her former position in Germany, pointed to this. A French victory—it was predicted by virtually all Austrian observers in the summer of 1870—would enable him to reach his goal with relative impunity. Of course the issue of neutrality versus intervention would first have to be settled, and here he could not avoid running afoul of the Russophobia that was so rampant in the Dual Monarchy and especially in Hungary. Because of it, he would be hard pressed to justify anything except a war in the east against the tsarist empire. However, if Russia did enter a Franco-Prussian struggle, then naturally Prussia too, as Russia's ally, would become a legitimate target for Austrian guns. Thus Vienna's policy, it seemed,

[1] Curtopassi to Visconti-Venosta, July 9, 1870, No. 210, MAE, AS, Serie politica (1867–1888), Austria-Ungheria, busta 1253: 1869–1871.

hinged exclusively on St. Petersburg's. Beust's problem was to
attenuate the overpowering character of this presupposition by
playing up the advantages of action in Germany and the west.
In the interview with Curtopassi, he was at pains to point
out that, on the subject of the Hohenzollern candidature, the
line his government had been taking in Berlin and Madrid
was quite indistinguishable from that of the French. He said
he was convinced that the danger to peace would be removed
thanks to the forced renunciation of the crown by Leopold. Alluding approvingly to the energy displayed by the French in
dealing with the crisis, he made no effort to conceal his satisfaction at the prospect of a humiliating defeat for Bismarck.[2]
Beust went on to indicate that his government would be willing to support the Bourbon prince of Asturias, who was reputed to be Napoleon's favorite candidate for the Spanish
throne.[3] The most significant feature of the conversation, apart
from the chancellor's stress on Franco-Austrian solidarity, was
his failure to do more than pay lip-service to Visconti-Venosta's
suggestion. He was obviously not consumed with eagerness to
help Great Britain and Italy cut the ground from under the
Franco-Prussian dispute. On the other hand, when he received
Kübeck's telegram—the one relaying Visconti-Venosta's com-
plaints about Napoleon's Roman policy—he seized upon it to
urge France to consider the evacuation of papal territory. In a
dispatch to the imperial ambassador in Paris, Prince Richard
von Metternich, Beust pointedly observed that if France se-
cured armed help from Italy in return for such a concession,
she would find it easier to obtain the same thing from Austria.[4]
This, more than anything else, indicated the direction of his
thoughts.

2

For some inexplicable reason, Curtopassi did not telegraph
his report. Instead, he sent it by ordinary diplomatic courier,

---

[2] *Ibid.*   [3] *Ibid.*

[4] Beust to Metternich, July 11, 1870, Oncken, III, No. 871, pp. 425–26.
This portion of Beust's lengthy letter has been deleted from the copy in
HHSA, PA, Frankreich, Weisungen 1870, Karton IX/97.

with the result that it did not reach Florence until July 12.
Visconti-Venosta heard much sooner from London. Cadorna
received the foreign minister's first telegram (suggesting multilateral mediation) on the eighth, the second (recommending
joint action by England and Italy) the morning of the next
day. Armed with these, Cadorna saw Granville around 2:00
P.M. on the ninth. A meeting of the British cabinet was due to
take place shortly, and so Granville agreed to a second interview later in the day. Cadorna, as Granville's record of their
first conversation testifies, came directly to the point:[5]

He said that the French Government had addressed themselves
to the Cabinet of Florence, with a request that they would use their
influence with Prussia [Malaret in actuality had asked for Italian
intervention not in Berlin but in Madrid] to prevent matters proceeding to extremity, and that the Italian Government being most
anxious that no disturbance of the general peace should take place,
were quite ready to act as requested by the French Government,
and desired to make known to the Government of Her Majesty that
they were prepared to join their efforts to those of Great Britain
for the maintenance of peace.

On this account M. de [sic] Cadorna was instructed to ascertain
the views of Her Majesty's Government on the present critical state
of affairs, and whether and to what extent any joint action should
take place between the two Governments.

Granville said he was happy to see such harmony in the aims
of Italy and Great Britain, then proceeded to give his own view
of the situation. He deplored Prim's conduct in the matter of
the Hohenzollern candidature, judging it discourteous and
heedless where France was concerned. The marshal should
have considered the well-known susceptibilities of the French
as well as the stake they thought they had in the solution of
the Spanish dynastic question. But Granville did not put all
the blame on Prim. He also found fault with Gramont's decla-

---

[5] Granville to Paget, July 9, 1870, No. 4, PRO, FO 45/160. The conversation with Cadorna was also reported to Lyons. The version that appears in *British and Foreign State Papers 1869–1870*, LX, 801–2, is slightly
inexact.

ration before the corps législatif, contending that such language could only impede a peaceful settlement.[6]

It seemed to him, the foreign secretary continued, that the French government was being very precipitate. After all, negotiations for the removal of the Hohenzollern candidature were still in a preliminary stage. On the other hand, however, it was quite understandable that the French government should feel constrained to do something to appease the inflamed emotions of its own people.[7] Cadorna made no comment on this. Instead, he inquired about the steps the British government might be planning to take in order to implement the accord which was now seen to exist between England and Italy. Granville answered that for the moment, at any rate, he could speak only for himself. The question of co-operation with other governments had not yet been discussed by the cabinet but was due to be taken up at the meeting that afternoon. He personally was of the opinion that a renunciation of the crown by Prince Leopold would be far and away the best solution. Unfortunately, King William seemed disinclined to put pressure on his kinsman. Someone therefore would have to caution the Prussians, point out to them what they themselves must have realized from the very beginning: that a war could grow out of the present dispute and that they would be assuming an enormous responsibility if they made no attempt to avert it. But while stressing the need for some very plain language in Berlin, Granville insisted that efforts from the outside to bring about a peaceful settlement must be concentrated on Madrid rather than on the Prussian capital. As the last person to countenance any breaches of a long-established rule among the nations, he readily admitted that it was a most delicate matter to interfere with the selection of a king. The right to choose belonged exclusively to the country concerned. But in view of the circumstances that had arisen as a consequence of this particular exercise of that right, the other powers could not very well be expected to remain passive. It did therefore

[6] Cadorna to Visconti-Venosta, July 9, 1870, No. 87, MAE, AS, Serie politica (1867–1888), Inghilterra, busta 1351: 1869–1870.

[7] *Ibid.*

seem proper to alert Prim and his associates to the difficulties
which already were pressing in upon their country from all
sides. They must be made to see how appalling the plight of
Spain would be and how terrible too the position of the dynasty if, in virtue of the very act of ascending the throne, the
monarch should prove the unwitting cause of dangerous complications.[8]

Was mediation likely to prove efficacious? Granville entertained some optimism on this score despite all the ominous
portents of the last few days. Cadorna too was inclined to take
a hopeful view of the situation but observed that confidence in
the efforts of the powers was bound to vary in accordance with
one's estimate of how sincere France and Prussia really were
when they disclaimed any desire to provoke hostilities. In his
reply Granville, leaving out Prussia because he knew so little
about conditions there, called attention to the divided state of
public opinion in France and ventured the guess that the imperial government had no wish to precipitate a war. Cadorna
solemnly concurred and, interestingly enough, cited Malaret's
démarche as proof.[9]

Around 5:30 P.M., immediately after the cabinet meeting,
Granville kept his appointment with Cadorna. He could now
confirm, with all the authority vested in him by the consensus
of his colleagues, what he had said earlier. The cabinet welcomed Italy's co-operative attitude. Henceforward the British
government would inform the Italians of everything it was
doing and hoped they would reciprocate in full measure.[10]
However, an interchange of information was hardly the same
thing as joint action, which Visconti-Venosta had recommended. Here, in effect, the two governments were not of one
mind. Granville was quite definite in saying that in their approaches to Madrid and Berlin, England and Italy should act
individually rather than in concert. By proceeding not in combination but along parallel lines, the two countries would enhance their chances of success.[11] The invitation from Visconti-

[8] *Ibid.*   [9] *Ibid.*
[10] Cadorna to Visconti-Venosta, July 10, 1870, No. 88, *ibid.*
[11] *Ibid.*

Venosta was thus politely but firmly rejected. To soften the blow, Granville assured Cadorna that the British government, "while acting separately," would be found "on all occasions" collaborating with the Italians "in the same spirit as that by which . . . the cabinet of Florence was now animated."[12]

Now that the question of procedure had been settled, Granville spent a little time recapitulating the steps he had already taken with an eye to staying the drift toward war. Naturally, he had said nothing to Prussia and Spain that they could construe as interference in their domestic affairs. While urging both countries to do what they could to prevent the situation from getting out of hand, he had left it to them to decide how they could be most helpful. To the Prussians he had suggested that their strength was so generally acknowledged and clearly proven that whatever they might do on behalf of peace could not possibly be misinterpreted as a sign of fear or weakness. He had made light of Gramont's declaration before the corps législatif, ascribing the vigor of its language to the uncomfortable position in which the French government had been placed by the pressure of public opinion. He had withheld his own opinion on the merits of the Hohenzollern candidature. But he had not hesitated to point out that the installation of a Germanic dynasty in Spain was bound to arouse France's enmity, with the result that the Spaniards, instead of being rescued from their current difficulties, would be thrown into even greater turmoil.[13] In addressing himself to the Spanish government, Granville had been careful to pass over the touchy subject of Leopold's qualifications. Posing instead the question of whether such a choice would be opportune, he had explained why it must be answered in the negative: Spain's inner life as well as her entire future would be jeopardized.[14]

Cadorna faithfully wrote down everything Granville said. For the most part he refrained from entering his own judgments. However, believing this would interest his chief, he

[12] Granville to Paget, July 9, 1870, No. 4, PRO, FO 45/160.

[13] Cadorna to Visconti-Venosta, July 10, 1870, No. 88, MAE, AS, Serie politica (1867–1888), Inghilterra, busta 1351: 1869–1870.

[14] *Ibid.*

recorded one purely personal impression: Granville, although understandably reticent on so delicate a topic, inclined to the belief that the Hohenzollern candidature was in itself too unimportant a matter to warrant all the fuss the French were making.[15] This was a view that Visconti-Venosta shared, but of course it was wholly academic: for cogent reasons of their own, the French had concluded that the presence of a Prussian dynasty on the other side of the Pyrenees would be intolerable. From that position nothing apparently could shake them.

3

Cadorna's full report of the conversation did not arrive until several days later, but his telegraphic résumé reached Visconti-Venosta very early in the morning of July 10.[16] Although Granville had rejected the proposal of joint action, the attitude of the British government was in every other respect so satisfactory and the sincerity of its desire to help so evident that Visconti-Venosta could not justly complain. However, the almost simultaneous arrival of a message from the king drove his thoughts to more immediate business. Victor Emmanuel, who loved to hunt, rejoiced that he would not have to return to Florence for the time being;[17] but despite his unabated enthusiasm for an Italian dynasty in Spain, he confessed he was in no mood to struggle with his son. Remembering only too well their last encounter—he and Aosta had almost come to blows— he anticipated no lessening of resistance now. So he begged off, declaring he could do no more. The duke was at present in Leghorn. If Visconti-Venosta wished to go there and try his luck, he was quite welcome to do so.[18]

In view of Aosta's lack of filial piety, the refusal of Victor Emmanuel to lend a hand could not have mattered greatly to Visconti-Venosta. The important thing was that he had the king's permission to go ahead. But the remainder of the tele-

[15] *Ibid.*

[16] Cadorna to Visconti-Venosta, July 9, 1870, No. 2367, MAE, AS, DTA.

[17] Mayor des Planches, p. 344.

[18] *Ibid.*, p. 345.

gram from Valsavaranche, which revealed anew the workings of the royal mind, was disquieting:[19]

As for the political question now under consideration, discuss it with the Austrian minister. Tell him that this time I would like to see the emperor and the Austrian government arrange a cessation of the French occupation of Rome. Otherwise neither an alliance nor an entente will be possible. Such an arrangement must come first. It would be best if a proposal to that effect were made as promptly as possible and permitted to produce satisfactory results. It would likewise be best if it were not demanded by us but volunteered by France. This she should do with an eye to what may follow.

After you have talked to the Austrian minister, telegraph me. Keep me posted on everything.

An entente with France always figured in Visconti-Venosta's calculations; in fact, owing to the pro-French orientation of his thinking on problems of international politics, he viewed it as essential to the well-being and security of Italy. But the idea of a military alliance, whether with France or any other power, continued to make little sense to this cautious diplomat. He hoped to steer clear of warlike complications while obtaining satisfaction in the Roman question and staying somehow on friendly terms with France. On the other hand, because he was temperamentally more vulnerable to royal pressure than his tough-minded colleague, Sella, it was quite conceivable that against his better judgment, he might still acquiesce in a policy whose dangers he saw all too clearly. The sincerity of his desire for peace and the logic of the course marked out by his prudent intelligence were unmistakable, but so was his irresolution.

However, for the moment there was complete certainty of purpose in his mind. Later in the morning of the tenth the cabinet met at his instance to consider the suggestion that the Aosta candidature should be revived. The king's consent was disclosed, but some of the ministers reiterated their opposition to involvement of any kind in the Spanish dynastic imbroglio. Arguing that peace might depend on the duke's willingness to

19 *Ibid.*

accept an offer of the crown, Visconti-Venosta finally had his way. One dissenter, according to some reports, was the prime minister. Now that he had the cabinet's authorization, Visconti-Venosta decided that not he but Govone should go to Leghorn and present the matter to Aosta. Secrecy was absolutely essential. At this stage of the international crisis, when diplomats rather than generals still occupied the foreground, the movements of the minister of war were less likely to attract attention than those of the foreign minister.[20]

4

If there was a prompt affirmative answer from Aosta, Visconti-Venosta evidently reckoned, a settlement of the Spanish dynastic problem might be reached before the French and the Prussians forsook diplomacy for the sword. The essential thing was to keep them at arm's length just a little longer. Visconti-Venosta must have begun to wonder whether any help could be expected from the Austrians. It was now almost three days since his telegram to Curtopassi and almost two since his conversation with Kübeck. The ominous silence from Vienna was partly offset by the tidings from St. Petersburg. Caracciolo, whose travel plans had been formally cancelled,[21] reported a conversation with the Russian foreign minister. True, Gorchakov said he disapproved of Gramont's declaration before the corps législatif and implied that Russia had no interest in France's grievance. But he also suggested that a peaceful solution was probable.[22] Since Russia was on the closest of terms with Prussia, this might portend the adoption of a less intractable attitude by King William and Bismarck.

[20] The above is based on information given Paget by Visconti-Venosta (Paget to Granville, July 11, 1870, No. 9, PRO [Ashridge], FO 170/163). For Lanza's reported dissent, see Layard to Granville, July 16, 1870, No. 37, PRO, FO 72/1235; Solvyns to d'Anethan, July 16, 1870, No. 87, Belgium, Archives du ministère des affaires étrangères, Correspondance politique, Légations: Italie, IV, 1868–1870.

[21] Visconti-Venosta to Caracciolo, July 10, 1870, No. 1186, MAE, AS, TS.

[22] Caracciolo to Visconti-Venosta, July 9, 1870, No. 2370, MAE, AS, DTA. This telegram reached Florence at 11:05 A.M. on the tenth.

However, that same morning brought yet another black report from Berlin. Launay had again talked with Thile, who said he appreciated the Italian government's friendly interest. But Bismarck's mouthpiece, obviously on orders from above, showed a total unwillingness to second Visconti-Venosta's efforts. With an almost mechanical monotony he repeated that Prussia washed her hands of the affair. She had had no official knowledge of the Hohenzollern candidature prior to the recent notification from the Spanish government. Like all the other powers, she had been taken by surprise. As for King William, he too was keeping completely aloof, being neither for nor against Leopold's elevation to the Spanish throne.[23] According to Launay, there was therefore no cheer to derive from the fact, which Thile mentioned, that Benedetti had been ordered to Ems for a direct confrontation with William. The purpose of the move was obviously to enlist the king's help in securing a retraction of the candidature; but, as was plain from Thile's remarks, the chances of success were infinitesimal. Besides, Leopold, on whom everything in the last analysis seemed to depend, appeared to be inaccessible, at least for the time being; it was believed that he was somewhere in Switzerland.[24]

Visconti-Venosta found it easy enough to subscribe to Launay's pessimism; however, a corner of his cool, calculating mind refused to rule out the possibility that either William or Leopold would yet heed the dictates of reason, especially if helped along by prodding from disinterested third parties. Accordingly, he urged Launay to pool his efforts with those of his diplomatic colleagues, especially the British ambassador, Lord Augustus Loftus, and in addition assured the envoy that he would continue to enjoy carte blanche in the choice of means. Should Launay perceive any advantage in doing so, he was even to go to Ems to see the king. A descent upon the royal headquarters would be particularly desirable if Loftus received authorization to do likewise.[25]

[23] Launay to Visconti-Venosta, July 9, 1870, No. 2369, *ibid.*

[24] Launay to Visconti-Venosta, July 9, 1870, No. 2368, *ibid.*

[25] Visconti-Venosta to Launay, July 10, 1870, No. 28, MAE, AS, Divisione politica, 1867–1888, registri copia-lettere in partenza, Prussia, busta

While he sought in this fashion to thrust the role of peacemaker upon the Prussian sovereign, Visconti-Venosta persisted in his efforts to push the Spaniards toward a quick cancellation of the Hohenzollern candidature. To prophecies of woe he could now, in the wake of the meeting of the Italian cabinet, add the promise of help in finding a substitute for Leopold. Early in the afternoon of July 10, around the time he was authorizing a journey to Ems, he summoned Montemar, who came at once. First Visconti-Venosta repeated his earlier warnings, but in more explicit terms. He predicted that the aftermath of a Franco-Prussian war fought over the Hohenzollern candidature would be anything but pleasant for Spain. Her interests would probably be sacrificed to those of the two belligerents, both of whom were great powers. In any event, she could not expect to profit. If France won, surely Leopold would never be king of Spain. If France lost, she would plague the new dynasty and encourage rival pretenders.[26] Having highlighted these dangers, Visconti-Venosta sounded a positive note. He observed that the powers now working for a peaceful solution ought not to confine themselves to the object of eliminating the Hohenzollern candidature; rather, they must help Spain to solve her dynastic problem. By so doing, they would give her a moral guaranty against attempts to restore the Bourbons, who had little popular support in the country.[27]

Visconti-Venosta said nothing to Montemar about Aosta. When he forwarded to Cerruti a résumé of what he had told Montemar and authorized similar language in Madrid, he maintained the same silence.[28] Govone had not yet left for Leghorn, and it was not clear just when he would leave. The lackadaisical way in which the general was permitted to dis-

---

1200: 7 gennaio 1867–14 febbraio 1871. Of course the authorization to go to Ems was likewise telegraphed: Visconti-Venosta to Launay, July 10, 1870, No. 1185, MAE, AS, TS.

[26] See Visconti-Venosta to Cerruti, July 10, 1870, No. 5, MAE, AS, Archivi di gabinetto (1861–1887), busta 219: guerra franco-prussiana e trattative segrete 8 luglio–14 settembre 1870, fascicolo 4; Visconti-Venosta to Cerruti, July 10, 1870, No. 1187, MAE, AS, TS.

[27] *Ibid.*   [28] *Ibid.*

charge a supposedly urgent mission underscored not only Visconti-Venosta's own tendency to procrastinate but also his proclivity to tolerate the same fault in others. Of course, with the mission as yet unaccomplished, it was too early to put Cerruti and Montemar to work. For some unaccountable reason, Cerruti later incorrectly claimed that he never did receive authorization to broach the matter to the Spanish government.[29] However, true it is that without waiting for instructions from Florence, but evidently certain that they would arrive at any moment, he took it upon himself to promote the Italian candidature. When Layard brought the subject up, Cerruti told him confidentially that "he had reason to believe that the Duke of Aosta would . . . be more inclined to accept the Spanish Crown at this time than he had been when the offer was first made to him."[30] Cerruti also assured his British colleague that Victor Emmanuel continued to favor Aosta's candidature.[31]

Cerruti's "disclosures," together with the manifest receptivity of the Spanish government, galvanized Layard into a new burst of activity. Assuming correctly that Cerruti had not yet been empowered to act, he sped the following telegram to Granville:[32]

I have reason to believe that the solution which I suggested yesterday [July 9] would be acceptable to all parties; that is, if the English Government could prevail upon the King of Prussia to refuse his consent to the election of Hohenzollern, and would promise to the Spanish Government their good offices to induce the Duke of Aosta to accept the Crown, the King of Italy, I am assured, would be favourable to this arrangement, and the Duke would be acceptable to Spain. If you are inclined to adopt this solution, and thought that I could be of use, I could go to Florence and assist Paget. My knowledge of the condition of Spain and of parties might be useful in removing impressions which may exist. In this case, I should be glad to see you first.

[29] Cerruti made this statement to Layard a few weeks later (Layard to Granville, August 1, 1870, No. 60, PRO, FO 72/1235).

[30] Layard to Granville, July 14, 1870, No. 22, *ibid.*

[31] *Ibid.*

[32] This telegram, which was sent on the afternoon of July 10, is reproduced in Layard to Granville, July 11, 1870, No. 11, PRO, FO 72/1234.

Layard's offer to help Paget was not taken up. The idea of reviving the Aosta candidature fared better. Granville and his chief, Gladstone, were agreed that the British government must do everything within reason to halt the drift toward war. If an Italian solution to Spain's dynastic problem could still be brought forward with some prospect of success—present indications suggested that the chances were good—Great Britain's support should of course not be withheld. But first a firm commitment must be obtained from Florence which would also bind Aosta. Neither Spain nor Europe could afford another fiasco. This being the prime minister's position as well as his own, Granville addressed the following telegram to Paget shortly before midnight on July 10:[33]

It appears from information received from Mr Layard that although Marshal Prim is firm in his language, he would not be indisposed to take steps to cancel the candidature of the Prince of Hohenzollern, if he was assured of the consent of a member of the Italian Royal family. Inform the King and his Government confidentially and ascertain whether for the great object of maintaining the peace of Europe His Majesty would consent to such an arrangement.

5

While Great Britain was thus preparing to lend her support to the Aosta candidature, in Paris the intrigue conducted by the French and Italian sovereigns seemed to be approaching a decisive phase. On the morning of the tenth, Napoleon received Vimercati at the imperial palace in St. Cloud. In the course of the conversation, which was obviously most cordial, the emperor said he expected to have Prussia's reply by the next day and asked Vimercati to telegraph this to Victor Emmanuel. He also told Vimercati that there would be no war if the candidature were renounced. On the other hand, if the anwer were either negative or evasive, he would dispatch troops to the frontier. In such an eventuality, he counted on the help of both Italy and Austria, but would await Visconti-

[33] Reproduced in Granville to Paget, July 11, 1870, confidential, No. 11, PRO, FO 45/160.

Venosta's definitive reply to Malaret's *démarche*. He explained
in this connection that the Hohenzollern affair had arisen so
suddenly that there had not been time to apprise Victor Emmanuel. As a consequence, Malaret had been authorized to
proceed without previous consultation or agreement between
the two sovereigns. The emperor indicated that he wished to
see the understanding with Italy concluded simultaneously
with the one between France and Austria. However, to show
that he had by no means abandoned hope for a peaceful solution, he pointed out that he had refrained from summoning
Nigra lest Italy be distracted from the effort, in which Austria
was likewise involved, to avert the outbreak of hostilities.[34]

The audience over, Vimercati telegraphed Victor Emmanuel.
Then he conferred with Nigra, who was faithfully executing
Visconti-Venosta's order to report the progress of the intrigue.
Vimercati recounted the interview, including some important
particulars that he had failed to mention in his telegram to the
king but which he obviously planned to convey in a subsequent
communication. Thus he noted that, if the reply from Prussia
turned out to be unsatisfactory, Napoleon would formally no-
tify Visconti-Venosta that France was relying on the "alliance"
with Italy. The French garrison would be immediately withdrawn from the papal state. Simultaneously, the Italian government would be called upon to dispatch via Hapsburg territory an army of 100,000 men (the military co-operation of
Austria, indispensable for an Italian invasion of South Germany, was taken for granted). In detailing these arrangements,
the emperor contended that hitherto Italy had been able to
count only on him. But once she had joined France in a comradeship of arms, she would command the loyalty of the entire
French nation.[35]

Victor Emmanuel's response, when he received this intelligence, left little to be desired. He promised Napoleon an im-

[34] For Vimercati's report of this conversation, see Nigra, pp. 107–8.

[35] Nigra to Visconti-Venosta, July 10, 1870, unnumbered private telegram, MAE, AS, Archivi di gabinetto (1861–1887), busta 219: guerra
franco-prussiana e trattative segrete 8 luglio–14 settembre 1870, fascicolo
4.

mediate contribution of 60,000 men whose mission it would be
to immobilize Bavaria. The operation was of course to be carried out jointly with Austria. If France decided to fight, Vimercati would hasten to Vienna to complete the necessary arrangements.[36] Thus, at the height of the crisis, Napoleon had every
reason to believe that Victor Emmanuel would not fail him.

At 1:20 P.M. on the tenth, Nigra relayed to Visconti-Venosta
everything Vimercati had reported. Despite his ardent Francophilism, Nigra viewed the sovereigns' intrigue with dismay.
He feared that its only effect would be to increase the likelihood of hostilities. He was of course aware that a Franco-
Prussian struggle could not fail to result in the freeing of
Rome from French occupation. But inasmuch as Italy, in
his estimation, was united to both countries by special ties,
she was bound to find herself deeply distressed if an armed
conflict broke out between them.[37] Worse, her involvement,
even without a prior pact with the French, was inevitable. In
one of his telegrams on the tenth, Nigra said as much. Noting
that France's military preparations were being suspended only
until the arrival of the Prussian reply, he entreated Visconti-
Venosta to spare no effort in trying to obtain a retraction of the
candidature by either William or Leopold. Otherwise, there
would be war within twenty-four hours, and Italy would be
dragged into it without fail.[38] After a short interval in which
he received further indications of the ugly mood around him,
Nigra telegraphed another supplication. He begged to know
whether, on the basis of information forwarded from Berlin,
Visconti-Venosta had reason to believe that the Prussian reply
would be favorable. Any answer which did not amount to a
removal of the candidature would be regarded by France as
justifying a declaration of war.[39]

[36] Metternich to Beust, July 11, 1870, No. 6653/175, HHSA, PA, Frankreich, Berichte 1870, Karton IX/95 (Oncken, III, No. 868, p. 418).

[37] So he told Lyons; see Lyons to Granville, July 11, 1870, confidential,
No. 730, PRO, FO 27/1805.

[38] Nigra to Visconti-Venosta, July 10, 1870, No. 2372, MAE, AS, DTA.
See also Nigra, pp. 96–97.

[39] Nigra to Visconti-Venosta, July 10, 1870, No. 2375, MAE, AS, DTA.

Much as Visconti-Venosta dreaded exciting Victor Emmanuel to the point of precipitating his return to Florence, he of course had no choice but to pass these warnings along to Valsavaranche. In doing so, he commented grimly that France might leave the mediating powers insufficient time to effect a settlement. In Madrid and Berlin Italy was exerting herself without stint, but the same could not be said of Austria. Reverting to one of the things that was uppermost in the king's mind as well as in his own, Visconti-Venosta pointed out that in a conversation with Kübeck two days before, he had underlined the difficulties which France, heedless of her own best interests, was creating for the Italian government by prolonging the occupation of Rome.[40] He wanted Victor Emmanuel to know that he had enlisted Austria's aid in seeking a speedy renewal of the September Convention. However, he also wished to make it clear to his sovereign that he was treating the Roman question not as the pivotal point of a partnership in arms but rather as an issue that could and should be divorced from military considerations. In his own thinking on the subject, Visconti-Venosta continued to keep before him the central truth that intervention in a Franco-Prussian war was anathema to Italian public opinion. He knew too that, although the nation was eager to see the Eternal City annexed, the time for serious discussions of *Roma capitale* had not yet come; first the September Convention would have to be unconditionally reactivated. On the other hand, it was equally plain that a Franco-Prussian war might break out at any moment; if it did, then the future of Franco-Italian relations and especially the ultimate fate of Rome would have to be taken up by the cabinet. The king's presence, however unwelcome from other points of view, was therefore indispensable. At 6:00 P.M. on the tenth, Visconti-Venosta disconsolately telegraphed Victor Emmanuel:[41]

I have received a telegram from Nigra concerning the communications which will be made to us by the emperor. If the reply of the king of Prussia, which is due to be delivered tomorrow, should not

[40] Mayor des Planches, p. 347.   [41] *Ibid.*

remove the danger of war, I shall telegraph Your Majesty . . . to
return to Florence.

This message was on its way when Victor Emmanuel decided
to proceed with his own plan for dragging the country into
war in return for the evacuation of Rome. He was overjoyed at
the probable renewal of the September Convention, which as
always he regarded not as the prelude to an indefinite prolongation of the Roman status quo but rather as a step toward the
eventual consummation of Italy's national program. Although
he of course knew, from what Napoleon had told Vimercati,
that it was presently the emperor's intention to recall the
French garrison if the current crisis was not surmounted, he
preferred to take no chances. He began to draft a telegram to
Visconti-Venosta. "I beg you," he wrote, "to tell me where the
question of the candidature presently stands and whether you
have seen the Austrian minister. Try so to arrange matters that
it will be the Austrian government which points out that, without a prior understanding about Rome, Italy will be unable to
aid France in the event of complications."[42] He had not quite
finished when Visconti-Venosta's latest message was handed to
him. Acknowledging its arrival, the king explained that he was
sending his telegram on all the same because it was urgently
necessary that Austria should make the position clear to
France.[43]

The obstinacy of Victor Emmanuel and the strong likelihood
that he would soon be back in the capital agitating in person
for a military alliance with France were not calculated to lift
the foreign minister's spirits. In addition, depressing news continued to pour in from Paris and Berlin. The French appeared
to be as determined as ever to brook no temporizing by the
Prussians, while the latter showed no inclination to stop acting
the part of indifferent bystanders. And would Aosta allow himself to be drafted as a candidate for the Spanish throne? The
possibility of a negative answer, which Visconti-Venosta could
not entirely discount, remained another source of painful uneasiness.

42 *Ibid.*, p. 348.   43 *Ibid.*

But there seemed to be a few small straws to clutch at. Count Giuseppe Greppi, the Italian minister in Stuttgart, noted the general belief there that warlike complications would be averted.[44] Similarly, Marquis Giovanni Antonio Migliorati, who was stationed in Munich, stressed the hopeful side of the picture by citing not only France's direct approaches to William in Ems but also a report that both Austria and Great Britain were supporting the attempt to elicit some co-operation from that reluctant sovereign. According to Migliorati, who evidently reflected the considered judgment of official circles, the position Bavaria would take in the days immediately ahead was by no means certain. This of course could be construed to mean that the largest and most powerful of the South German states was trying to keep open an escape hatch to neutrality despite its military ties to Berlin. If such an interpretation had any validity, then it was conceivable too that whatever influence Bavaria could muster in the Prussian capital would be exerted on the side of restraint. Migliorati himself pointed out that although the numerically small pro-Prussian faction in Munich had assailed Gramont's declaration before the corps législatif, stigmatizing it as provocative, the much more powerful conservative party and the government which it controlled inclined to the view that Bismarck had intended all along to play a trick on France—in other words, to goad her into some overt act of hostility. In any case, no decision on basic questions of policy would be reached by Count Otto von Bray, Bavaria's premier and foreign minister, until France had received William's reply.[45]

The slender comfort that could be derived from these crumbs was scarcely visible in Visconti-Venosta's own evaluation of the Prussian attitude.[46] Fluctuating between pessimism and a very faint hope, he continued to seek the closest possible liaison with the British in Berlin. In carefully phrased instructions, he specified that if for some reason Loftus should not go to Ems,

[44] Greppi to Visconti-Venosta, July 10, 1870, No. 2373, MAE, AS, DTA.

[45] Migliorati to Visconti-Venosta, July 10, 1870, No. 2377, *ibid.*

[46] Visconti-Venosta to Nigra, July 10, 1870, No. 1189, MAE, AS, TS. See also Nigra, p. 98.

Launay was also to stay away. In any case, Launay was to contact Loftus immediately, so that the two of them might concert a joint *démarche*.[47] Of course Visconti-Venosta anticipated that this might not tally with Loftus' instructions, and so he appealed to Granville to reconsider the British stand and agree to a total pooling of Anglo-Italian efforts in place of the parallel but separate action preferred by the Gladstone cabinet. In this connection he called attention to the wide powers he had given Launay and noted especially the authorization to make direct contact with the Prussian sovereign.[48]

Thereafter Visconti-Venosta did not mention Ems again either to Launay or the British. Loftus was never empowered to go to William's summer headquarters,[49] and the Italian foreign minister had no choice but to consider other expedients for achieving maximum collaboration between the two governments. At all events, Launay, who did not have ambassadorial rank, fastened on this as a reason for staying away from Ems, claiming that it barred him from asking the king for an audience unless he first took the matter up with the Prussian foreign office.[50] Even before he discovered that Loftus was without the necessary authorization, he decided not to raise the question. Instead, he sounded Thile on the possibility of obtaining clearance for a quick journey to Varzin to see Bismarck, who reportedly was still ailing.[51] The idea of substituting Varzin for Ems originated with Launay, and he acted on it without informing Visconti-Venosta. An ardent Prussophile, Launay evidently counted on the cordiality of his relations with Bismarck. However, this plan too came to nought. Thile, who knew his chief's aversion to such intrusions, advised

[47] Visconti-Venosta to Launay, July 10, 1870, No. 1188, MAE, AS, TS.

[48] Visconti-Venosta to Cadorna, July 10, 1870, No. 1190, *ibid.*; Visconti-Venosta to Cadorna, July 10, 1870, No. 51, MAE, AS, Divisione politica, 1867–1888, registri copia-lettere in partenza, Inghilterra, busta 1167: 22 maggio 1869–29 luglio 1872.

[49] Launay to Visconti-Venosta, July 11, 1870, No. 2490, MAE, AS, DTA.

[50] Launay to Visconti-Venosta, July 11, 1870, No. 2480, *ibid.*

[51] Launay to Visconti-Venosta, July 11, 1870, No. 2490, *ibid.*

Launay that the moment was not "opportune" for a visit to Varzin.[52]

6

In Ems, Benedetti waited for William's answer, which was expected almost hourly. In Florence, Visconti-Venosta waited for Govone to contact Aosta, exhibiting once again that lack of hurry which seemed to characterize his behavior in emergencies as well as in ordinary situations. Meanwhile, he continued to warn the Spaniards of the dire things that would happen if the Hohenzollern candidature were not withdrawn.[53] A brief message from Cerruti indicated that the atmosphere in Madrid was somewhat calmer than it had been,[54] but what this might mean in the context of the crisis as a whole was not clear. Then, just before midnight on the tenth, important news arrived from Nigra. The king's reply had been transmitted by Benedetti. William admitted that he had given his consent to Leopold's candidature, but also let it be known that he was arranging a conference with the prince. The meeting was expected to take place immediately, and the French government had decided to await the result before announcing the mobilization of its armed forces. On the other hand, certain secret preparations that were already in progress would continue.[55]

Apart from the short respite won on the diplomatic front, what benefits would flow from William's willingness to see Leopold? According to Lyons, whose opinion Nigra cited, the situation was hopeless: war could no longer be averted.[56] Nigra feebly disagreed, declaring that he still put his trust in Leo-

[52] Launay to Visconti-Venosta, July 11, 1870, No. 2487, *ibid.*

[53] Visconti-Venosta to Cerruti, July 10, 1870, No. 1191, MAE, AS, TS. See also Visconti-Venosta to Cerruti, July 10, 1870, No. 5, MAE, AS, Archivi di gabinetto (1861–1887), busta 219: guerra franco-prussiana e trattative segrete 8 luglio–14 settembre 1870, fascicolo 4; Visconti-Venosta to Cerruti, July 10, 1870, No. 26, MAE, AS, Divisione politica, 1867–1888, registri copia-lettere in partenza, Spagna, busta 1212: 13 febbraio 1867–31 luglio 1873.

[54] Cerruti to Visconti-Venosta, July 10, 1870, No. 2378, MAE, AS, DTA.

[55] Nigra to Visconti-Venosta, July 10, 1870, No. 2479, *ibid.*

[56] *Ibid.*

pold's wisdom![57] However, he went on to urge that if there
were any way, in conjunction with the British, of exerting pressure on the prince, Visconti-Venosta should not overlook it. In
any case, speed continued to be essential: twenty-four hours
and no more remained in which to do something.[58]

William's involvement in the launching of the Hohenzollern
candidature came as no surprise to Visconti-Venosta; he already knew it from Launay. But the belated admission under
French pressure, after so many protestations by the Prussian
government that it had known absolutely nothing about the
affair and that the question of the succession was the exclusive
concern of Leopold and the Spaniards, would of course make
a very bad impression in Paris. The readiness of the French
to postpone the announcement of mobilization therefore
seemed to count for little against the fact that secret military
preparations were not being suspended. Nevertheless, their decision to wait until William and Leopold had conferred represented for Visconti-Venosta another straw to clutch at;
perhaps it was something more than a purely tactical move
intended to absolve France from blame for whatever might
follow. In any case, a reprieve had been won, and Visconti-
Venosta could see no better way of using it than to bring every
possible pressure to bear on Leopold. Instructions in this sense
were dispatched to Launay.[59] The denouement in Ems now
seemed only hours away, yet there was still no word from
Govone. Visconti-Venosta must have wondered about the delay
but so far had done nothing about it.

[57] *Ibid.*   [58] *Ibid.*

[59] Visconti-Venosta to Launay, July 11, 1870, No. 1193, MAE, AS, TS.

CHAPTER SIX

DUEL WITH THE LEFT

In the midst of all his other preoccupations, Visconti-Venosta found himself confronted with the necessity of engaging in a verbal duel with spokesmen for the Left. In the chamber of deputies the opposition was preparing to censure the government. It had been infuriated by the statement Ollivier was reported to have made to the clerical delegation, and it was sure that Visconti-Venosta had not reacted with sufficient vigor. Above all, it was concerned over recurrent rumors that, if and when the September Convention was renewed, Italy would pay by undertaking to give military aid to Napoleon. Naturally Visconti-Venosta did not relish the prospect of a public discussion at a moment when delicate negotiations were still in progress. The Sinistra, however, had no intention of holding its fire to suit the convenience of the foreign minister. Its leaders were obviously eager to embarrass the government and make political capital. But partisan considerations were not the sole determinants. Genuinely alarmed, the men of the Left considered it a patriotic duty to mount their offensive and to bring the issue out into the open before it was too late. Since parliament was the only place where they could hope to corner the government, they decided to force a debate that would clear the air once and for all.

The opposition was served by a large number of newspapers, but unquestionably its two leading organs were the *Riforma* and the *Diritto* of Florence. The *Riforma* had been founded in 1867 by Francesco Crispi, Benedetto Cairoli, Agostino Bertani, and other Sinistra stalwarts. It was directed by Crispi and

Antonio Oliva, later also by Luigi Miceli and Giuseppe Lazzaro.[1] Reflecting above all the outlook of Crispi, the *Riforma* stood closer to the party's militant wing than did the *Diritto*. Of Garibaldian fame and an erstwhile republican, Crispi was a very influential figure as well as a tempestuous and colorful one. Because of the Roman question, which literally obsessed him, he was violently anti-French. But there was a second reason: he detested Bonapartism and the "tyranny" of Napoleon III, author of the "infamous" coup d'état of December 2, 1851.[2]

Just before the sensational tidings from Madrid reached the Italian press, Florence buzzed with reports of negotiations for the evacuation of Rome. The *Riforma* seized upon them to charge that the French were again imposing conditions that could not be squared with Italy's sovereignty and honor. With tongue in cheek it professed to have not the slightest doubt about the patriotism of Visconti-Venosta and labeled as "foolish" any assumptions that he could not be trusted. But in the same breath it admonished him to abstain from imitating his immediate predecessors in the foreign office who, it alleged, had not hesitated to betray the national interest in the hope of obtaining concessions from France. Specifically, it cautioned against a *"modus vivendi,"* by which it meant an offer of guaranties to France in order to induce her to carry out her obligations under the September Convention. Such guaranties, if translated into a formal commitment, would signify that Italy was renouncing Rome indefinitely. But the inhabitants of the peninsula could not and would not accept any solution that failed to give full satisfaction to their national aspirations. In other words, the city must be liberated unconditionally, without any restrictive stipulations that clashed with the principle of sovereignty. Should it prove impossible to reach agreement with the French on this, the government must give up trying to avoid the inevitable; it must halt forthwith its conspiracy against destiny and desist from a "policy of half-measures."[3]

[1] Chabod, p. 49.

[2] *Ibid.*, pp. 26, 27.

[3] *La Riforma*, July 4, 1870.

Twenty-four hours after the *Riforma* issued this warning, all Italy knew that a Hohenzollern prince had accepted Prim's offer of the Spanish crown. But while most of the Italian press devoted column after column to the news, the *Riforma* completely ignored it. On the other hand, true to the Francophobia of the Sinistra radicals, it raged for three days over Ollivier's remarks to the clerical delegation. Terming this latest "insult" no surprise, it renewed its familiar attacks against the September Convention. In the last analysis, that agreement was merely a trick to substitute Italy for France as the military protector of the temporal power. In lending itself to so nefarious a maneuver, the Italian government had behaved strangely, to say the least.[4]

What was to be done? There was but a single answer, argued the *Riforma*: for the sake of the "dignity" of the government and the "integrity" of the nation, it was imperative to declare once and for all that the September Convention was null and void.[5] Italy would have to act unilaterally; it was delusory to expect anything from the French. Their foreign policy could never free itself from the influence of the Catholic party, whose support Napoleon needed. Without that support the imperial regime, which rested on the ignorance and superstition of the rural masses, would crumble.[6] If the Lanza government were to agree now or later to a renewal of the September Convention, it would be abdicating reason and will, with results that were bound to be fatal. Since the men of the Right who composed the cabinet were not likely of their own accord to do what was necessary, they would have to be told time and again to put an end to this "indecent comedy" whose sole effect was to vest in a foreign power control over the administration and police of Italy.[7]

Apart from this anxiety about the fate of Rome, ideological considerations led the *Riforma* to lash out repeatedly against the Second Empire. For similar reasons it found much to praise in the camp of France's rival. Thus, early in the July crisis, it lauded the Prussian Progressives as champions of freedom as

---

4 *Ibid.*, July 6, 1870.   6 *Ibid.*
5 *Ibid.*   7 *Ibid.*

well as national unity and voiced the confident hope that their
democratic, antimilitarist, and socially enlightened program
would prove acceptable to all "liberal" Germans.[8] The contrast
between the fervor of this tribute and the venomous tone of
the references to Napoleonic "despotism" could hardly have
been sharper.

Finally, on July 8 the *Riforma* took notice of the growing
threat to peace, and in doing so poured out more wrath against
France. It denounced Gramont's declaration as completely warlike and took the imperial government to task for resorting to
threats. If the honor of France had been affronted, such behavior would be pardonable. But she had not been insulted;
her rage was purely the result of mortification at having been
taken by surprise and outwitted. With mock concern, the
Riforma advised Gramont that he should have been more
careful. After all, Bismarck was not an Italian who could be
bullied with impunity. Nor was he the kind of man who over-
looked anything. He had probably calculated all the possible
consequences of his acts and even foreseen what was happening now. He must have guessed how excited the French would
be, how they would react to an affair hatched with such adroit-
ness under their very eyes but of which they had had no ink-
ling. "Poor imperial diplomacy," the *Riforma* lamented in the
same caustic vein, "only Italy has provided you with . . . easy
triumphs! Sadowa, Luxemburg, and now the Hohenzollern
candidature; this is really something to be sad about! And to
think that only a few days ago Émile Ollivier was proclaiming
that after the plebiscite [of May 8, 1870], the diplomats of the
empire reported that henceforward they would be able to im-
pose the will of France everywhere!"[9]

Relying on its own estimate of Bismarck's methods and goals,
the *Riforma* decided that there was more to the present crisis
than met the eye. The Spanish question was really only a side
issue, a pretext, so far as Prussia was concerned. Bismarck had
known all along that a German dynasty could not be perma-
nently installed in a country as fiercely nationalistic as Spain.

[8] *Ibid.*   [9] *Ibid.*, July 8, 1870.

He was using the Hohenzollern candidature to set the stage for something bigger: a final showdown with France. Prudent calculation on the part of the French would have led them to postpone the evil day, but Gramont's outburst proved that they had taken leave of their senses.[10] On the question of Italy's role the *Riforma* was of course quite outspoken. It noted an Austrian report which claimed that the cabinets of London, Vienna, and Florence were disposed to unite their diplomatic efforts with those of France for the purpose of resolving the crisis. If the report meant that Italy, together with Great Britain and Austria, was siding with France in the present controversy, the Lanza government would have to do a good deal of explaining. The Sinistra, for which the *Riforma* felt qualified to speak, would refuse to allow the country to be stripped of its neutrality and dragged into a struggle for supremacy between France and Germany. To be sure, Italy must be vigilant and prepared for all emergencies, but she must bind herself to no one.[11]

During the next few days, the *Riforma* exhibited increasing fury against the French and their supposed collaborators in Italy. From its Paris correspondent it received a vivid picture of the hysteria that had gripped the city. Everybody, he reported, was talking about revenge for Sadowa. Ollivier was quoted as saying that within two months, either France would have the Rhine or Prussia would have France.[12] This, the *Riforma* complained, was not facilitating the task of those who were striving for a peaceful solution. If war broke out, the fault would lie squarely with France, with her "intolerable" insistence on the right to meddle in the affairs of other countries. In Italy, by means of armed intervention, she was blocking the last step toward unification; in Spain she was vetoing whatever did not suit her. True, the Napoleonic dream of a Latin empire had ended in smoke; but France still wanted to exercise a "high sovereignty," a "quasi-arbitral function," a "preponderant influence" in lands where the masses disliked her tyrannical system of government. Little wonder that she now found herself isolated: the blame was entirely her own.[13]

10 *Ibid.*   12 *Ibid.*, July 10, 1870.
11 *Ibid.*   13 *Ibid.*

The culpability and folly of the Second Empire were thus plain to the *Riforma*. Equally incontrovertible in its view was the danger inherent in the "unpredictable" behavior of the Lanza government. The overwhelming majority of Italians wanted the country to proclaim its non-interventionist position as often as might be necessary. They wished to see Italy heed the dictates of her innermost essence: "unitary, independent, sovereign nationality." For this "positive, realistic, effective" value some deluded individuals desired to substitute the "vague, fantastic, fallacious, utopian" idea of a Latin race in inescapable and eternal conflict with the Germanic race. In contrast to such "quasi-Hegelian" nonsense about Latin and Germanic races, the principle of nationality excluded "a priori" ties to other peoples. According to it, every nation was juridically a state and every state had a personality that was absolutely unique and autonomous. At the present moment, Italy had two vital problems of her own that required immediate attention. One was the Roman question; so long as it remained unresolved, the national revolution would be a stunted affair. The other was internal reorganization. Nothing must be permitted to divert the country from either of these problems. It was therefore essential that Italy should adopt and maintain a neutral policy.[14] If, instead, she sided with France, she would be committing suicide.[15]

It was on this note that the *Riforma* attacked the *Italie*, another Florentine daily that claimed to be in the confidence of Visconti-Venosta. The *Italie* argued that the country had everything to gain from a French victory and everything to lose by Prussian preponderance. The *Riforma* tartly retorted that the effect on Italy of French preponderance was already much too apparent. About the alleged perils of Prussian supremacy the editors of the paper professed total unconcern. There was no reason to worry: the country had only to adopt a policy that was worthy of a great nation. When it did—and this would surely happen as soon as the Destra had been removed from power—all foreign influence would be banished forever from the peninsula.[16]

[14] *Ibid.*   [15] *Ibid.*, July 13, 1870.   [16] *Ibid.*

2

Like the *Riforma*, the *Diritto*[17] used its columns to set the stage for a trial of strength in the chamber of deputies. Directed by a coterie that included the future boss of the country, Agostino Depretis, it too trained its guns on the French "allies" of the Lanza cabinet. It recalled some recent discussions in the corps législatif in order to illustrate the pernicious character of French chauvinism. First there was the uproar over the Saint Gotthard tunnel. Then came the diatribes against Prussia during the debate on the annual military contingent; they showed that the leaders of the Second Empire still regarded the destruction of Prussia as the primary goal.[18] Gramont's declaration was of a piece with these and other infractions of international decency. The French government knew very well that, according to a measure enacted by the Cortes not long ago, only the legally elected representatives of the Spanish nation could settle dynastic problems. Therefore, should a majority of these deputies decide, for whatever reason, to elevate a Prussian prince to the throne, the imperial government would have no right to stand in the way. If it did, it would contravene those justly celebrated principles of public law of which France herself claimed exclusive authorship.[19]

The *Diritto*, like so many of its confreres, insisted that the Spanish affair was nothing more than the old "Franco-Prussian question" in a new guise. But who had initiated this tension between the two countries? And who was trying by every conceivable means to perpetuate it? Obviously France, the entire French nation, and not just the government, which merely reflected the attitude of the country. For as long as anyone could remember, the French had been denouncing the treaties of 1815. Then, strangely enough, they had taken it into their heads that Sadowa, which by destroying a large part of the Vienna settlement accomplished the very end they had been trying to promote, was a defeat not for Austria but for France. Intent on revenge ever since 1866, they had marked Prussia

---

[17] On the standing of the *Diritto*, see Chabod, p. 347.

[18] *Il Diritto*, July 6, 1870.   [19] *Ibid.*, July 8, 1870.

out for punishment, even going so far as to consider dismembering her and seizing the Rhineland.[20] It was only natural that Bismarck should seek to defend himself with any weapons that he had or could improvise. In this connection the *Diritto* admitted it did not know how much truth there was to the French charge that the Prussian statesman had been instrumental in instigating the Spanish revolution of 1868. However, it could scarcely deny that the revolution had provided him with a splendid opportunity to hit back which was now being put to use. At all events, France was receiving her just deserts.[21]

Enlarging on this theme, the *Diritto* charged that France had been attempting to keep other countries—Germany, Italy, Spain—in a state of subjection. Of course it went without saying that it was all very well, even "noble," to aspire to be the foremost nation in the world. But the French would have to put their minds and energies to achieving this ambition some other way. First they must set their own house in order and cultivate their potentialities. This meant establishing true and lasting freedom at home, raising the level of their intellectual and spiritual life, and developing to the utmost the immense resources which a bountiful nature had bestowed upon them. If France followed this advice, she would be, if not the foremost, at least one of the leading nations on the face of the earth, and as such she would have nothing to fear from anyone. On the other hand, if she persisted in her present practices, she would not only harm herself; she would also find it impossible to prevent Germany, Italy, and Spain from reaching those goals that had been preordained for them by "invincible natural laws." She would, into the bargain, sow even more antipathy where today she might be harvesting gratitude, and she would saddle herself with responsibility for disasters which, it was to be hoped, could still be averted.[22]

Unhappily, moral principles and values no longer seemed to matter to the French, but the sheer instinct of self-preservation should have impelled them to postpone their long meditated war against Prussia until certain points had been cleared up. However, even that instinct appeared to be moribund in

[20] *Ibid.*   [21] *Ibid.*   [22] *Ibid.*

France. With evident approval the *Diritto* cited a statement from the semiofficial *Norddeutsche Allgemeine Zeitung* of Berlin deploring France's precipitancy. Why, asked the *Diritto*, had Paris moved with such furious haste to take up a position from which retreat would be impossible without loss of face? After all, the German people had no direct interest in the Spanish dynastic problem, and a mutually satisfactory solution should not have been hard to find. The failure so far to arrive at one could be only too easily explained: France was determined to prevent the unification of Germany; she was making a tremendous fuss over Leopold's candidature because of this ulterior objective. Her actions now as in the past were animated by the "miserable" fear that other countries might become too powerful. How would she feel if her neighbors decided that she must be dismembered because in her present form she was too strong?[23]

Would French belligerence lead to war? Although manifestly far from optimistic, the *Diritto* ventured the opinion that the answer was not necessarily yes and that the powers might still succeed in resolving the crisis before one side or the other did something irreparable. Thinking ahead to the confrontation in the chamber of deputies, it insisted that Italy must put her shoulder to the wheel. Like Prussia, she wanted peace. To achieve it, she must make a maximum effort, especially with the French, who needed to be told that their conduct could not be condoned.[24] Should such plain language fail of its purpose and war ensue, Italy would have to steer clear of military entanglements; under no circumstances was she to become the ally of France. This was the nation's fixed resolve.[25] It was hardly necessary to add that even if self-interest were not enough justification for this attitude, the merits of the dispute could also be adduced. Prussia had carefully avoided giving provocation to anyone; despite her splendid successes, she had shown remarkable restraint. The French, on the other hand, had constantly harassed her. Little wonder then that the Italian people wished to see an end to such bullying. National

[23] *Ibid.*, July 10, 1870.
[24] *Ibid.*, July 11, 1870.   [25] *Ibid.*

policy must take this into account. If the Lanza cabinet refused to heed the country's demands, parliament would have no option but to take matters into its own hands and to proceed to whatever action the situation might require.[26]

On July 9, the Sinistra set the stage for its exposure of the alleged shortcomings of the government's foreign policy. Five of its deputies—Giovanni Nicotera, Clemente Corte, Abele Damiani, Miceli, and Oliva—descended upon Giovanni Biancheri, the president of the chamber. All of them formally petitioned for permission to interrogate Visconti-Venosta. Miceli had a question about the Spanish affair. Nicotera and Corte fixed their sights not only on the position that the government was taking in the Franco-Prussian dispute but also on Ollivier's controversial remarks to the clerical delegation. The third query, which bore the signatures of Oliva, Damiani, and Miceli, alluded to the current state of Italy's foreign relations but emphasized the Roman question. Biancheri, who belonged to the Destra, made no objection and scheduled the discussion for the eleventh.

As the moment for the debate drew near, the Sinistra leaders felt they could rely increasingly on a ground swell of popular support. The nation was worried and restive. During the first few days of the crisis, most Italians had assumed that a peaceful solution would be found. Now they feared that the Spanish issue was being supplanted by the question of whether France or Prussia would dominate Europe. If this was really what was happening, diplomacy might well prove powerless to prevent the outbreak of hostilities.[27]

3

A few minutes past noon on the eleventh, Visconti-Venosta hurried to the chamber of deputies. He dreaded what lay ahead but still hoped he would be able to forestall a full debate. As soon as he appeared, Biancheri asked him to speak.

[26] Ibid.

[27] See the observations on this in Malaret to Gramont, July 12, 1870, No. 51, AMAE, Italie, janvier–juillet 1870, tome 378 (OD, XXVIII, No. 8451, p. 280).

His first care, on ascending the rostrum, was to implore a delay.
He warned his listeners on the Left that a public scrutiny of
foreign policy would be inopportune. However, because he
understood and respected the "legitimate" anxiety that motivated the interpellants, he would try to allay it with a brief
declaration.[28] He addressed himself first to Ollivier's remarks.
They had been made in a private conversation and as such
were not a proper subject for diplomatic exchanges. Nevertheless, in view of the special interest that attached to the matter
allegedly discussed by Ollivier, the Italian government had
asked Gramont for an explanation. In his reply the duke had
stated that the reports published in the French press were
false, that Ollivier had uttered neither the words attributed to
him nor any like them.[29]

Visconti-Venosta went on to make plain that, since the incident was related to the French occupation of Rome, he was
mentioning it now in order to underline the need for caution
as well as firmness. Reiterating statements previously made by
him in both the chamber of deputies and the senate, he asserted
that the Italian government had not yet raised the question
because it believed that a waiting, reserved policy was indicated; to proceed otherwise would not be in the best interests
of Italy. There had therefore been no negotiations, and none
were in progress. What some newspapers were saying on this
score was consequently quite inaccurate. On the other hand,
the existing situation could not be prolonged indefinitely; diplomatic action of some sort would have to be taken. But it was
to be hoped that the members of parliament, mindful of the
government's heavy responsibilities, would leave it free to
choose the right moment.[30]

The deputies on the ministerial benches evidenced their approval while the opposition sat in stony silence. Visconti-
Venosta, speaking guardedly, turned from the Roman question
to the "grave complications" produced by the Hohenzollern

[28] *Rendiconti del parlamento italiano. Sessione del 1869–70 (seconda
della legislatura X): discussioni della camera dei deputati* (Florence,
1870), III: dal 4 giugno al 12 luglio 1870, p. 3218.

[29] *Ibid.*   [30] *Ibid.*, pp. 3218–19.

candidature. He emphasized the necessity of reticence. So much, however, he would say: the Italian government was following the only possible course, the one marked out for it by the kind of circumstances that had arisen. It was uniting with other powers that shared its interest in the preservation of international tranquillity. Peace was Italy's paramount need, just as it was essential to the rest of Europe. Negotiations were presently under way. It was therefore obvious why he could not elaborate. Were he to say anything more, he would do the nation a disservice and make a mockery of the responsibilities of his office. He trusted that his brief remarks would suffice, but he was confident at all events that the patriotism and wisdom of the interpellants would deter them from insisting on a debate at this time.[31]

Amid cries of "Bravo!" from the Right, Visconti-Venosta returned to his place next to Lanza's on the bench reserved for members of the cabinet. Biancheri took his cue from the foreign minister and ruled that the discussion of foreign policy would have to be postponed until a more suitable moment. But this the majority of the Sinistra would not tolerate. Their emotions had been inflamed over the past several days by persistent reports that the Italian government was siding with France against Prussia, and Visconti-Venosta's laconic statement failed to pacify them. Clearly, they were in no mood to be kept waiting until the foreign minister should "condescend" to afford them a glimpse of what was happening behind the portals of secret diplomacy. Brushing Biancheri's objections aside and ignoring the audible signs of displeasure on the Right, Miceli strode to the rostrum and launched a bitter attack on the government. It was all very well, he sneered, for Visconti-Venosta to say that the moment was inopportune for a discussion of Italy's foreign relations. Europe was reacting to grave threats of war. Public opinion in Italy, France, Germany, Spain, and elsewhere was deeply perturbed. With the continent teetering on the brink of a great catastrophe, could there be a better moment than the present for such a debate? Was it the government's intention to make the country mark time until some

[31] *Ibid.*, p. 3219.

irrevocable step had been taken, when it would be too late for parliament to say or do anything? As for Rome, it was quite amazing that almost three years after the reoccupation of the city by the French, and after so many genuflections by Italy before her powerful neighbor, so many examples of abnegation, not to say apathy and even cowardice on her part, the country should now be told that it must wait a little longer and keep silent.[32] After almost three years, a disgraceful state of affairs that was absolutely incompatible with Italy's rights and needs was being ruled out as a subject for discussion. To acquiesce would be suicidal as well as insufferable. A nation which over a long period of time failed to speak up in its own behalf was bound to be taken for dead and treated as such.[33]

At this point Biancheri, spurred by indications of mounting impatience on the Right, decided to intervene. A long procedural wrangle between him and Miceli followed. Biancheri insisted that Miceli must stop and await a formal vote by the chamber on whether or not he should continue. To this Miceli retorted that he was entitled to comment on Visconti-Venosta's declaration and that if the chamber wished to vote, it should do so later. With Biancheri's grudging consent, and in the midst of much restiveness on the ministerial benches, Miceli resumed. He stubbornly maintained that his interpellation was indispensable as well as opportune and demanded a debate on the questions it raised. Lashing at Ollivier's remarks, he ridiculed the "new conception of political wisdom" propounded by Visconti-Venosta. Ollivier presided over the French cabinet. The visiting delegation consisted of members of a public body, the corps législatif. When Ollivier talked to such people in his official capacity, he was not performing a private act. Yet, in the face of these plain facts, Visconti-Venosta contended otherwise. How, then, could the country and the chamber of deputies resign themselves to his "wretched arguments"? How could they accept his line of reasoning when it was being used to throttle discussion of a matter that brought so much pain to all patriotic Italians?[34]

Miceli was merely warming to his theme. But the ministerial

---

[32] *Ibid.*   [33] *Ibid.*   [34] *Ibid.*, p. 3220.

benches became angrier and noisier, and once again Biancheri tried to silence him. Encouraged by shouts of "Speak! Speak!" from his friends on the Left, Miceli asked the chamber to hear him out; what he proposed to say concerned the nation's "vital interests."[35] Biancheri objected, but Miceli continued as if the procedural question had been settled in his favor. Reverting to the statements ascribed to Ollivier, he impugned Gramont's denial. The press reports had never been contradicted by any member of the clerical delegation, and the attempt to exonerate Ollivier was not the first example of mendacity on the part of a high-ranking French official.[36] According to one account, Ollivier had said that the French would not leave Rome and that Italy was unable to guarantee public order. This version was accurate.[37]

Apparently savoring every minute, and treating Biancheri with the same disregard as before, Miceli now prepared to launch into a discussion of the Spanish affair. In desperation, Biancheri called for a vote by the chamber. Deaf to Miceli's protests, the Destra majority ruled that he would have to desist.[38] He finally gave way, but only after flinging out a double warning: if the chamber insisted on deriding the Sinistra's questions, the responsibility for whatever might follow would fall squarely on the Destra; if the Lanza cabinet continued to travel the road on which it was presently embarked, and if in the interim parliament should be prevented from speaking its mind, the Sinistra deputies would have no recourse but to leave the chamber.[39]

Before quitting the rostrum, Miceli asked that a date be set for the discussion of his interpellation, but Visconti-Venosta suggested that the chamber do nothing until the railway conventions, which were on its agenda, had been disposed of. At these words, the ministerial benches, thinking he was being sardonic at Miceli's expense, burst into loud derisive laughter. Appearing not to notice, Visconti-Venosta went on to say that he would agree to an earlier date only if the European situation took a turn for the worse.[40]

[35] *Ibid.*   [37] *Ibid.*   [39] *Ibid.*, p. 3221.

[36] *Ibid.*   [38] *Ibid.*   [40] *Ibid.*

When the foreign minister, never verbose, finished with an abruptness that was unusual even for him, Biancheri ruled that Urbano Rattazzi was entitled to speak to a point of order. Rattazzi, the controversial former premier, had friends in both parties but sympathized with the Sinistra militants on the Roman question. On this occasion he began gently enough. He could understand, he said, that for official reasons Visconti-Venosta must be extremely cautious. He also conceded that parliament could not compel the foreign minister to go into particulars which his conscience and his responsibilities forbade him to divulge. Then, with a sudden change to asperity, Rattazzi emphasized that Visconti-Venosta was not the only one with rights and duties. Deputies had them, too. As elected representatives, they were entitled and obligated to interpellate the government if they thought the national interest so required. Considered from this point of view, the silencing of Miceli was inexcusable.[41] The foreign minister had heard that certain questions were to be put to him. Giving his interrogators no opportunity to explain, and quite obviously determined to forestall them, he had hurried to tell the chamber only what he wanted it to know. Instead of avoiding his interrogators, he should have given them a chance to be heard. Afterward the chamber could have decided whether to stage or forgo a full debate. To postpone the discussion until action had been completed on the railway conventions was equivalent to denying the interpellants the right to perform their duty.[42]

Stung by this charge, Visconti-Venosta retorted with unwonted sharpness. He had hoped that Miceli would relent after hearing his declaration, which stated everything that could be said for the present, and which in any case made it clear that the government would not dream of playing fast and loose with the country's interests. This hope, he could now see, was entirely futile. But at any rate the chamber must remember that it would be consulted without fail in the event of serious complications. He himself was quite content to let the deputies judge and decide the procedural issue, although for the reasons

41 *Ibid.*   42 *Ibid.*

he had indicated, he still preferred to wait until a full report could be presented.[43]

Returning to the rostrum for a point of order, the irrepressible Miceli stoutly defended his conduct. It was essential, he insisted, that the chamber be afforded an opportunity to offer its counsel before irrevocable steps were taken. Otherwise, it could find itself confronted with an ugly situation that it had had no hand in creating. This was a completely unassailable position, yet the majority of the deputies were holding their tongues and resigning themselves to whatever the future might bring. At this very moment, in fact, some new disgrace or misfortune might be in the making. Then, brushing aside murmurs of protest from the Right, Miceli converted this insinuation into a definite accusation, charging that the government was pursuing in Spain a course of action that violated the principle of national sovereignty and alienated the good will of Prussia, a country to which Italy was bound by important interests.[44]

Vowing vengeance against Biancheri for the way he had been treated, Miceli subsided,[45] whereupon a host of Sinistra deputies, all clamoring for permission to speak, besieged the harassed president. After a slight hesitation, Biancheri awarded the floor to Oliva, one of the original interpellants. Affecting a mildness that his words belied, Oliva said he could not accept Visconti-Venosta's plea for a postponement of the discussion. After all, the foreign minister himself admitted that Italians were justified in feeling anxious about the current international crisis.[46] Because the Roman question was involved in these complications, he had joined his friends, Miceli and Damiani, in asking for information. He had allowed himself to believe that Visconti-Venosta's reply would dissipate the fears of the Italian people. Unhappily, it had failed to do so, and to point this out was not a pleasant duty. The foreign minister preferred a policy of reserve and restraint for reasons of expediency. This seemed plausible enough. However, it was disturbing to note that with the aid of such words as "until now," "if," and "but,"

[43] *Ibid.,* p. 3222.

[44] *Ibid.*

[45] *Ibid.*

[46] *Ibid.,* pp. 3222–23.

he had left himself so many loopholes that concern about the immediate future was bound to grow rather than lessen.[47]

To underscore this point, Oliva started to say something about an incident in the senate. But Biancheri broke in to warn that he would have to stop at once. Oliva refused. While the ministerial benches noisily supported Biancheri, Oliva's friends egged him on. One Sinistra stalwart called out: "They don't want to give anyone on our side a chance; only people on their side are allowed to speak."[48] When Biancheri retorted that he would not be influenced by such outbursts, another of Oliva's comrades shouted: "This is a shameful example of intolerance!"[49] And a third raised the banner of revolt with this exhortation: "Let us leave the chamber *en masse* and appeal to the country."[50] Biancheri suddenly relapsed into helplessness, and Oliva reverted to the incident in the senate. There, not long ago, Visconti-Venosta had been praised by his predecessor, Menabrea, for following the same policy with regard to the Roman question. Oliva continued:[51]

Now, gentlemen, when I recall Menabrea's policy on the Roman question; when I recall that far from pursuing a reserved and restrained policy he was negotiating a *modus vivendi* that would have guaranteed the integrity of the papal territory; when I hear the present foreign minister say that he reserves the right to depart in future from the restraint he claims he has preferred until now—then, in the face of such a contradiction, I feel it is permissible, even necessary, not only to distrust but to dread the direction in which he may be pushing us.

That is why . . . I cannot consent to the retraction of the interpellation, why I am asking the chamber to fix a day on which parliament will be permitted to say to the government that the country absolutely refuses to allow the Roman question to be . . . sacrificed to French policy. This is a matter of such importance that we cannot ignore it without abdicating our rights, our duties, our dignity.

The next speaker was Nicotera, the only topflight politician among the interpellants and a leader of the Sinistra's moderate wing. He reluctantly agreed to a postponement of the debate

---

[47] *Ibid.*, p. 3223.   [49] *Ibid.*

[48] *Ibid.*   [50] *Ibid.*   [51] *Ibid.*

on the Roman question. However, he demanded immediate
clarification of one aspect of the Spanish affair. There was a
report from Paris that the Italian government was vigorously
supporting the French point of view in the current crisis. Confirmation of this report would mean that Lanza and his colleagues were no longer working for the maintenance of peace,
that they had adopted as their own the warlike course on
which France was embarked.[52] Needless to say, such a policy
would be repudiated by the entire membership of the chamber. Would Visconti-Venosta therefore be good enough to say
whether the report was true or false?[53] The foreign minister
sprang to his feet to complain that his declaration could not
possibly leave room for the interpretation which Nicotera had
put on the report from Paris. To assist Nicotera, Visconti-
Venosta recalled what he had said: Italy's principal concern in
the current crisis was to see that the tranquillity of Europe was
not disturbed; she had joined others similarly disposed in an
attempt to achieve a peaceful solution. Such was the path that
had been and was being followed, and it was to be hoped that
Nicotera would accept this reaffirmation as completely satisfactory.[54]

Just how Nicotera reacted to the foreign minister's explanation could not be immediately ascertained because Corte, the
fourth interpellant to be recognized by Biancheri, was on the
rostrum as soon as Visconti-Venosta had stepped down. After
praising Nicotera, Corte harked back to the remarks attributed
to Ollivier. With heavy sarcasm he thanked Visconti-Venosta
for clearing up that mystery. Of course he had far too much
esteem for the members of the Lanza cabinet to suppose even
for a moment that they would suffer a foreign statesman to
charge that order did not reign in the country they governed.
That such an offensive statement should have been ascribed to
Ollivier was scarcely surprising, for in actuality he had made
it. After all, the man was nothing but a repentant republican
trying to atone for earlier sins. But since he had been exoner-
ated by Gramont, Italians would have no choice but to regard
him as innocent. Corte took some comfort in the thought that

[52] *Ibid.*, pp. 3223–24.   [53] *Ibid.*, p. 3224.   [54] *Ibid.*

Gramont's gesture represented "a good and handsome apology," and as such he was pleased to accept it.[55]

On this note he finished, and Nicotera, who had been signaling Biancheri, was granted a few minutes to make a special declaration. Once again the Sinistra chieftain admitted that it would be inopportune to go into the Roman question; the fate of the city could not be discussed freely because of the international crisis and the situation in which Italy was placed as a consequence of this exceptional state of affairs. But everything would be rectified when the chamber got around to scrutinizing the behavior of the Lanza government. The proper course—as Nicotera said this he appealed to Miceli for concurrence—was to wait a little longer, to see what would happen in the Spanish affair, and then to have a wide-ranging debate on the country's foreign policy.[56]

Thus Visconti-Venosta had achieved his purpose: Nicotera, a member of the Sinistra's directorate, was prepared to mark time for at least a few days, to refrain from asking any more questions about Italy's role in the crisis, and this could not fail to influence his comrades. That all of them did not share Nicotera's patience was evident from the acrid comments of the next speaker, but the *élan* of the opposition had been broken, and this was quite enough even for Biancheri. Acting for once with dispatch, he had little trouble closing the proceedings.

The reaction of the press followed the usual party lines. Of the ministerial papers, the *Opinione* was the most reflective. After dwelling on the unmitigated gravity of the crisis, the authoritative daily recalled that some twenty years earlier, when it was advocating the unification of Italy, it had prophesied that all sorts of wonderful things would come to pass in the wake of that consummation: expansion of the nation's wealth, consolidation of internal tranquillity, orderly progress toward ever higher levels of morality, and the achievement of peaceful as well as self-respecting relations with those countries that had been accustomed to regard Italy as a place where outsiders competed for spheres of influence. All these high hopes had not

55 *Ibid.*, pp. 3324–25.   56 *Ibid.*, p. 3225.

been fulfilled, but it was a fact that today no nation on the face of the earth was more interested than Italy in the preservation of peace. England used to boast that she was the world's most peace-loving country. Now Italy surpassed her. The distance that separated them could be explained by the disparity between Italy's financial deficits and England's "scandalous prosperity."[57] The formula of "peace at almost any price," which best expressed the feelings of the cabinet majority, could hardly have been stated more candidly.

Alluding to the proceedings in the chamber, the *Opinione* gently yet firmly observed that the government could not speak its mind. Difficult negotiations were in progress, and they must not be jeopardized. The foreign minister had been very clear about this. But because he appreciated the considerations which had prompted the action of the interpellants, he had offered a brief explanation. Although it had failed to satisfy Miceli and Oliva, Nicotera had seen the need for caution and conceded the advisability of deferring a discussion of the Roman question. Leaning over backward in an effort to be fair, the *Opinione* charitably concluded that everyone realized the gravity of the situation and understood why Visconti-Venosta had had to be so laconic. In any case, the foreign minister was not given to talking too much; rather, he possessed "the art of saying no more than he deemed opportune and of using the language of diplomacy with great precision."[58]

Turning its attention to the dispute between France on the one side and Spain and Prussia on the other, the *Opinione* insisted that although the difficulties were enormous, they were by no means insurmountable. The Prussians were at the Rhine, but France was not proposing to dislodge them; she was objecting only to the introduction of Prussian influence on the other side of the Pyrenees. Prussia, concerned with problems of internal consolidation, had in the last analysis neither the desire nor the means to wage war on behalf of Leopold's candidature. Such a struggle would not be over principles or the idea of nationality; and even from Prussia's own point of view, it

[57] *L'Opinione,* July 12, 1870.   [58] *Ibid.*

would be genuinely dynastic in character only to a limited degree. As for the Spaniards, they could scarcely entertain any great liking for Leopold, whereas they had ample reason to desire a continuation of the traditional friendship with France. A war over the succession, no matter how it ended, could only do them harm. It was therefore incumbent on all three disputants to move toward an agreement. The only sensible solution was to drop Leopold and offer the Cortes some other candidate who would be acceptable to all the great powers as well as to the Spanish people. International diplomacy was now hard at work on the problem. Would France allow enough time? This was the overriding question.[59]

[59] *Ibid.*

CHAPTER SEVEN

THE FALSE PEACE

The parliamentary session of July 11 ended at about 3:00 P.M. Approximately a half hour later, Visconti-Venosta was back in the foreign office. A number of messages had arrived during his absence. The one of greatest immediate interest—nothing new had come in on the drama at Ems—was contained in a telegram from Cerruti. He reported that Serrano and Sagasta fully appreciated the seriousness of the situation and would welcome a voluntary withdrawal of Leopold's acceptance. This, in their opinion, was the only solution that could be reconciled with the honor of Spain.[1] Visconti-Venosta passed the message on to Launay, who could be expected to redouble his efforts against the Hohenzollern candidature.[2]

Help from the people in Berlin seemed more remote than ever. As for the attitude of the Spaniards, although it was encouraging, it obviously needed to be fortified. With this in mind, Visconti-Venosta decided now to let Madrid know how much Italy was prepared to contribute. He instructed Cerruti to inquire confidentially whether the Spanish government would be willing to renew its offer to Aosta if it had some assurance that he would accept.[3] Nothing as yet had been heard from Govone. So far as the foreign office knew, he was still in Florence. Visconti-Venosta had not seen the general since the

[1] Cerruti to Visconti-Venosta, July 11, 1870, No. 2481, MAE, AS, DTA.

[2] Visconti-Venosta to Launay, July 11, 1870, No. 1194, MAE, AS, TS.

[3] Visconti-Venosta to Cerruti, July 11, 1870, unnumbered private telegram, MAE, AS, Archivi di gabinetto (1861–1887), busta 219: guerra franco-prussiana e trattative segrete 8 luglio–14 settembre 1870, fascicolo 4.

cabinet meeting and was apparently unaware of the reason for the delay. He still thought it probable but by no means certain that Aosta, when exhorted to sacrifice his own personal inclinations for the sake of the peace of Europe, would take the larger view and consent to do the right thing.

Early that evening the best news since the start of the crisis reached Florence. A report from Nigra stated that King William's reply, expected momentarily in Paris, might announce Leopold's withdrawal.[4] This roseate prospect appeared to diminish the urgency of Govone's mission. However, a telegram from Cadorna, which arrived a few minutes after Nigra's, noted that Granville attached great importance to the Aosta candidature and that Paget had been instructed to so inform the Italian government. Great Britain's predilection for an Italian prince was of course no news to Visconti-Venosta; but what he had not known and now learned for the first time was Granville's reluctance to intensify the pressure on Leopold. When Cadorna, following his instructions, had raised the question, Granville had replied that the decision to withdraw was one that only Leopold himself could ultimately make.[5] Visconti-Venosta was naturally disappointed. With the French making saber-rattling gestures, the authorities in Berlin quite loath to smooth away any of the difficulties, and the Spaniards more than willing to take Aosta if he would consent, it seemed imperative to make a maximum effort against the Hohenzollern candidature despite the hope held out in Nigra's report; and because of the family ties between Queen Victoria and the Hohenzollerns, the British seemed in the best position to influence Leopold through King William.

Hoping to induce Granville to reconsider, Visconti-Venosta looked forward to the visit from Paget, who shared his feeling that absolutely nothing should be left undone to halt the drift toward war. They met during the night of the eleventh and had a long and cordial chat. Visconti-Venosta recounted the developments in the Aosta candidature since they had last conversed two days before. Victor Emmanuel, although unwilling

[4] Nigra to Visconti-Venosta, July 11, 1870, No. 2483, MAE, AS, DTA.

[5] Cadorna to Visconti-Venosta, July 11, 1870, No. 2484, *ibid.*

to have a hand in the affair because of his previous discom-
fiture, had authorized an approach to his son, who was staying
in Leghorn. Some members of the cabinet, "strongly imbued
with their former prejudices," had objected, but only until they
were shown that the question of war and peace might depend
on the duke's response to a second invitation from the Spaniards. Because the movements of the foreign minister would
excite too much attention at this time, the mission to Leghorn
had been intrusted to the minister of war.[6]

To stimulate a greater effort by the British, Visconti-Venosta
decided then and there on a change of strategy. He told Paget
that, in view of London's interest in an Italian candidature, he
would attend to the matter personally instead of allowing it to
remain in the hands of Govone. In the morning he would go to
Leghorn and "leave no stone unturned to induce the Duke of
Aosta to agree to accept the crown in the event of its being
offered to him."[7] However, even if all went well, success might
not come soon enough. The immediate danger stemmed from
the fact that the imperial government had "displaced the question from Madrid to Berlin." The latest reports indicated that
unless King William's reply, due after his conference with
Leopold, was considered satisfactory by the French, they would
initiate hostilities within forty-eight hours. This made a quick
retraction by Leopold mandatory, and here the British could
help. Visconti-Venosta urged Paget to put the matter strongly
to Granville. He for his part had telegraphed Launay to join
Loftus in any moves, including a descent on Ems, that might
contribute to the preservation of peace.[8]

The foreign minister and his visitor parted shortly before
11:00 P.M. with the understanding that they would meet again
the following afternoon, after Visconti-Venosta's return from
Leghorn.[9] As soon as Paget had left, Visconti-Venosta turned
his attention to a telegram from Cerruti which had arrived a
few hours earlier but which he had barely had time to skim.

[6] Paget to Granville, July 11, 1870, No. 9, confidential, PRO (Ashridge),
FO 170/163.

[7] *Ibid.*   [8] *Ibid.*

[9] Paget to Granville, July 11, 1870, No. 6, PRO, FO 45/164.

It was an important communication. After noting that Sagasta and his colleagues were saying that for the sake of peace they would accept any solution that was consonant with the dignity of their country, Cerruti pointed out that they were now ready to take concrete steps to ease the crisis. Specifically, they proposed to ask the Cortes to postpone the election of the king and promised to do everything in their power to secure the adoption of this request. However, a minimum of co-operation by the French was indispensable. Just a few more days of waiting should be enough. Once the necessary arrangements had been completed in Madrid, the other capitals could do the rest.[10]

Thus the need for a slowing down in Paris, which he himself appreciated so intensely, was again brought home to Visconti-Venosta. A few minutes past midnight he telegraphed Cerruti's message to Nigra and added:

It is our duty to point out earnestly to the imperial government the responsibility it would assume and the embarrassment it would cause its best friends if it precipitated complications and refused to allow sufficient time for a solution which in London, Madrid and Florence is regarded as possible. I beg you to communicate this without delay to the government of the emperor. We count on its friendship for a proper understanding of a step that is forced upon us by the obligation, which we share with everyone, of doing whatever we can for the maintenance of peace.[11]

Simultaneously, he took care to inform Granville of Spain's helpful attitude. Naturally assuming, in the absence of any decisive break in the deadlock, that a negotiated solution continued to hinge, not only on France, but also on those who could sway Leopold, Visconti-Venosta reiterated in effect the point he had stressed in his last conversation with Paget. The British government, he insisted, was "better placed than any other" to influence the decisions of the prince at this critical moment.[12]

[10] Cerruti to Visconti-Venosta, July 11, 1870, No. 2482, MAE, AS, DTA.

[11] Visconti-Venosta to Nigra, July 12, 1870, No. 1197, MAE, AS, TS.

[12] Visconti-Venosta to Cadorna, July 12, 1870, No. 1196, *ibid.*

2

Early in the morning of the twelfth, there was a further albeit slight improvement in the news from abroad. Visconti-Venosta was about to leave for Leghorn. But at the last moment, concern lest his absence from the chamber of deputies should attract too much attention led him to postpone his departure until 4:00 P.M., when the sitting of the lower house would presumably be over. Paget was apprised and also invited to drop in for another chat.[13] Visconti-Venosta intended to explain the reason for the delay, but the arrival meanwhile of a disquieting telegram from Berlin[14] so dismayed him that when he and Paget met again at 1:00, he dwelt mainly on this communication. Launay reported Thile as "not very hopeful" about the decisions that were being hammered out by the Prussian cabinet. Although orders for mobilization had not yet been issued, "everything was ready for war." The military preparations under way in France "were producing their very natural effect on the feeling in Prussia."[15] This being so, and in view of Spain's conciliatory mood, Visconti-Venosta urged the necessity of again cautioning France not to obstruct a diplomatic settlement. He for his part had already let Paris know that in the opinion of the British, Spanish, and Italian governments an accommodation could still be worked out if only Napoleon and his ministers would help by displaying a little patience. He had also warned the imperial government that France would place herself in a "bad position . . . even in the eyes of her best friends, if by her conduct she shows that she is not only not inclined to favour a peaceful solution, but is determined on provoking war."[16] The French must be persuaded to wait a few more days, and here London could help.[17]

Paget returned to his legation, sent off a telegram to Granville, and then began drafting his report. He had not yet

[13] Paget to Granville, July 12, 1870, No. 16, PRO, FO 45/164.

[14] Launay to Visconti-Venosta, July 11, 1870, No. 2487, MAE, AS, DTA. This telegram reached the Italian foreign office at 10:15 A.M. on the twelfth.

[15] Paget to Granville, July 12, 1870, No. 16, PRO, FO 45/164.

[16] Ibid,   [17] Paget to Granville, July 12, 1870, No. 15, ibid.

finished when he was interrupted by another message from
Visconti-Venosta, who wished to see him immediately.[18] He
found the foreign minister, fresh from a conversation with
Govone, both nettled and pleased: nettled because Govone had
gone to Leghorn and seen the Duke of Aosta the day before
without informing him in advance; pleased because the general's visit had proved quite productive. According to Govone,
Aosta showed an appreciation for the considerations that had
led the Italian government to approach him, and he had indicated a willingness to discuss the terms on which he might
accept a second offer from the Spaniards. To be sure, there was
as yet no commitment on his part, but Visconti-Venosta suggested that the British government, in its communications to
Paris, might nevertheless cite the duke's response as still
another reason why the French should allow time for negotiation.[19] On the question of whether there was now any point in
his going to Leghorn, Visconti-Venosta seemed rather undecided, although inclined to feel that Aosta should not be
approached again until the British and Italian governments
had formally agreed on what to do next. Paget, however,
thought otherwise. He urged Visconti-Venosta to go, if for no
other reason than to encourage the duke in his accommodating
attitude.[20]

In any case, the journey could not be undertaken before the
following morning. In the meanwhile, there was a new rash of
alarming reports. One, from Launay, relayed intelligence
which, even if premature or inaccurate, was nonetheless especially ominous because it was being taken seriously in Berlin.
According to Launay, the Prussian government claimed to have
"positive information" that the movement of French troops toward the eastern frontier had already begun. The South German states, bound to Prussia by military alliances, had been
alerted. Despite the continued absence of both Bismarck and
King William, the Prussian cabinet had decided to meet in
order to consider the situation; and in the opinion of Thile,

18 Paget to Granville, July 12, 1870, No. 16, *ibid.*
19 Paget to Granville, July 12, 1870, No. 17, confidential, *ibid.*
20 *Ibid.*

who was not given to exaggeration, there would be war in a matter of days.[21] As if this were not enough, Visconti-Venosta had before him a report from Nigra which noted that a military bill was already on the agenda of the corps législatif.[22] Visconti-Venosta knew that his counsels of moderation had been duly passed on to Gramont,[23] but apparently they were being ignored; and it was likewise evident that the Prussian government, far from heeding Italy's pleas, was preparing for combat.[24]

Thus, it must have seemed to Visconti-Venosta that all his exertions, as well as those of anyone else, for that matter, were foredoomed for the simple but overwhelming reason that neither Paris nor Berlin really preferred a diplomatic solution. In the face of such a massive will to fight, the Aosta candidature appeared to be a preposterously puny expedient; at all events, Leopold had not yet withdrawn, and there was still no word on his meeting with King William. The most disturbing aspect of the crisis of course continued to be the danger of Italian involvement in a life-and-death struggle between France and Prussia. In addition to Victor Emmanuel, ready as always to spring into the fray if the French would oblige him by evacuating Rome, there was Beust, whose interventionist proclivities posed a deadly threat to the preservation of Italian neutrality. The scheming, restless chancellor of the Hapsburg empire apparently anticipated a French declaration of war; in the meantime he was proceeding on the assumption that anything which helped to throw the blame on Prussia would improve the chances of Austrian participation quite apart from whatever Russia might decide to do. From the very outset he had been "neither displeased nor surprised" by the eruption of the Franco-Prussian dispute; and as it progressed he specu-

[21] Launay to Visconti-Venosta, July 11, 1870, No. 2490, MAE, AS, DTA. This telegram arrived at 1:49 P.M. on the twelfth.

[22] Nigra to Visconti-Venosta, July 12, 1870, No. 2491, *ibid.*

[23] Nigra to Visconti-Venosta, July 12, 1870, No. 2494, *ibid.*

[24] See, for example, Greppi to Visconti-Venosta, July 12, 1870, No. 2493, *ibid,*

lated "on the prospect of contingent gain in a general scramble."[25]

Fresh evidence of the way Beust's mind was working was presented by Kübeck during the afternoon of the twelfth. The Austrian envoy visited the foreign office for a few minutes to read a short communication from his chief. It was in reply to the telegram of the eighth summarizing the long conversation Kübeck had had with Visconti-Venosta immediately after Malaret's *démarche*. The chancellor insisted that he was in complete agreement with Visconti-Venosta. However, it was plain from what Beust went on to say that he was thinking not so much of the best way to prevent war but rather of how France could make sure of the good will of the non-belligerents. After repeating that he was supporting France's diplomatic moves in Berlin and Madrid and would continue to do so, he explained that he was also cautioning against "precipitate steps" and advising a line of conduct less likely to create the impression that France was the aggressor.[26]

When Kübeck had finished reading Beust's message, Visconti-Venosta responded with his usual tact. He professed to believe that the chancellor shared his passion for peace. Austria, he observed, was the friend of France. So was Italy, and that was why he was greatly pleased to learn that Beust was counseling Paris to follow a moderate line and shun hasty moves. The voice of the chancellor was more likely to be heeded in French governing circles than that of anyone else.[27] However, Visconti-Venosta had to confess that he was not sanguine. France might decide to push ahead even if King William's reply, about which nothing was known in Florence, should give some but not total satisfaction.[28]

Kübeck left a little before 4:00. Several hours later, another

---

[25] So Lord Bloomfield, the British ambassador in Vienna, reported: see Hammond to Lyons, July 11, 1870, private and unnumbered, PRO, FO 391/13.

[26] Beust to Kübeck, July 10, 1870, No. 557, HHSA, PA, Italien, Weisungen 1870, Karton XI/79.

[27] Kübeck to Beust, July 13, 1870, secret and unnumbered, HHSA, PA, Italien, Varia 1870, Karton XI/79.

[28] Kübeck to Beust, July 12, 1870, No. 7242/706, HHSA, PA, Italien, Berichte 1870, Karton XI/77.

facet of Beust's attitude, and by no means an unfamiliar one, was re-created for Visconti-Venosta as he read a lengthy telegram from Curtopassi. The Italian chargé saw the chancellor on the twelfth. Evidently convinced that war could not be delayed much longer, Beust made no secret of his desire to see the Italian government accept France's proposal of a military alliance against Prussia. He suggested that once the partnership was an accomplished fact, Italy could be sure of a satisfactory settlement of the Roman question, which greatly interested him too for reasons of internal policy.[29] Although Beust of course kept this to himself, he apparently hoped that even the staunchest champions of non-intervention among the members of the Lanza cabinet would waver at the prospect of such a reward. To render the alliance still more attractive, he dangled before Curtopassi the possibility of a rectification of the Austro-Italian frontier in accordance with the aspirations of Italian nationalism. The transparent allusion to the cession of the Trentino seemed to indicate—Custopassi carefully recorded this impression in his report—that France's efforts to set the stage for Austrian participation in a war against Prussia were gaining ground. According to Curtopassi's information, it would be easy to mobilize an Austrian army corps; a sizable sum was available in the public treasury for this purpose. As to the other military and financial measures that would require, under the terms of the *Ausgleich* of 1867, the approval of both the Austrian and Hungarian delegations, it was assumed that they could be expedited by convoking those bodies within three weeks at the latest. The main obstacle continued to be the opposition of the Magyars. However, if they persisted in their refractory attitude, France would not hesitate to coerce them by creating difficulties in the Danubian Principalities.[30]

3

Curtopassi's report underscored anew the possibility of Austrian and hence Italian involvement. But already, at 7:40 P.M. on that same unforgettable day, July 12, an electrifying

[29] Curtopassi to Visconti-Venosta, July 12, 1870, No. 2496, MAE, AS, DTA.

[30] *Ibid.*

message had been received from Nigra. It read: "A telegram from the father of the Prince of Hohenzollern addressed today to General Prim announces that the candidature has been withdrawn. War has been averted."[31] Nigra's categorical statement that the crisis was over was supported by the tidings from Berlin. Bismarck, who had just arrived in the Prussian capital, was not going on to Ems, as he had originally planned to do. Instead, he was returning the very next morning to the seclusion of his Varzin estate.[32] This could only signify that Prussia regarded the Spanish affair as ended. On the night of July 12, Lanza jubilantly telegraphed Victor Emmanuel: "The danger of war seems to have been eliminated for the present."[33]

Despite his modesty, Visconti-Venosta was persuaded that his own efforts, together with Great Britain's parallel activities and Austria's show of solidarity with France, had given pause to the Prussians and thus helped to bring about the retraction of Leopold's candidature. Naturally, he experienced a sense of personal triumph that added to his gratification. In this happy state of mind he reviewed the situation with Paget the following morning. The two men of course saw no need to maintain the tempo of the last few days. They agreed that "in view of the renunciation of Prince Hohenzollern and the danger of war being consequently removed," the Aosta candidature was "no longer of that immediate importance which would render further action upon it for the moment a pressing necessity." And now that the emergency was a thing of the past, Visconti-Venosta also felt free to assure Paget that if any other solution to the Spanish dynastic problem should be thought "more suitable," Italy would not hold to the Aosta candidature even for a single moment. After all, she had permitted it to be revived only because it represented a means of inducing the Spanish government "to take a step in the interests of the peace of Europe." On the other hand, if Spain should evince an unmistakable desire to have Aosta, Italy would do her utmost to per-

[31] Nigra to Visconti-Venosta, July 12, 1870, No. 2495, *ibid.*

[32] Launay to Visconti-Venosta, July 12, 1870, No. 2603, *ibid.*

[33] The full text of this wire is in *Le carte di Giovanni Lanza,* V, No. 1691, pp. 203–4.

suade him to accept[34]—a task which could hardly be classed as formidable in view of the outcome of Govone's mission.

The gladness that filled the foreign office overflowed in the columns of the *Opinione*. That faithful mouthpiece sang the praises of Italy, England, and Austria. The three powers, serving in the crisis just ended as the right arm of international diplomacy, had saved Europe from a calamity of incalculable proportions. Leopold and his father had co-operated, and so had the Spaniards, with their assurance to the French that at no time had they intended to weaken the traditional ties between the two peoples. Under the circumstances, it was to be expected that France would be fully satisfied. In the general rejoicing at the avoidance of war, Italy wholeheartedly shared. No country surpassed her in dedication to peace and international conciliation.[35]

The *Opinione* was by no means alone in lauding Italy's contribution. Virtually every important newspaper of the Right joined in the paeans of praise. Malaret heartily concurred. In a dispatch which he addressed to Gramont shortly after learning of the retraction of the Hohenzollern candidature, he wrote:[36]

Your Excellency is aware . . . of the active role played by the cabinet of Florence in the swift negotiations which have apparently resolved the current difficulties. At no time did Visconti-Venosta cease to stimulate the zeal of his agents in Prussia and Germany. In conversations with me during this week of anxiety and tension, his language, although inspired by a very natural desire for peace, was always markedly sympathetic to France and the government of the emperor. . . . To sum up, the attitude of the Italian government . . . has been everything it could and should be: basically friendly to us, officially impartial, and very active on behalf of the maintenance of peace.

4

Visconti-Venosta's relief was short-lived. No sooner had he savored the satisfaction of success than a small dark cloud

[34] Paget to Granville, July 13, 1870, confidential, No. 21, PRO, FO 45/164.

[35] *L'Opinione*, July 14, 1870.

[36] Malaret to Gramont, July 13, 1870, No. 52, AMAE, Italie, janvier–juillet 1870, tome 378 (*OD*, XXVIII, No. 8485, pp. 324, 325).

appeared in his firmament and began to mar his contentment. When he returned to his desk very early in the morning of the thirteenth, he found a telegraphic report from the Stefani news agency. Dated the evening of July 12 and filed by the agency's Paris office, it quoted at length from an article which had just been printed in *La France,* a semiofficial newspaper of considerable standing that claimed to be particularly well informed on questions of foreign policy. This was the gist of the article: France had informed the king of Prussia that Leopold must renounce the candidature and in addition had asked William, as head of the Hohenzollern family as well as head of the state, to disavow it. The king had agreed to the first of these conditions but had balked at the second, refusing to give France the guaranty she required. His reply was not acceptable; it failed to remove the germs of future complications.[37]

At 8:15 A.M. Visconti-Venosta dispatched the following telegram to Nigra: "Let me know whether there is any truth to the article in *La France* regarding the new guaranties which the French government is demanding."[38] The Stefani report suggested that Paris would not be content until France had won a more complete diplomatic victory over the Prussians. On the other hand, Nigra had stated flatly that the crisis was over, and he was an experienced, extremely well-informed, and reliable observer. This should have been enough. Nevertheless, the Stefani report weighed heavily on Visconti-Venosta's mind; it apparently brought to the surface certain latent misgivings of his own about the real aims of France in the current conjuncture. When he saw Kübeck later in the day, the cheerfulness of a few hours before was gone. He did express the hope that no new incidents would mar what had been achieved by France's vigorous stand and even more by the conciliatory yet firm action of the powers. But he admitted that he did not feel optimistic; a Franco-Prussian war could still come overnight.[39]

[37] The text of this Stefani report, which reached Visconti-Venosta before the Italian press could print it, was published in Florence the following day.

[38] Visconti-Venosta to Nigra, July 13, 1870, No. 1198, MAE, AS, TS.

[39] Kübeck to Beust, July 13, 1870, secret and unnumbered, HHSA, PA, Italien, Varia 1870, Karton XI/79.

Several hours dragged by without further word from Nigra. Finally, at 2:40 P.M., the reply to Visconti-Venosta's telegraphic inquiry reached the foreign office. On the twelfth, Nigra explained, Napoleon had told him that the withdrawal of the Prince of Hohenzollern met France's requirements and that war had been averted. Therefore, Nigra added, there could be no question of guaranties, at least for the moment. To be sure, the emperor "was not content, for he had preferred war." But he recognized that the retraction of the candidature represented a satisfactory solution.[40] The allusion to Napoleon's dissatisfaction, to his predilection for war, was of course not lost on Visconti-Venosta. But the important thing was that temporarily, at any rate, the storm signal in *La France* could be ignored.

[40] Nigra to Visconti-Venosta, July 13, 1870, No. 2604, MAE, AS, DTA. On July 12, Metternich had reported: "Tomorrow . . . he [Napoleon] will decree the first stage of mobilization . . . , and he believes that this will make war inevitable. . . . [France] wants to march, in the correct belief . . . that she will never find a better opportunity: the German question has not been touched, and she has a ten-day start on Prussia" (No. 78, HHSA, PA, Frankreich, Berichte 1870, Karton IX/95).

CHAPTER EIGHT

THE DENOUEMENT

At 6:00 P.M. on the thirteenth, another telegram arrived from Nigra. It shattered the hope that even a reprieve was in the offing. For, armed with additional information, the envoy now told a different story. France, it appeared, no longer had any quarrel with Spain; the Spanish ambassador in Paris had officially notified Gramont of the retraction of Leopold's candidature. Negotiations with Prussia were continuing; the French government was asking King William to guarantee that Leopold would stay away from Spain.[1] Although hardly surprising in view of the article in *La France* and the emperor's frustrated mood, France's decision to keep on disputing with Prussia over the Spanish issue was nevertheless a cruel blow to the Italian government. Nigra attempted to soften it by pointing out that the French were couching their new demand in language that was both conciliatory and friendly,[2] but the unpleasant truth remained that William was being asked to do something which all of Germany would resent as a gratuitous humiliation. If, as was to be expected, he refused to comply, war was certain to follow, and the danger of Italian involvement would have to be wrestled with all over again.

A heavy gloom pervaded the foreign office. Reflecting this melancholy, the *Opinione* lamented the continuation of the Franco-Prussian dispute. The emperor himself was on record as admitting that France's requirements had been met, yet he was now demanding guaranties against a renewal of the candi-

[1] Nigra to Visconti-Venosta, July 13, 1870, No. 2605, MAE, AS, DTA.

[2] Nigra to Visconti-Venosta, July 13, 1870, No. 2608, *ibid.*

dature. This was an extremely grave development.[3] Reviewing
the situation on the evening of the thirteenth, Visconti-Venosta
could see only one faint ray of hope: Napoleon might be de-
terred by the prospect of alienating everyone, including his best
friends. Until now France had had a real grievance. Even
those who most loudly deplored her intemperate language conceded that she had suffered provocation. But by refusing to
accept Leopold's withdrawal as a full and final settlement, by
spurning the very object for which she had supposedly striven,
she would condemn herself in the eyes of all Europe.

On such matters, Beust could be considered a reliable indi-
cator. Visconti-Venosta was therefore particularly interested to
learn from Curtopassi that the chancellor disapproved of the
new French line. Concerned as always about the reaction of
other governments, he had apparently decided that the Hohenzollern candidature had outlived its usefulness as a pretext for
war with Prussia and that France in consequence would have
to bide her time and look for another *casus belli*. Certain it was
that he was telling Paris that, in view of the retraction of the
Hohenzollern candidature, all the South German states would
stand firmly with Prussia against fresh French demands.[4] This
was also an oblique warning that public opinion in the Dual
Monarchy, especially among the Austrian Germans, would become even more difficult now that France had so flagrantly put
herself in the wrong. In any case, as Curtopassi pointed out,
Magyar opposition to intervention showed no sign of abating.[5]
Beust's alarm, together with the resoluteness of the Hungarians, augured well for the role Austria might be expected to
play from now on, and Visconti-Venosta was naturally eager to
have all the information Curtopassi could collect.[6] He also instructed the chargé to express Italy's confidence that Austria
would advise the French to be satisfied with the very considerable diplomatic victory they had won. For good measure

[3] *L'Opinione,* July 15, 1870.

[4] Curtopassi to Visconti-Venosta, July 13, 1870, No. 2607, *ibid.*

[5] *Ibid.*

[6] Visconti-Venosta to Curtopassi, July 14, 1870, No. 1206, MAE, AS, TS.

Curtopassi was to add: "Public opinion in Italy is unanimous in desiring the maintenance of peace."[7]

The news from Vienna continued to suggest a sharp lessening of the chances of Austrian involvement. In addition to the dogged recalcitrance of the Hungarians, the lack of a bellicose (*i.e.*, anti-Prussian) spirit among the army leaders appeared to be having a perceptible effect. Another factor, it seemed, was the bait held out by the old rival in the north. General Hans von Schweinitz, the Prussian ambassador in Vienna, had reportedly hinted at substantial rewards for the Hapsburg empire if it adopted a policy which, if not hostile to France, would at least be impeccably neutral. However, when Beust again talked with Curtopassi, he gave the impression of having recovered from the shock produced by France's *gaffe* in refusing to be satisfied with the cancellation of Leopold's candidature. He told Curtopassi confidentially that his government, while abstaining from warlike preparations, continued to distrust Prussia and was anxious to retain a completely free hand. It was eager too to collaborate closely with Italy. As if to underscore the nexus between French, Austrian, and Italian policy, he called attention to a rumor that Rome was about to be evacuated. Curtopassi, who knew nothing about it, answered evasively.[8]

Reminded of the need to talk realistically to the French, Beust insisted that he had done his best. Throughout the crisis, he had preached calm and moderation. After the retraction of Leopold's candidature, he had urged France to let well enough alone. But it was now apparent that his efforts, like those of the British, were quite futile. If France should surprise everyone by taking a more reasonable position, she would do so not because of his representations but rather because she had failed to get what she wanted in Vienna.[9] Her behavior was admittedly trying, but Beust hoped it would not lead to any change in Italy's present policy. A declaration of neutrality would be a

7 Visconti-Venosta to Curtopassi, July 14, 1870, No. 1212, *ibid.*

8 Curtopassi to Visconti-Venosta, July 14, 1870, No. 2619, MAE, AS, DTA.

9 Curtopassi to Visconti-Venosta, July 15, 1870, No. 2630, *ibid.*

mistake. "Because of Austria's geographical proximity to Prussia and Italy's to France," such a declaration by either Austria or Italy would amount to a demonstration of hostility toward France. Speaking for himself alone rather than for his emperor and the government, Beust suggested that the evacuation of Rome, as well as Russian participation in a Franco-Prussian war, "could singularly modify the attitude of Austria"[10]—that is, decide her to cross the line between passivity and belligerency. This was typical of the chancellor's deviousness. Small wonder, therefore, that Visconti-Venosta, despite all the signs pointing the other way, should have been unable to rid himself of the fear of Austrian intervention; it was to haunt him until the menace to Italian neutrality had been definitively removed.

2

Of course, if King William were to accede to France's latest request, the specter of war would once again be exorcised. But Visconti-Venosta did not suppose such a reply probable, and it was therefore without any illusions that he turned to Launay for whatever precise information might be to hand.[11] The expected came early in the afternoon of the fourteenth, in a report from Launay recounting the result of a meeting between William and Benedetti in Ems. Complying with his instructions, Benedetti had asked for authorization to telegraph the following message to Paris: His Majesty would oppose any attempt by Leopold to revive the candidature. William had avoided a direct reply, but subsequently had let it be known through his aide-de-camp that he had nothing more to say to Benedetti. The semiofficial organ of the Prussian government had blazoned the story in a special edition.[12] Additional proof of the hardening of Prussia's attitude was to be found in Bismarck's change of plans. Instead of returning to Varzin, he had decided to remain in Berlin.[13]

Although quite sure that the die was cast, Visconti-Venosta

[10] *Ibid.*

[11] Visconti-Venosta to Launay, July 14, 1870, No. 1207, MAE, AS, TS.

[12] Launay to Visconti-Venosta, July 14, 1870, No. 2613, MAE, AS, DTA.

[13] *Ibid.*

persisted in his attempts to find an escape route. Once again he addressed himself to London. Cadorna was instructed to see Granville immediately and ascertain what he thought of the latest turn of affairs. Did the foreign secretary perceive any way of procuring for France the guaranty she wanted?[14] Visconti-Venosta's telegram crossed with one from Cadorna, who had hastened to the British foreign office without waiting for instructions. From Granville he had learned that public opinion in Prussia had begun to rise up in indignation against the concessions already made by King William.[15] This of course was a reference to the sovereign's willingness to confer with Leopold. Granville's implication that William could hardly be expected to complicate his own personal situation by giving in on the question of a guaranty was spelled out to Cadorna by Count Albrecht von Bernstorff, the Prussian ambassador in London. According to Bernstorff, Prussia had done everything she possibly could on behalf of peace, and she would make no more concessions. Her conscience was clear.[16]

Visconti-Venosta's melancholy brooding was interrupted by Paget, who brought the information which the query to Cadorna had been designed to elicit. The British envoy read a telegram from Granville which revealed that London was irate over the prolongation of the crisis. On behalf of his government, the foreign secretary had bluntly told France that the request for a guaranty was indefensible because she had already obtained the substance of her demand. At the same time, however, Granville had implored William to contribute to a relaxation of the tension by stating in advance that he would comply if he were asked by France to associate himself with Leopold's withdrawal.[17] It was obvious that the British felt

14 Visconti-Venosta to Cadorna, July 14, 1870, No. 1210, MAE, AS, TS. See also Visconti-Venosta to Cadorna, July 14, 1870, No. 53, MAE, AS, Divisione politica, 1867–1888, registri copia-lettere in partenza, Inghilterra, busta 1167: 22 maggio 1869–29 luglio 1872.

15 Cadorna to Visconti-Venosta, July 14, 1870, No. 2615, MAE, AS, DTA.

16 Ibid.

17 Visconti-Venosta to Cadorna, July 14, 1870, No. 54, MAE, AS, Divisione politica, 1867–1888, registri copia-lettere in partenza, Inghilterra, busta 1167: 22 maggio 1869–29 luglio 1872.

they had gone as far as they could. They would not press Prussia to grant a demand which they themselves regarded as unjustifiable, but they evidently believed that the substitute gesture they were urging on the king might satisfy the French. But it seemed altogether unlikely that this plea would have any effect on the Prussians. As for the French, they were apparently not to be diverted from their reckless, irresponsible course. Nevertheless, more from a sense of duty to the cause of peace than from any hope of success, Visconti-Venosta turned to Paris. First he telegraphed the text of Launay's report on the outcome of the meeting between William and Benedetti[18] so that Nigra would know exactly how desperate the situation was. Next he conveyed a thinly concealed warning that was intended to counteract the impression produced at the Tuileries by Vimercati's statements on the subject of a Franco-Italian alliance. Nigra was to tell the imperial government that its warmest partisans in Italy would be unhappy if war should break out after the retraction of the Hohenzollern candidature.[19] In an accompanying dispatch to Paris, Visconti-Venosta stated that even at this late hour, the Italian government preferred to believe that its counsels of conciliation, coupled with those of other powers, would be heeded and the threat of war removed.[20]

While waiting to hear, he puzzled over the dreadful disparity between Nigra's "war has been averted" and the belated confirmation that France was asking for guaranties. He could not explain it and asked for light from the legation in Paris.[21] In his reply, Nigra began by recalling the emperor's initial reaction, which was that the withdrawal of Leopold had put an end to the crisis. Nothing whatever, Nigra repeated, had been said then about guaranties of any kind.[22] As for the subsequent course of events, Nigra could offer only this: the council of

[18] Visconti-Venosta to Nigra, July 14, 1870, No. 1208, MAE, AS, TS.

[19] Visconti-Venosta to Nigra, July 14, 1870, No. 1211, *ibid.*

[20] Visconti-Venosta to Nigra, July 14, 1870, No. 59, MAE, AS, Divisione politica, 1867–1888, registri copia-lettere in partenza, Francia, busta 1144: 20 luglio 1869–14 febbraio 1871.

[21] Visconti-Venosta to Nigra, July 14, 1870, No. 1209, MAE, AS, TS.

[22] Nigra to Visconti-Venosta, July 14, 1870, No. 2622, MAE, AS, DTA.

ministers had been convoked, and it had decided that some
sort of assurance would have to be obtained from Prussia.[23]
Actually, Nigra's information was quite inaccurate. The decision to demand guaranties was reached by Napoleon and Gramont; they did not consult the council of ministers. Even
Ollivier, although agreeing after an initial show of satisfaction
that the retraction of Leopold's candidature by the elder Prince
of Hohenzollern rather than by the king or government of
Prussia was, from the point of view of form, not enough of a
triumph to appease the aroused nation, knew nothing about
the new instructions to Benedetti until after they had been
telegraphed. However, in regard to the emperor's motives and
intentions, Nigra was on firm ground: Napoleon wanted from
Prussia, not from Spain, something that would suffice to satisfy
France's *amour propre*. If he could not get it, he would go to
war.[24]

A few hours after he had sent off this explanation, Nigra returned to the subject in a supplementary telegram. At the
meeting on the twelfth, he noted once again, the emperor had
stated that the matter was settled. In the corridors of the build-
ing that housed the corps législatif, Ollivier had said the same
thing. Afterward, however, when no confirmation of the retraction came from Prussia, there had been a change of attitude
and the demand for guaranties was put forward. The fact of
the matter, Nigra continued, was that Napoleon "considers the
occasion to be favorable and desires to profit by it." In addition, public opinion in Paris was not content with the renunciation, since Prussia was not a party to it, and as a consequence
the city was showing itself to be more and more bellicose.[25]

3

By this time, such analyses were of academic interest only.
Early in the evening of the fourteenth, Florence saw the last

[23] *Ibid.*   [24] *Ibid.*

[25] Nigra to Visconti-Venosta, July 15, 1870, unnumbered, MAE, AS,
Archivi di gabinetto (1861–1887), busta 219: guerra franco-prussiana e
trattative segrete 8 luglio–14 settembre 1870, fascicolo 4. This telegram
was sent at 1:05 A.M.

ray of hope seemingly extinguished. A telegram from Nigra announced that in view of King William's refusal to receive Benedetti, the French government was expected to declare war at any moment.[26] Launay for his part reported that William was expected to arrive in Berlin some time that night. It was believed that he would promptly convoke the North German parliament, and the portents left no room for uncertainty: war was inevitable if France persisted in her new demands.[27] Violently Francophobe, Launay was glad to pass along the views of Gorchakov, who had stopped over in Berlin on his way to a summer vacation at Wildbad. According to Gorchakov, France would find herself completely isolated if she continued to insist on guaranties. As for what the Italians should do, he had this bit of advice to offer: the situation which France seemed intent on creating presented them with an opportunity to demonstrate by their language that they were a great power in fact as well as in name.[28] The Russian statesman's suggestion that this was a time for stern warnings to France dovetailed with Launay's own conception of Italy's proper role. He urged his chief to exert pressure on Paris, not on Berlin. Any attempt, however friendly, to persuade Prussia to give in could accomplish nothing; worse, it would boomerang. Prussia was bound to resent it as another gratuitous affront. She had done her fair share, as evidenced by the retraction of the candidature; it was now up to the French to stop being so aggressive.[29]

On the heels of this telegram came another from Launay in which he again criticized the French and defended the Prussians. Bismarck was a genuine friend of peace who still hoped that the efforts of England and the other great powers would restore sanity in France. As yet, Berlin had ordered no special military preparations, but the Prussian cabinet, having learned

[26] Nigra to Visconti-Venosta, July 14, 1870, No. 2616, MAE, AS, DTA.

[27] Launay to Visconti-Venosta, July 14, 1870, No. 2620, *ibid*. Launay's informants on the movements of the king were mistaken. William did not leave Ems until the morning of the fifteenth. He arrived in Berlin about thirteen hours later.

[28] *Ibid*.   [29] *Ibid*.

that France was readying her navy for action, decided it would be prudent to take some precautionary measures in the port of Hamburg in order to forestall a surprise attack.[30] Paraphrasing Thile but without identifying him as the source, Launay recounted a conversation between Gramont and the Prussian ambassador, Baron Karl von Werther, who had returned to Paris on the twelfth. Launay quoted Gramont as saying that the best solution would be a letter from William to the emperor containing an apology for past behavior as well as a promise about the future. Werther agreed to transmit this message to his superiors. When William read Werther's dispatch, he was deeply offended and notified Bismarck. The latter acted at once. Werther was instructed to say that, after reflecting on the matter, he had decided he could not pass the message along. But instead of doing as he was told, Werther demurred, explaining that he had promised the French he would comply with their request. By way of punishment for accepting this undignified role, he was relieved of his duties and ordered to quit Paris on a leave of unspecified duration. To be sure, diplomatic relations with France had not been broken off. But official circles in Prussia were resentful, and they viewed the future with undisguised pessimism.[31]

4

The demand for guaranties had already alienated William, and now the almost incredible request for a letter of apology threatened to close every remaining avenue of conciliation. The deadlock seemed complete. Nevertheless, Visconti-Venosta's spirits must have risen a little when he learned that the British were not yet prepared to concede defeat. According to a telegram from Cadorna that arrived shortly before 6:00 A.M. on the fifteenth, Granville still clung to the belief that a way out might be found. He had suggested that William should send the French a message approving Leopold's withdrawal.

---

[30] Launay to Visconti-Venosta, July 15, 1870, No. 2623, *ibid*. This telegram was dispatched at 1:10 A.M. and arrived in Florence three and a half hours later.

[31] *Ibid*.

He was waiting for the answer and thought there was a chance that it would be affirmative. However, he made no attempt to conceal from Cadorna just how uneasy he really was.[32]

Visconti-Venosta for his part did not rule out, as a last resort, the idea of a collective guaranty by the powers which might be offered to France as a substitute for the purely unilateral guaranty she was demanding of Prussia. Blanc told Wesdehlen that London had been queried about this.[33] But Visconti-Venosta had so little confidence in the idea that he refrained from mentioning it when he conferred with Paget on the morning of the fifteenth. Besides, like every other statesman and diplomat, he found it difficult to think about anything except the declaration that Gramont was scheduled to make in the corps législatif that afternoon. In the meanwhile, however, something would have to be done about the Aosta candidature, which took on a new significance in the light of the latest developments. To be sure, both Visconti-Venosta and Paget realized that even if that candidature were to give France the equivalent of the guaranty she was now demanding from the Prussians, war might eventually break out anyway. But at least "it would have to be grounded on some other pretext" than the one put forward by the French government in the past few days;[34] and for a span of time that could conceivably be extended, hostilities would have been averted. Paget could see no flaw in this reasoning. To him it was quite clear that "no more positive guarantee against the return of the Hohenzollern Candidature could have been found than that which would have resulted from the election of another Prince to the Throne of Spain." Consequently, the Spanish government "should immediately be urged to proclaim the Duke of Aosta, and to summon the Cortes to ratify the choice." Paget asked Visconti-Venosta for permission to telegraph this advice to Granville. He also suggested that Italy could expedite matters by guaranteeing Aosta's acceptance of

[32] Cadorna to Visconti-Venosta, July 14, 1870, No. 2621, *ibid*.

[33] Wesdehlen to Bismarck, July 15, 1870, Lord, No. 233, p. 256.

[34] Paget to Granville, July 16, 1870, No. 25, most confidential, PRO, FO 45/164.

the crown.[35] Visconti-Venosta readily agreed, even though he was afraid "that things had now gone too far" and that Gramont's announcement "would prevent further negotiations."[36] The two men decided to await word from Paris, with the understanding that, if it "left the smallest door open," they would proceed at once with the plan outlined by Paget.[37]

What Visconti-Venosta feared seemed on the verge of coming true. Shortly after the conversation with Paget, telegrams arrived from Paris[38] and Brussels[39] which indicated that France would declare war that afternoon. In the midst of this nerve-racking interlude, Visconti-Venosta saw Wesdehlen, who came to recount the grim events at Ems. Exhibiting his usual calm, the foreign minister deplored the gravity of the situation. After Leopold's withdrawal, he said, he had regarded the issue as settled. Although expressing regret, he refrained from passing judgment on the behavior of the disputants. The only power he mentioned, but in a complimentary vein, was Great Britain: she was still urging a compromise on France and Prussia.[40]

The conversation with Wesdehlen ended without Visconti-Venosta's having disclosed what further moves, if any, he might be contemplating. But as a matter of fact, he was already planning a special assignment for Isacco Artom, Italy's minister to Baden and Blanc's prospective successor as general secretary of the foreign office. A man of first-rate ability and impeccable finesse and discretion, Artom had worked closely with Cavour in Turin and with Nigra in Paris. More recently, he had represented his country in Copenhagen and had been intrusted with several confidential missions.[41] With a Franco-Prussian

---

[35] *Ibid.*   [36] *Ibid.*

[37] *Ibid.* See also Paget to Granville, July 18, 1870, No. 31, *ibid.*

[38] Nigra to Visconti-Venosta, July 15, 1870, No. 2625, MAE, AS, DTA.

[39] Barral to Visconti-Venosta, July 15, 1870, No. 2626, *ibid.*

[40] Wesdehlen to Bismarck, July 15, 1870, Lord, No. 233, pp. 255–56.

[41] See the observations on Artom in Gordon to Granville, July 17, 1870, No. 17, PRO (Ashridge), FO 163/42. One well-informed observer noted: "M. Artom, qui appartient à une famille israélite de Piémont, est un de ceux qu'employait le plus fréquemment le Comte de Cavour dans les circonstances importantes. La sûreté de son coup d'œil, la netteté de son

war virtually certain, the role of Vienna was bound to become crucial. It was almost axiomatic that Italy's neutrality would depend on Austria's; a redoubled effort would have to be made to promote the second in order to insure the first. The Magyars and France's bullheadedness were having a sobering effect in the Hapsburg capital, but it would be criminally remiss not to do everything in reason to assist the process. Yet at this juncture Italy's legation in Vienna was still without a chief. To fill this lacuna, and because he was not at all sure that Curtopassi would measure up to the situation, Visconti-Venosta decided to avail himself of Artom's services the moment war broke out.

The Belgian minister in Florence, Solvyns, described that city as being in the grip of a veritable panic. The general opinion was that, if a war should ensue, the country's recent efforts to escape financial bankruptcy would be nullified. Public anxiety at this moment was even greater than it had been during the critical days of 1866.[42] Solvyns also reported that the Italian government apparently had no intention of increasing its armaments. On the contrary, the minister of war was presumably very determined to continue the policy of drastic retrenchment. If hostilities broke out, he was supposed to have said, they would take place far from Italy's frontiers. The government would therefore be spared the necessity of enforcing respect for its neutrality. Inside the country, all attempts to sow disorder would be easily suppressed. Govone's attitude, according to these sources, could be summed up as follows: "With a storm impending, we should lighten the ship, not arm her."[43]

5

Early in the afternoon of the fifteenth, the French government, acting through Gramont and Ollivier, went before the two chambers of parliament with a request for war credits.

---

esprit, sa parfaite connaissance des intérêts européens, font de lui un agent précieux" (Solvyns to d'Anethan, July 21, 1870, No. 95, Belgium, Archives du ministère des affaires étrangères, Correspondance politique, Légations: Italie, IV, 1868–1870).

[42] Solvyns to d'Anethan, July 15, 1870, No. 83, *ibid.*

[43] *Ibid.*

Although the statement read by both men was not a formal declaration of war against Prussia (the two countries were not officially at war until the nineteenth), it amounted to the same thing, and as such it was universally and correctly interpreted. The senate voted the credits quickly and without demur. The corps législatif, with Orleanist and republican critics of the regime speaking up, followed suit late in the night, after prolonged and stormy debates. The struggle between France and Prussia, in the making ever since 1866, was about to begin. How long it would last, where it would lead, and whom it would engulf, no one could say.

This was a bitter moment for Visconti-Venosta. His efforts on behalf of peace had proved utterly fruitless, and what the morrow might hold for Italy seemed at the mercy of events beyond her control. The French declaration, wailed the *Opinione*, had upset the calculations of Europe's statesmen. The Hohenzollern candidature could hardly be blamed; thanks to Leopold and Spain, it had been removed betimes from the arena of conflict. The one incontrovertible fact in an otherwise obscure sequence of events was the sudden change in the attitude of Napoleon. He had professed to be satisfied; there had been no mention of guaranties. Diplomacy had apparently triumphed on July 12. Then the French government, impelled perhaps by the excitement and bellicosity of its people, had decided to push matters to a point from which there was no turning back. For four years, the threat of a Franco-Prussian contest for supremacy had kept Europe in a state of fear and uncertainty. Finally the war had come, and it was a catastrophe for everyone, including Italy, which had barely begun to restore her sickly finances.[44]

Although Visconti-Venosta was feeling anything but a success, his handling of the crisis won commendation from a pair of observers who were in the best position to judge. In one of his reports to Beust, Kübeck insisted that it was impossible to praise Visconti-Venosta enough. He stressed among other things the foreign minister's "straightforward character," the "soundness of his views," and his "evident desire" to maintain

[44] *L'Opinione*, July 16, 1870.

the closest possible accord between Austria and Italy.[45] No less enthusiastic but far more expansive was Paget. In an appreciative vein, he wrote Granville:[46]

Although Your Lordship will have had adequate proof from my previous correspondence and in other ways of the hearty desire of the Italian Government to do everything which lay in their power towards the maintenance of peace, I nevertheless feel it due to the Foreign Minister of this country to revert once more to this subject, and to state that from the very beginning of the present crisis up to the moment of the declaration of war becoming known here . . . , Visconti-Venosta has consistently expressed not only his readiness, but his desire to cooperate with Her Majesty's Government in any course which might be thought desirable for the purpose of warding off the dire calamity with which Europe is now about to be afflicted.

Similarly, in a letter to his good friend Edmund Hammond, the permanent undersecretary in the ministry of foreign affairs, Paget remarked: "I don't think any one could behave better than Visconti has done and is doing."[47]

[45] Kübeck to Beust, July 13, 1870, secret and unnumbered, HHSA, PA, Italien, Varia 1870, Karton XI/79.

[46] Paget to Granville, July 16, 1870, most confidential, No. 25, PRO, FO 45/164.

[47] Paget to Hammond, July 16, 1870, private and unnumbered, *ibid.*, FO 391/23.

CHAPTER NINE

WHICH WAY ITALY?

Now that France and Prussia were to all intents and purposes at war, what should Italy's policy be? As before, Victor Emmanuel favored Italo-Austrian intervention on the side of France provided Rome was evacuated. He was supported by some prominent military leaders and by a goodly number of right-wing politicians who regarded intervention as an ineluctable necessity, as the price that would have to be paid for the ultimate attainment of *Roma capitale*.[1] Public opinion, however, was overwhelmingly in favor of neutrality[2] and, in its anxiety to see it prevail, adopted a preponderantly pro-Prussian attitude.[3] The Sinistra, as partial to Prussia as it was hostile to France, demanded an official and public declaration of absolute and unconditional neutrality as the only way to preclude a later backdoor alignment with Napoleon. The most militant elements of the Left were on this occasion resolved to stop at nothing in their efforts to prevent Italy from "placing herself at the disposal of the assassins of Mentana."[4] Spearheaded by Mazzini and Garibaldi,[5] the agitation threw ordinary people into such an uproar that even Beust, watching anxiously from

---

[1] Nola, p. 416.

[2] This emerges clearly from the editorials of leading Destra and Sinistra press organs. The newspapers consulted include the *Opinione, Nazione, Riforma*, and *Diritto* of Florence and the *Perseveranza* of Milan. See also Chabod, p. 33.

[3] Chabod, pp. 31–32.

[4] Valsecchi, p. 192.   [5] Nola, p. 416.

Vienna, wondered whether the Italian cabinet would be able to have its way if it decided in favor of intervention.[6]

In actuality the leaders of the Destra, including spokesmen for its Francophile wing, were second to no one in appreciating the need for neutrality, but they insisted that such a policy must not be regarded as unalterable. Their position was stated by Ruggero Bonghi, editor of the Milanese daily, the *Perseveranza*, and political chronicler for the country's outstanding periodical, the *Nuova antologia*. Bonghi maintained that so long as the war remained confined to France and Prussia, Italy should not ally herself with either. If Austria did not move, Italy would be well advised to remain passive. If Austria intervened, however, Italy would have no choice but to follow suit. It was plain that Austria could not side with Prussia against France, and this fact would undoubtedly help to determine Italy's alignment. But even if Germanic national sentiment should force Austria to become the ally of Prussia—a most unlikely eventuality, to be sure—Italy would still have to side with France. The reason was not far to seek: whereas a German victory due to Prussian prowess alone could not harm Italy, the same would not be true of a triumph effected by an Austro-Prussian combination. Therefore Italy must not only strive to remain neutral so long as other powers were not involved; she must also try by every possible means to keep the war from spreading.[7] Sinistra extremists, whose hatred of Napoleon knew no bounds, took a very different line. These revolutionaries reiterated their readiness to collaborate with Bismarck, to offer him the aid of insurrectionary movements within the peninsula if the Lanza government, for whatever reason, should contemplate intervention on the side of France.[8]

Within the diplomatic corps, the most forceful and insistent champion of neutrality was Launay, whose Savoyard origin (he could neither forget nor forgive the loss of his native land to Napoleon) contributed to his intense Francophobia and predilection for Prussia.[9] Convinced of his own superior wis-

[6] Valsecchi, pp. 192–93.

[7] *Nuova antologia*, XIV (1870), 880–81.

[8] Chabod, p. 28.   [9] *Ibid.*, p. 7.

dom and impatient of delay, he even usurped the prerogatives of the government by formulating policy instead of merely transmitting it. A glaring instance of this occurred on the night of July 12, when Launay saw Bismarck, who was still unnerved by the news of Leopold's withdrawal. The conversation turned to the diplomatic situation, and Bismarck, despite his distraught condition, made the most of his opportunity. He told Launay that it was being bruited about that Italy would help France with an army of 80,000 men. To be sure, by mentioning the fact that the report had come via the rumor factory in Bavaria, the South German stronghold of anti-Prussianism, Bismarck implied that the story was open to suspicion, to say the least. Yet, because he was nonetheless worried, he called Launay's attention to this report, as well as to a second which portrayed Italy as still undecided about the course she would follow.[10]

In his reply, Launay held nothing back. First he recapitulated the instructions he had received from Visconti-Venosta ever since the beginning of the crisis. Next he described the moves he had made on his own initiative, including a suggestion to the Prussian foreign office that he should pay a visit to Varzin. Italy, he went on to emphasize, had worked honestly and without *arrière-pensée* for the preservation of peace. Why? Because it was her duty to do what she could to prevent a clash between her former comrades in arms.

A point that Launay was at great pains to stress was that he was known to be a "serious" diplomat. Consequently, Visconti-Venosta would never have consented to employ him as a mere errand boy—the word Launay used was "marionette." In any case, no one could have induced him to play such a role. Besides, if Italy were already planning to fight on the side of the French in a Franco-Prussian war, she would have enjoined upon her envoy in Berlin an attitude of the utmost reserve. Certainly she would not have given him a species of carte blanche, subject of course to the understanding that he would refrain from

<hr>

[10] The conversation, as reported by Launay, is recounted in S. William Halperin, "Bismarck and the Italian Envoy in Berlin on the Eve of the Franco-Prussian War," *Journal of Modern History*, XXXIII (1961), 35–37.

doing anything that conflicted with his country's very clear determination to contribute to a peaceful resolution of the crisis. As for the rumor that an Italian army of 80,000 would be put into the field, it came from Bavaria; and any report originating there was too unbelievable to be merely suspect. Was it not rather a deliberate maneuver to deter Prussia from asking her South German allies to fulfil their treaty obligations?

How much credence could be put in the other story, which depicted Italy as still undecided about what she would do if all efforts to prevent a Franco-Prussian war should fail? Absolutely none, Launay insisted. One had only to glance at the present state of affairs in Italy. That should be quite enough to convince even the most incredulous that, in the event of a Franco-Prussian war, the Italian government could pursue but one policy: scrupulous and absolute neutrality; and in thus doing what was unavoidable, it would have the approval of the great majority of the nation.

Launay had boasted that in the game of diplomacy he would never be a mere puppet. On this occasion, he proved, at least to himself, that he was not exaggerating. For in reassuring Bismarck about Italy's future intentions—the best the Prussian statesman had ever hoped for was of course her neutrality—Launay exceeded his instructions by a long chalk. No doubt, he had been empowered by Visconti-Venosta to do whatever he could to promote a peaceful settlement of the Franco-Prussian dispute. He had also been given very wide latitude as to the choice of means. But he had never been authorized to indicate what Italy's policy would be in the event of a Franco-Prussian war.

True, Visconti-Venosta himself was just as anxious as Launay to see Italy remain neutral, just as prone to assume that any other course was fraught with deadly peril; and most of the cabinet agreed with him. But the issue had not been clarified beyond the certainty, which Visconti-Venosta had conveyed to Malaret on July 8, that Italy would not be found among France's enemies. This meant that Italy would surely not fight on the side of Prussia; but it was by no means equally sure that she would be able to avoid a military partnership with France.

The situation was complicated by Victor Emmanuel's enthusiasm for a Franco-Italian alliance. Hitherto he had been stymied by France's refusal to evacuate Rome; but presumably
this roadblock would be removed once France was at war with
Prussia. In addition, there was the ever-present possibility that
a struggle between two major powers would spread as a consequence of developments that were of no direct concern to
Italy. If that were to happen, in all probability the Italian government would be forced to intervene, despite the antiwar
sentiment of public opinion. Thus, all things considered, Launay's attribution of an unshakably neutral posture to Italy was
not only premature; it was grossly irresponsible.

But he was apparently unperturbed by such considerations.
Intent on preventing Italian involvement and worried by Visconti-Venosta's well-known Francophilism, he literally bombarded the foreign minister with unsolicited reminders of the
need to avoid the meshes of France. On the fourteenth he
forwarded an analysis of the military strength of the prospective combatants. Aiming to show that a French triumph could
not be taken for granted, he cited the British military attaché
in Paris as his source in estimating the French army at 700,000,
but gave no authority for his flat statement that the North
German Confederation had at least an equal number of soldiers at its disposal. If all the German states were included—
and the indications were that they should be—the total would
be considerably higher. Moreover, Prussia had three surplus
rifles for every man under arms. Thus the chances of victory
on land could be deemed about the same for both sides
(France, with an army rated man for man the best in Europe,
was generally regarded as the stronger of the two). But the
chances of a Prussian victory would be appreciably enhanced
if the fighting came to a head in a few months (a prolonged
struggle was expected to benefit France because of her greater
resources), and as a matter of fact the war was likely to be
brief owing to recent improvements in the military art.[11]

<hr />

[11] Launay to Visconti-Venosta, July 14, 1870, confidential, No. 588,
MAE, AS, Serie politica (1867–1888), Prussia, busta 1328: 1867–1870.

Launay went on to quote an unnamed Prussian general whom he described as "most distinguished":[12]

No one can predict which side will score the initial successes. But in the end we too shall win our laurels. France forgets that in most of her victorious wars against us, she owed her triumphs in part to German allies who this time will not be available.

On the other hand, Launay readily conceded that the naval power of France was distinctly superior. No country in the world had a better maritime transport service, and France's fleet of steam-propelled warships was much more formidable than Prussia's. However, this was somewhat offset by the fact that the disembarkation of troops was an extremely difficult operation, and Prussia had made it no easier by strengthening her defenses in the most exposed coastal areas.[13]

Turning next to an assessment of the diplomatic assets and debits of the two powers, Launay concurred with the Prussians in seeing but little likelihood of Hapsburg intervention on the side of France. They expected Austria to remain passive, at least at the outset, and relied on the Russians to paralyze any inclination toward active participation that she might entertain later in the contest. As for Italy, the Berlin cabinet desired her "perfect" neutrality, and Bismarck was counting on it. In this connection, Launay did not mention the unequivocal assurance he had given Bismarck two days before. Instead, he cited Loftus, who had told the Prussian crown prince that Italy would steer clear of complications because of the state of her finances, the memories of 1859 and 1866, and a distaste for risky enterprises. Saying that he quite agreed, Launay described non-intervention as "the only line of conduct we can choose if France should stubbornly persist in wanting war at any price."[14] Some people, of course, were afraid that self-proclaimed neutrals might be overwhelmed or victimized by the victorious side. But this could happen only to secondary states, not to a power which, once aroused, would prove strong enough to do as it pleased.[15]

[12] *Ibid.*
[13] *Ibid.*
[14] *Ibid.*
[15] *Ibid.*

Launay returned to the charge on the afternoon of the fifteenth, just before he learned of the virtual declaration of war. He telegraphed Visconti-Venosta to urge once again that in the event of hostilities, neutrality would be the only wise and prudent course for Italy.[16] He promptly followed this up with another lengthy dispatch in which, among other things, he reverted to an earlier suggestion: the Italian government should tell the French that, if war came, it would be prepared to take over the handling of their current business in Berlin and look after the safety of their nationals. Launay believed that such an offer would be the "best proof" that Italy intended to remain aloof.[17] He expressed the hope that the Lanza cabinet, certain to be subjected to many pressures, would be guided solely by the national interest. There must be no capitulation to the "generous impulses" of the army, which was eager for an opportunity to demonstrate its worth. There must also be no surrender to the "seductions" of those who would drag the country into foreign adventures. The French would offer Italy the moon in order to get her help, but if they won the war, they would keep none of their promises.[18]

According to Launay, the "old traditional school," which objected to the growth of other nations, was now rising to a dominant position in France. The emperor, who almost alone among his countrymen was friendly to Italy, had no option but to yield to this trend. The "policy of the Restoration" would be resurrected if Italy showed the slightest inclination to aid the French, if she failed to convince them that her blood would be expended only for the defense of her own interests and her own territory. The debt of 1859 had been largely liquidated by the loss of Savoy and Nice. Besides, in helping Italy against the Austrians, the French had been thinking of themselves. Their aim had been to supplant Austrian influence in the peninsula and to make Italy a mere appendage of France. It was

[16] Launay to Visconti-Venosta, July 15, 1870, No. 2362, MAE, AS, DTA.

[17] Launay to Visconti-Venosta, July 15, 1870 (Launay inadvertently wrote June instead of July), No. 589, confidential, MAE, AS, Serie politica (1867–1888), Prussia, busta 1328: 1867–1870.

[18] Ibid.

easy enough to perceive both of these intentions, and if until
now the attempt to carry out the second had lagged somewhat,
the explanation could be found in the salutary influence of
Napoleon. Henceforward, however, it would be impossible to
hold the French back, especially if Italy forfeited her best protection by alienating the powers that hoped to localize the
imminent conflict. These states (Launay must have been thinking primarily of Bismarck's ally, Russia) would not forgive her
if she betrayed what to them represented her *raison d'être*. In
their view, she could have but a single goal: to prove that she
was independent of both France and Austria. "Therefore,"
exhorted Launay, "let us be *ourselves;* let us remain outside
the struggle, if there should be one, not because of weakness
but rather in order to demonstrate that we feel strong enough
to say no to those who insist that we should throw our sword
into the scales. We shall be all the more respected for it."[19] If
the French triumphed without Italy's help, they would still
have to treat her with consideration; for otherwise she might
turn against them when Germany launched the inevitable war
of revenge.[20]

Conversely, Launay contended that if Prussia rather than
France won the war, Italy would be in the enviable position of
having nothing to fear. It was absurd to think that a Germany
united under Hohenzollern rule and extending even as far as
Trieste would represent a danger to Italy. Besides, if any peril
should arise, it would be so remote that Italy would have ample
time to meet it. At all events, Austria seemed for the moment
quite loath to allow Prussia to expand in the direction of the
Adriatic. It was primarily against the supremacy of France that
Italy must take precautions. If the Lanza cabinet failed to do
so, if instead it formed a close partnership with France and
placed troops at her disposal, there would be trouble at home,
especially in central and southern Italy. Acquired only recently by the House of Savoy, these regions were bound to react
strongly against "anti-national" policies; and in the process,
"demagogic passions" would be stirred up, and these could do

[19] *Ibid.*   [20] *Ibid.*

neither the monarchy nor the party of the Right any good.[21]
The French vote of July 15 intensified Launay's anxiety
about Italy's future course. On the seventeenth, he had more
to say about the need for a clear-cut enunciation of neutrality.
It was important, he felt, to forestall any attempt by France to
entice Italy into the war by "deceitful allurements." He also
dwelt on the need to act betimes in any effort to curb Austria's
interventionist velleities and thus prevent the war from spreading.[22] A neutral stand by Italy would represent ingratitude
toward France, whereas intervention would signify ingratitude
toward Prussia. Launay so defined the choices, and it was of
course obvious which of these he preferred. Indeed, he even
went so far as to argue that ingratitude toward France, far
from being the lesser of two evils, could actually prove profit-
able. On the other hand, ingratitude toward Prussia would
estrange from Italy all of Germany without bringing any coun-
tervailing gain in terms of French good will.[23]

Convinced that in the contest now about to begin, Prussia
would prove the stronger,[24] Launay continued to impress upon
Visconti-Venosta that a French victory was far from certain.
It was well known that Victor Emmanuel and his military ad-
visers regarded the defeat of Prussia as inevitable, and Launay
was especially concerned to correct this erroneous assumption.
Mustering additional evidence, he cited the attitude of the entire German nation, whose manpower and resources would be
at Prussia's disposal. On this subject, the French had not only
misled others; they had also deceived themselves. Likening the
diplomacy of the Second Empire to Russian diplomacy under
Tsar Nicholas I, Launay maintained that the French foreign
office had received from its agents in Central Europe a false
impression of the intentions of the South German states. Dealing for the most part with trivial issues, these diplomats had
not dared to tell the truth; they had hidden from their superiors
the certainty that if Germanic territory were attacked or even

[21] *Ibid.*

[22] Launay to Visconti-Venosta, July 17, 1870, confidential, No. 592, *ibid.*

[23] *Ibid.*   [24] Chabod, p. 9.

merely threatened with or without cause, the German people
would rise up as one to safeguard their national independ-
ence.[25]

2

Launay's anxiety was understandable. There was not only
the king; there was also Visconti-Venosta's irresolution. To be
sure, the foreign minister's hardheadedness left nothing to be
desired; and his wish to keep Italy neutral could not have been
more sincere. But his vulnerability to pressure from the king
could result in his being deflected from the course he knew to
be right. Meanwhile, however, he allowed no ambiguity to
creep into the dispatches he addressed to Italy's representatives
abroad. An opportunity to underscore the present position of
the cabinet was provided by a telegram from Migliorati, which
arrived simultaneously with the news of the French declaration. In addition to pointing out that France's latest demands
had made a very unfavorable impression in Bavaria and that
this most important South German state would consequently
fight on the side of Prussia, Migliorati called attention to a
report that was causing considerable alarm in Munich. It was
to the effect that Italy planned to enter the war as France's
ally. Bray had asked about it, but Migliorati could only say
that he had received no information from his government.[26]

Visconti-Venosta hastened to clarify the matter. Especially
mindful of Launay's concern, he addressed his first denial to
the legation in Berlin. Italy, he said, was free to do as she
pleased; she was bound by no engagements and had no intention of contracting any. The report circulating in Munich was
entirely without foundation. Public opinion throughout the peninsula had hoped, until the fifteenth, that peace would be
preserved. Now that Italy's efforts to save it had proved un-
availing, she, together with other non-belligerents, must endeavor to circumscribe the conflict, to keep it confined if pos-

[25] Launay to Visconti-Venosta, July 18, 1870, No. 593, MAE, AS, Serie
politica (1867–1888), Prussia, busta 1328: 1867–1870.

[26] Migliorati to Visconti-Venosta, July 15, 1870, No. 2627, MAE, AS,
DTA.

sible to the present combatants.[27] A few days later Visconti-
Venosta conveyed the same message to Munich and Stuttgart.
It was absolutely untrue, he asserted, that Italy had offered
military assistance to France.[28] In a separate dispatch to
Greppi in Stuttgart, he characterized his policy as one of "waiting and vigilant observation."[29] No doubt, if circumstances
beyond his control made it impossible for him to maintain such
a policy, he would be prepared to take the country into the
French camp.[30] It was precisely this that distressed Launay.
Sure that the future belonged to Germany, he felt constrained
to protest with all his might against the "worst of sentimental
policies, that of siding with the vanquished."[31]

This of course was a clash of views about how to deal with
future contingencies. As for the present intentions of the foreign minister, they could no longer be misconstrued even by
Launay. Paget, who knew them well, gave an accurate summary in a letter to Hammond. Visconti-Venosta, he wrote,
wanted only "to march along with us on the road of neutrality."
The supposition, entertained in some quarters, that Italy had a
secret military understanding with Prussia, was "too absurd."
There could be no doubt that the "Revolutionary party" in
Italy did wish to exploit a French defeat, and with this in mind
hoped to see the country join Prussia "with the view of getting
Rome." Visconti-Venosta, however, "will never go in for anything of the kind." From the little he was saying, it was plain
that even if France were soundly beaten, he would not move
against her. Conversely, if he and his colleagues sided with

[27] Visconti-Venosta to Launay, July 16, 1870, No. 1213, MAE, AS, TS;
Visconti-Venosta to Launay, July 16, 1870, No. 32, MAE, AS, Divisione
politica, 1867–1888, registri copia-lettere in partenza, Prussia, busta 1200:
7 gennaio 1867–14 febbraio 1871.

[28] Visconti-Venosta to the legations in Munich and Stuttgart, July 19,
1870, No. 1217, MAE, AS, TS.

[29] Visconti-Venosta to Greppi, July 19, 1870, No. 3, MAE, AS, Divisione
politica, 1867–1888, registri copia-lettere in partenza, Baviera, Baden,
Württemberg, busta 1116: 2 febbraio 1867–18 marzo 1875.

[30] Chabod, p. 8.

[31] Ibid.

anyone, "it must be France," but their prime concern was to avoid involvement in the war which was now beginning.[32]

They faced a severe test. Paget described their plight to Hammond:[33]

You must remember however that their position is not ours, that they do not inhabit an Island although they do a Peninsula; that they have got a question of great national anxiety, and consequently if France was to come some day & say "look here, if you will give us a couple of hundred thousand men which we'll pay for, we will withdraw our troops for ever from Rome & let you settle with the Pope as you like," under such circumstances you must remember that human nature is human nature & that this would be a very tempting offer. I repeat however that as long as Visconti is in he will do what he can to be neutral, & if the fight can be confined to France & Prussia he will succeed in doing so,—although you are aware of course that H.M. Victor Emmanuel is no joke under these circumstances and is rather prone, as Lord Russell was wont occasionally to observe, to be making scores off his own bat.

Kübeck, who knew the foreign minister's tendency to vacillate, noted at this time that he seemed firm in his determination to avoid commitments of any kind. On the morrow of the French declaration, the Austrian envoy found the members of the Lanza cabinet "very preoccupied with events and eventualities that threaten to upset all their plans and measures . . . for meeting the needs of the country's disordered finances."[34] Visconti-Venosta himself exhibited as usual "a prudent reserve," holding that the condition of the country and the temper of public opinion made it imperative for the government to move carefully and slowly. In any case, Italy's interests could be safeguarded only by preserving "the greatest possible freedom of action."[35] When Kübeck mentioned a rumor that Victor Emmanuel had ordered Menabrea, a staunch advocate of

[32] Paget to Hammond, July 16, 1870, private and unnumbered, PRO, FO 391/23.

[33] *Ibid.*

[34] Kübeck to Beust, July 16, 1870, No. 53, HHSA, PA, Italien, Berichte 1870, Karton XI/77.

[35] *Ibid.*

Franco-Italian military co-operation, first to Turin and then to Paris, Visconti-Venosta drily remarked that he knew nothing about this. However, he did indicate that "important decisions" might be in the offing.[36] In the meanwhile, as Kübeck pointed out in his report, the Lanza cabinet was making no military preparations. It hoped to bring the sessions of parliament to a quick close in order to be at liberty to deal as it saw fit with any emergencies that might arise.[37]

It was from Vimercati, who decided to tarry in Paris until the completion of his conversations with the emperor, that Victor Emmanuel had received the news that despite Leopold's withdrawal, Napoleon continued to entertain "warlike ideas."[38] In an obvious state of excitement, the king telegraphed Visconti-Venosta:[39]

I believe he [Napoleon] is wrong and hope he will change his mind. But as the situation is very tense and complications may develop from one minute to the next, I should like to know quite confidentially, and without dwelling at this point on any settled plan, whether you have discussed with Lanza and Sella the project of a triple alliance, and what they have said about it. Remember that in this grave matter, regardless of how it may come up, I do not want to find myself embarrassed by ministerial obstacles. The events which lie ahead will be our guide, and I believe that it will soon be necessary to arrive at a decision. I hope that there will be no misunderstanding among us as to the path that should be followed.

Visconti-Venosta consulted his colleagues, who agreed that the king should return to Florence. Late in the night of the fourteenth, Lanza sent a telegram to Valsavaranche. He referred to the "negative and proud" answer given by King William to Benedetti and noted that Paris regarded a rupture of relations with Prussia as "inevitable and imminent." The council of ministers took a very serious view of the situation, which could become more threatening at any moment and require speedy decisions on the part of the government. Con-

[36] *Ibid.*   [37] *Ibid.*

[38] See the reference to this in the king's telegram of July 14 to Visconti-Venosta (Mayor des Planches, p. 351).

[39] *Ibid.*

sequently, His Majesty was herewith requested to come back to the capital "as soon as possible."[40]

The next morning, when word of the French declaration was expected almost momentarily, Visconti-Venosta replied to Victor Emmanuel. He disclosed that he had spoken with Lanza and Sella more than once about Napoleon's proposals for a triple alliance. Both men had emphasized that everything would depend on the terms granted by France and that the national interest was their sole concern. Implying that they opposed any commitment at this time, Visconti-Venosta pictured them as ready "to remove the difficulties" in which the king might find himself as a consequence of his negotiations with Napoleon. At all events, under the present circumstances, it would be best if Victor Emmanuel cut his holiday short.[41]

A showdown loomed between king and cabinet. A majority of the ministers, with varying degrees of firmness, opposed intervention, while Victor Emmanuel clung obstinately to the idea of a triple alliance, stipulating as before the evacuation of Rome. The stage for the trial of strength in Florence was set on the fifteenth, when Napoleon and Vimercati met again in St. Cloud to review the situation. The emperor was now prepared to order the immediate withdrawal of his Roman garrison.[42] The evacuation, he naturally assumed, would clinch the alliance with Italy. He also took it for granted that Austria would sign at the same time—he had been conferring with Count Vitzthum, Francis Joseph's special emissary for the tripartite negotiations who was then in Paris. To Vimercati, Napoleon confided that he intended to send Victor Emmanuel a letter suggesting that the integrity of the papal territory should be intrusted to the honor of the king[43]—a euphemistic way of saying that the September Convention, so distasteful to many

[40] *Le carte di Giovanni Lanza*, V, No. 1692, p. 204.

[41] Mayor des Planches, p. 351.

[42] This information was relayed by Nigra to Visconti-Venosta in an unnumbered telegram of July 16: MAE, AS, Archivi di gabinetto (1861–1887), busta 219: guerra franco-prussiana e trattative segrete 8 luglio–14 settembre 1870, fascicolo 4.

[43] *Ibid.*

of Victor Emmanuel's subjects, was to be given a new lease of life. When Vimercati left, Napoleon briefed Gramont, who as an ardent supporter of the temporal power had continued to oppose the idea of evacuation.[44] The emperor explained to his foreign minister that the war would require the use of all of France's available forces. It was therefore "indispensable" to recall the troops now on duty in Rome and Civitavecchia. Before such action was taken, however, notice would be given the Italians that they must guarantee the existing papal frontier.[45] On the sixteenth, Napoleon's telegram to Victor Emmanuel[46] was on the way. So was Vimercati, who departed in high hopes for Florence to report to the king.

Although the emperor was the last person on earth to need reminders of how much importance the Italians attached to the Roman question, he was convinced that far more was at stake for them as well as for the Austrians. A few days before the virtual declaration of war, Gramont reproduced his master's views when he wrote as follows in reply to Malaret's lengthy account of the conversation with Visconti-Venosta on the eighth:[47]

If there is a country which more than any other must guard against the ambitions that are manifesting themselves in Berlin, it is Italy. Her entire history shows how dangerous for her would be the reestablishment under the Prussian scepter of the great empire that for so long dominated her. If, therefore, the current developments should lead to a war with Prussia, we are in advance persuaded that the political instinct of the Italian nation will indicate to it that its interests are bound up with our cause.

[44] As late as July 12, Gramont wrote Malaret that the recall of the French garrison "is obviously subordinated to considerations which would not permit its inclusion in an agreement in return for which we would obtain the alliance of Italy" (AMAE, Italie, janvier–juillet 1870, No. 19, tome 378 [OD, XXVIII, No. 8445, p. 269]).

[45] Napoleon III to Gramont, July 15, 1870, OD, XXVIII, No. 8526, p. 383.

[46] Napoleon III to Victor Emmanuel II, July 16, 1870, ibid., XXIX, No. 8571, p. 11.

[47] Gramont to Malaret, July 12, 1870, No. 19, AMAE, Italie, janvier–juillet 1870, tome 378 (OD, XXVIII, No. 8445, p. 268).

On a subsequent occasion Napoleon himself observed that the well-being of the peninsula would be threatened by a Prussian victory, for then all of Central, South, and East Europe would fall under the yoke of the "powers of the North," meaning of course Russia and Prussia. For reasons of self-preservation, then, Italy, like Austria, would have to give maximum aid to France.[48] As for the military arrangements, the plan proposed by the French envisaged an Austrian invasion of Saxony and Silesia. The Italians for their part were to move through the Tyrol into Bavaria in order to prevent the South Germans from effecting a junction with the Prussians.[49]

While Napoleon and Vimercati were putting the finishing touches to their blueprint for Franco-Italian collaboration, the Sinistra, restive again despite the reasonableness of men like Nicotera, did not remain idle. In an effort to eliminate once and for all the danger of military intervention, it sought to force another discussion in the chamber of deputies. It hoped in this way to crystallize public support for its uncompromisingly neutralist position. Twice, on the thirteenth and fifteenth, it had attempted to set the stage for a comprehensive and searching debate. Both times it had failed. In a carefully worded editorial written immediately after the French declaration became known in Florence, the *Opinione* elucidated the ministerial position. It noted that many members of the chamber were finding it very difficult to preserve "that serenity of mind and tranquillity of spirit which are essential for a discussion of serious proposals." They were worried about the kind of policy the government might be planning to follow now that war had broken out. Mindful of this alarm, the Sinistra was seeking to pin Visconti-Venosta down. However, the time was hardly right for an official statement. Anything said now would only fetter the government's freedom of action and thus endanger the interests of the state. No one knew whether the

[48] For the emperor's views, see Oncken, III, No. 935, p. 493.

[49] In military conversations held prior to July 1870, the Austrians had suggested that all three members of the proposed alliance should concentrate their main armies in South Germany before striking north to Berlin (Michael Howard, *The Franco-Prussian War: The German Invasion of France, 1870–1871* [New York, 1961], p. 46).

war would spread or remain limited to France and Prussia, whether it would be over quickly or drag on for an indefinite period. Yet it was precisely considerations like these that had to figure in the government's calculations. Besides, the situation could change from one day to the next, so that if a debate were held at this moment, the foreign minister would have no choice but to say as little as possible. Only the unfolding of the war and the concomitant developments in international politics could induce him to dispense with such reserve.[50]

Finally, on the sixteenth, with the entire country reaching an apogee of anxiety over the possible repercussions of the Franco-Prussian conflict, and with rumors floating about that a cabinet crisis was imminent,[51] the government relented. A Sinistra interrogation was put at the very top of the agenda for the next regular sitting of the chamber.[52] Meanwhile, the pressure of public opinion grew ever more pronounced. Although some of the traditional Francophilism still lingered among the upper classes, most Italians supported the Sinistra's position on the question of war guilt. They had disapproved of France's latest demands[53] and now blamed the impending breach of peace entirely on her. Besides, the memory of Mentana was still fresh in their minds, and they could not see why their country should contribute to a victory whose only effect would be to block the national program. Napoleon barred the way to Rome; to aid him meant to postpone indefinitely, perhaps forever, the acquisition of Italy's predestined capital. The organs of the Sinistra coupled their denunciations of France with expressions of fervid appreciation for Prussia, and this sharp differentiation between the two contestants coincided with the feeling that surged through the peninsula. So strong was the tide of anti-French, pro-Prussian sentiment that

[50] *L'Opinione*, July 16, 1870.

[51] Solvyns to d'Anethan, July 16, 1870, No. 86, Belgium, Archives du ministère des affaires étrangères, Correspondance politique, Légations: Italie, IV, 1868–1870.

[52] *Rendiconti del parlamento italiano. Sessione del 1869–70 (seconda della legislatura X): discussioni della camera dei deputati* (Florence, 1871), IV: dal 13 luglio al 25 agosto 1870, p. 3417.

[53] See Wesdehlen to Bismarck, July 15, 1870, Lord, No. 233, p. 256.

even a few Destra newspapers found themselves carried along by it. But none of them approached the ferocity of the Left, which of course damned the cabinet as well as the French, holding it up to obloquy as the "servant" of Napoleon. Demonstrations in favor of strict neutrality occurred in various cities, and there resounded such cries as "Long live Prussia!" "Long live Rome, capital of Italy!" "Down with French tyranny!"[54]

In Florence itself the opposition issued a proclamation which excoriated France and warned that the government was traitorously negotiating an alliance with her. Patriotic citizens were urged to protest against this betrayal of the country's interests. They were reminded of the many grievances against France and the advantages reaped from the partnership of 1866 with Prussia. The Sinistra summed up its position in the following manifesto:[55]

Whereas the services rendered by the Second Empire to Italy in a just cause . . . do not obligate Italy to cooperate in an unjust one, all the more so as those services . . . have been requited at a usurious rate . . . with blood, money and territories; whereas the consummation of the alliance [with France] . . . would profoundly shock the national sentiment, mindful of so many bloody humiliations and insults; whereas an aggrandizement of French power would strengthen our yoke for many years; whereas the French alliance would never be based upon the recognition of Rome but would, instead, perpetuate its renunciation . . . we hold that Italy must observe neutrality.

These Francophobes obviously did not know how much Visconti-Venosta sympathized with their conclusion. Nor did they realize that in view of the attitude of Victor Emmanuel and the need to await a declaration by Austria, it was as yet too soon for the government to proclaim that there would be no intervention. In any case, Visconti-Venosta was strongly of the opinion that he and his colleagues should not be "fettered" by

[54] S. William Halperin, *Italy and the Vatican at War: A Study of Their Relations from the Outbreak of the Franco-Prussian War to the Death of Pius IX* (Chicago, 1939), p. 6.

[55] *Ibid.*, p. 7.

demonstrations in the streets and interpellations in parliament. Complete freedom of action was necessary for those who bore the responsibilities of office. This was what foreign diplomats were given to understand.[56]

Just how intolerable the cabinet found the Sinistra's tactics was made plain by the *Opinione*. Policy, it warned, could not be formulated in a public square. Naturally, the government was always under obligation to preserve public order, but this was especially true at difficult, trying moments like the present. When a war between two great military powers, one of them Italy's neighbor, was about to begin, demonstrations simply could not be permitted because they were political acts, expressions of feeling or passion that were bound to antagonize one or the other of the combatants. They were imprudent, to say the least. At all events, such partisan outbursts were not only incompatible with neutrality but also unworthy of mature men.[57] Henceforward the government would take action to forestall them, in order to spare itself embarrassment and because it needed no reminders of the drawbacks of war. The present conflict was already having a bad effect on the national economy, and agitation would only make matters worse.[58]

On the morning of the seventeenth, Victor Emmanuel was back in Florence. He reacted as expected to the telegram from Napoleon proposing the renewal of the September Convention.[59] One of his first acts was to dispatch the following wire to Napoleon:[60]

The delay in my answer . . . is due to the fact that I was en route to Florence. I desire with all my heart to be agreeable to Your Majesty while seeking at the same time the true interest of the

[56] See, for example, Kübeck to Beust, July 17, 1870, No. 3239/616, HHSA, PA, Italien, Berichte 1870, Karton XI/77.

[57] *L'Opinione*, July 17, 1870.

[58] *Ibid.*, July 18, 1870.

[59] For his formal reply, which was sent a few days later, see Victor Emmanuel II to Napoleon III, July 20, 1870, *OD*, XXIX, No. 8686, p. 129. The exchange of communications paved the way for the renewal of the pact of 1864. The French troops sailed from Civitavecchia on August 5.

[60] Mayor des Planches, p. 353.

Italian nation. I should like to know the attitude of Austria and whether she has already committed herself. I am awaiting the arrival of Vimercati for details. I shall write Your Majesty a letter about the Roman affair. Sire, my friendship will never fail you.

With the French preparing to carry out their part of the bargain, the king vowed he would unite with them. He supposed of course that Francis Joseph would do likewise. On that score he was evidently reassured when he saw Vimercati a bit later in the day. Vimercati reported not only the confidences of Napoleon but also what he had learned from Vitzthum in Paris.

Leading members of the cabinet had ideas of their own. This became apparent at a meeting convoked by Victor Emmanuel a few hours after his return to the capital. Sella, a rock-ribbed advocate of neutrality,[61] proved the king's most formidable adversary. Unlike Destra Francophiles of the stamp of Visconti-Venosta and Bonghi, Sella was strongly pro-German, an admirer of Bismarck, and one of the few Italians who foresaw a Prussian victory. Ever since his student days he had harbored the conviction that French influence represented a danger for Italy; thus his opposition to Victor Emmanuel's interventionism had deep roots.[62] Lanza, although less firm than Sella and unquestionably Francophile in his sympathies,[63] was nevertheless inclined to support the minister of finance. Visconti-Venosta, less resolute than Sella but on this occasion more so than Lanza, bulwarked the two of them with the enormous prestige he enjoyed in Destra circles. In turn, he received indispensable help from Sella in his efforts to gain time and preserve Italian neutrality.[64]

The king, however, made intervention a question of honor. He chided Sella for his tradesman's outlook, his "merchant's psychology." In reply Sella declared: "To be sure, I am a merchant, but one whose signature has always been honored, whereas Your Majesty wishes to sign a promissory note that cannot be redeemed."[65] Reason was on the side of Sella. But

[61] Chabod, p. 20.
[62] Ibid., p. 21.
[63] Ibid., pp. 114, 652.
[64] Ibid., p. 108.
[65] Valsecchi, p. 192.

Victor Emmanuel was insistent; Visconti-Venosta and Lanza gave ground. Toward the close of its meeting on the seventeenth, the cabinet voted to call up two classes of reservists. This meant increasing the army by about 70,000 men. The impending renewal of the September Convention and the military problems which would thus be created for Italy undoubtedly influenced the decision of the ministers;[66] but they challenged the king's suggestion that the recall of the garrison should be made the first article of a treaty of alliance with France. In their view, the renewal of the September Convention and the conclusion of an alliance were entirely separate and must be treated as such.[67] Nevertheless, conceding that the situation was too volatile to permit a do-nothing policy, they assented to an enlargement of the armed forces. Even Sella could justify the increase on the ground that the possibility of the war's spread required a state of instant readiness. Besides, the cabinet's action would expedite a swift transition to total preparedness should that become really necessary.[68]

When the Sinistra criticized the move, the *Opinione* hastened to assure the country that it did not represent a step toward war. "One must have a rather vague notion of neutrality," the paper contended, "to believe that the calling up of two classes of reservists is proof of a bellicose attitude. The two classes merely restore the army to its full peacetime strength."[69] The king and Vimercati took quite a different view. Through Kübeck, Vimercati jubilantly reported to Vitzthum in Vienna that all was going well and asked for information about the plans of the Austrian government.[70] Victor Emmanuel assumed that the ministers, having yielded on the question of partial re-

[66] The cabinet was understandably concerned about the danger of a Garibaldian expedition against Rome and wished to be ready to meet it (Solvyns to d'Anethan, July 20, 1870, No. 93, Belgium, Archives du ministère des affaires étrangères, Correspondance politique, Légations: Italie, IV, 1868–1870).

[67] Nola, p. 427.

[68] See Mayor des Planches, p. 353.   [69] *L'Opinione*, July 20, 1870.

[70] Kübeck to Beust, July 18, 1870, No. 3795/829, HHSA, PA, Italien, Berichte 1870, Karton XI/77.

armament, would be forced to make additional concessions. But the neutralists in the cabinet had every intention of standing firm on the central issue. They took heart from the example of Sella, who threatened to resign if armed neutrality were made into a springboard for intervention.[71] They counted on Visconti-Venosta's help and were justified in doing so. Although not nearly as steadfast as Sella in resisting the kind of pressure Victor Emmanuel could bring to bear, the foreign minister was sustained by his conviction of what was good for his country at this critical juncture. Intending to strive for the localization of the war, he had already set about to achieve it.

[71] According to reports circulating in Florence, a cabinet crisis was narrowly averted (Solvyns to d'Anethan, July 19, 1870, No. 89, Belgium, Archives du ministère des affaires étrangères, Correspondance politique, Légations: Italie, IV, 1868–1870).

CHAPTER TEN

THE LEAGUE OF NEUTRALS

Late in the afternoon of the fifteenth, shortly after learning from Paris that a virtual state of war existed between France and Prussia, Visconti-Venosta summoned Paget. The two men quickly agreed that it was now too late to push ahead with their plans for the Aosta candidature.[1] But the foreign minister was more concerned about other matters, and it was these he wanted to discuss. Adverting to what was uppermost in his mind, he engaged Paget in a strictly confidential conversation about "the future policy of Italy and other Powers not now directly involved in the War." Explaining that he had not yet had an opportunity to consult the king and the cabinet, he stressed that what he was about to say "was not in the name of the Italian Government but rather the reflection of his own ideas." Inasmuch as all the means of averting hostilities had vanished, it was his conviction that "every endeavour should now be directed to limiting the war to the two Powers immediately engaged." He believed that "the possibility of succeeding in this attempt depended for the most part upon Austria." If she remained neutral, "other Powers might do so too." But if, on the contrary, she took part in the war,

it was to be apprehended (though he had no other reason for saying so than the very natural reflections which suggested themselves in contemplating the probable course of events) that Russia would join the other side, and with these four colossal Powers engaged,

[1] Paget to Granville, July 18, 1870, No. 31, PRO, FO 45/164.

what other Power could be sure of being able to maintain its neutrality?[2]

This was the problem that confronted Italy, and Visconti-Venosta urgently invoked Paget's assistance. He was perfectly aware, he said, that it was the policy of the British government and people "to avoid mixing up Great Britain in conflicts on the continent, but in keeping too much aloof, might not the unavoidable result be that England would ultimately find herself drawn into the strife?" He asked this question in order to obtain the answer to another, namely: if the British agreed with him that the possibility of confining the war to France and Prussia depended upon the attitude of Vienna, would they be prepared to conclude a pact of neutrality with Austria and propose the same arrangement to the other non-belligerent powers?[3] England's reply would enable him "to examine with more precision and to decide with greater certainty upon the policy to be adopted by Italy." He hastened to add that he "did not by any means intend to say that if Austria did not remain neutral, Italy would follow her example and join in the conflict." On the contrary, it was his "firm conviction that the most vital interests of this country made it desirable that she should abstain, if possible, from taking any part in hostilities." But in contemplating the future, "it was impossible . . . not to foresee that circumstances might occur, by the war becoming general, which might perhaps place the Italian Government under the necessity of reconsidering its position, unless that position were definitely fixed by arrangements with other Powers." In short, it would help him if he knew the views of the British government. Inasmuch as the interests of the two countries seemed to be "identical," he hoped that Italy's policy could be shaped in accordance with England's.[4]

Paget of course had to consult Granville, but he was sure that his government would welcome Visconti-Venosta's views on the subject of Italian neutrality and co-operation with Great Britain. According to him, England was ready not only to do

[2] Paget to Granville, July 16, 1870, most confidential, No. 25, *ibid.*
[3] *Ibid.*   [4] *Ibid.*

everything she could to preserve her own neutrality but also to urge other powers to emulate her example.[5] There was one bit of information, in the meanwhile, he was anxious to have: what was Austria planning to do? Visconti-Venosta replied evasively, saying he "had no knowledge of the intentions of the Austrian Government in regard to the present war." However, Paget thought he detected some apprehension that Vienna "might be already compromised with France." The only thing that Visconti-Venosta admitted knowing was that the Magyars were very much opposed to intervention.[6]

When Paget left, Visconti-Venosta composed a long dispatch to Cadorna. The Italian government, he wrote, now had but a single resort: to act with others to prevent the interests of neutral states from being drawn into or compromised by the war. The struggle must be restricted to the present contestants. To achieve this object, it would be necessary first of all to make sure of Austria. Accordingly, Paget had been asked to inquire of the British government whether it would be disposed to seek a neutrality agreement with that country. Afterward, the other non-belligerents could be approached.[7] Thus, anxiety to localize the Franco-Prussian War, to keep it from becoming general as a consequence of decisions that might be reached in Vienna and St. Petersburg, continued to be the motive force of Visconti-Venosta's policy; for, if a multilateral struggle were to ensue, it seemed more and more certain that it would engulf Italy and threaten her very existence as a state.[8] To be sure, he knew that even Beust had been disheartened by France's demand for guaranties, and that this almost certainly foreshadowed a declaration of neutrality on the part of the Hapsburg monarchy. But an element of real doubt nevertheless remained, and he did not want to say anything that might deter England from playing an active role to reinforce the present dispositions in Vienna. Above all, he wished, through a close

[5] *Ibid.*   [6] *Ibid.*

[7] Visconti-Venosta to Cadorna, July 15, 1870, confidential, No. 55, MAE, AS, Divisione politica, 1867–1888, registri copia-lettere in partenza, Inghilterra, busta 1167: 22 maggio 1869–29 luglio 1872.

[8] Chabod, p. 108.

liaison with the British, to strengthen Italy's position as a non-belligerent in advance of the expected pressure from the French.

One of the indispensable conditions of success was the planned Italian *démarche* in Vienna. A telegram sent off post-haste in the wake of the dispatch to Cadorna informed Artom that he was to leave unobtrusively for the Austrian capital. There, at the Italian legation, a courier with a letter would be waiting for him; and he was to keep his presence as secret as possible.[9] The letter was on its way during the night of July 15. Visconti-Venosta's object in writing it was of course to explain as fully as possible the purpose of Artom's mission.

Italy, he began, was very much in need of peace. She desired it passionately, and during the diplomatic crisis she had worked hard for it, in concert above all with Great Britain.[10] From the very outset a war between France and Prussia had been regarded by the Italian government as something supremely frightful and dangerous. In the midst of the grave problems precipitated by its outbreak, Italians were sure about one thing: so long as the war remained confined to France and Prussia, their country should and could preserve its neutrality. On this, so far as the Italian government was concerned, there was no room for discussion.[11]

Visconti-Venosta briefly reviewed the secret alliance negotiation to which Artom was privy, noting that under the terms of the agreement which had never been signed, Italy was to have contributed troops for a war against Prussia in return for such rewards as the Trentino, the line of the Isonzo, and an establishment in Tunis. Against this background he set Napoleon's current request for aid. The emperor wanted Italy to dispatch an army of 100,000 men into Austria. Simultaneously, he would recall his troops from the papal state in order to pave

---

[9] Visconti-Venosta to Artom, July 15, 1870, private and unnumbered, MAE, AS, Archivi di gabinetto (1861–1887), busta 219: guerra franco-prussiana e trattative segrete 8 luglio–14 settembre 1870, fascicolo 4. See also Artom, p. 38. The secret was not well kept: there was something about the Artom mission in the *Opinione* of July 21, 1870.

[10] Artom, pp. 38–39.   [11] *Ibid.*, p. 39.

the way for a return to the September Convention. A communication incorporating these proposals was expected momentarily from Paris. Beust for his part was urging an affirmative response, insisting on the advantages *in re* the Roman question which the Italian government would derive from such an arrangement. On the other hand, Curtopassi's reports laid bare the difficulties encountered by Beust in his attempt to conclude a military alliance with France. Specifically, these reports underscored the resolute opposition of the Magyars to the chancellor's policy.[12]

It was plain, Visconti-Venosta continued, that Austria represented the key to the situation. Napoleon was using her in trying to drag Italy into the war, just as he was attempting to make sure of Austrian aid by his maneuvers in Florence. Artom was therefore to convey to Beust and Andrássy the hope of his government that Austria would stay out of the war or at least declare that for the time being she intended to remain neutral.[13] It was unnecessary to dwell on the difficulties, quite apart from the pacific attitude of public opinion and parliament, which a policy of belligerence would create for the Italian government. In any event, Austria was acquainted with the commitments that France was demanding of Italy, whereas the Italian government had no knowledge of the obligations which the Austrians might have already assumed. Italy would find it impossible to fix her own course of action unless Vienna and Florence kept each other apprised of their respective plans, and both would have to take care in the process to exclude the interested intermediation of France. An independent Austro-Italian agreement to exchange information was thus to be the immediate object of Artom's conversations with Beust and Andrássy.[14]

In a subsequent telegram to Artom, Visconti-Venosta reemphasized Italy's position on the localization of the war. Since Austria apparently thought that she might be drawn into the conflict, it was essential, he repeated, that she should keep Florence fully acquainted with her intentions. In any

[12] *Ibid.*, pp. 39–40.   [13] *Ibid.*, p. 40.   [14] *Ibid.*, pp. 40–41.

case, Beust and Andrássy must be made to understand that Italian military action would be "paralyzed" if the Roman question did not progress beyond a mere renewal of the September Convention. That pact was "onerous for our army and insufficient to satisfy the country in time of war."[15] Visconti-Venosta knew that, although Beust was in favor of allowing Italy to occupy the papal territory, Napoleon would strongly object. By making Italian intervention dependent on concessions in the Roman question that were manifestly not in the offing, Visconti-Venosta hoped to discourage the Austrians from committing themselves to France if they had not already done so.

The foreign minister's outlook and program were spelled out in forceful fashion by the *Opinione*. Addressing itself to the apprehension that tormented every well-informed Italian, it posed the following question: would the various non-belligerent powers remain on the sidelines indefinitely? An answer was admittedly difficult. The start of wars was plain enough; the same could not be said about their unfolding. The vicissitudes of great struggles were always unpredictable; the injection of new interests and passions could confound every expectation. However, there was some ground for believing that, if the war could be ended quickly, it would remain confined to the present contestants. But to help shorten it, the non-belligerent powers must set about to form a league of neutrals. If three or four great powers, acting in concert, were to invite the French and the Prussians to give ear to the counsels of peace and lay down their arms, it was unlikely that their urgings would go unheeded.[16]

While counting heavily on Granville's assistance in Vienna, Visconti-Venosta attached considerable importance to his own efforts there. Early in the morning of the sixteenth, he learned that Artom was leaving Karlsruhe for the Austrian capital.[17] He immediately informed Curtopassi of Artom's impending

[15] *Ibid.*, p. 46.   [16] *L'Opinione*, July 21, 1870.

[17] Artom to Visconti-Venosta, July 15, 1870, private and unnumbered, MAE, AS, Archivi di gabinetto (1861–1887), busta 219: guerra franco-prussiana e trattative segrete 8 luglio–14 settembre 1870, fascicolo 4.

arrival and reiterated the need to keep the mission as secret as possible. Curtopassi was to present Artom to Beust and Andrássy as an emissary who enjoyed the full confidence of the Italian government.[18] A telegram from the legation in Vienna suggested that the Austrians were backing away from the idea of intervention. Fear of their "allies" was even causing them to indulge in some openly anti-French talk. They seemed to be afraid that Napoleon would stir up trouble in the Danubian Principalities—indeed, that he might go so far as to provoke a Russian attack. At the same time the Austrian government appeared to be setting greater store by its unavowed neutrality, and all the information reaching Curtopassi led him to believe that as yet not a single step had been taken with a view to mobilizing the armed forces of the empire. This was tremendously encouraging. But on the debit side Curtopassi noted that the Magyar press, anticipating Russia's entry into the fray, had begun to exhibit an accentuated sympathy for France.[19] This could portend a weakening of the chief pillar of Austrian neutralism. To make matters worse, unforeseen delays slowed Artom's journey to Vienna. He did not reach the Austrian capital until the night of July 18.[20]

2

In Italy the clamor for a proclamation of neutrality reached a new crescendo. The universality of this sentiment was plain enough to the foreign minister,[21] and he scarcely needed to be reminded of it. But of course the Sinistra would not desist. A chance to lash out against the government's "procrastination"

[18] Visconti-Venosta to Curtopassi, July 16, 1870, private and unnumbered, *ibid.*; Artom, p. 43.

[19] Curtopassi to Visconti-Venosta, July 16, 1870, private and unnumbered, MAE, AS, Archivi di gabinetto (1861–1887), busta 219: guerra franco-prussiana e trattative segrete 8 luglio–14 settembre 1870, fascicolo 4.

[20] Artom, p. 47.

[21] See, for example, Visconti-Venosta to the Italian minister at The Hague, July 16, 1870, No. 7, MAE, AS, Archivi di gabinetto (1861–1887), busta 219: guerra franco-prussiana e trattative segrete 8 luglio–14 settembre 1870, fascicolo 4.

came on the eighteenth, when one of the spokesmen for the
Left, Luigi La Porta, developed a previously announced interrogation in the chamber of deputies. An ardent critic of the
alleged Francophilism of the government, La Porta recalled
that Visconti-Venosta's declaration of the eleventh had failed
to satisfy the opposition. However, the chamber had tolerated
the pronouncement on the ground that extreme reserve was
unavoidable. Delicate negotiations were then in progress, and
it was thought that they might avert war between France and
Prussia. This hope had proved illusory. Under the circumstances, it was altogether natural that the government should
be asked to explain the basis on which the negotiations had
been conducted and why they had failed. But this was not all.
La Porta wanted the government to indicate the stand it proposed to take in regard to the war, which was creating difficulties for all the powers and especially for Italy.[22] Despite the
removal of the Hohenzollern candidature, France insisted on
fighting. Why? Was the war being waged for dynastic reasons?
Or was it a struggle for supremacy in Europe? Was the object
to keep Germany from achieving unity, or to seize the Rhineland? In deciding what policy to pursue in such a contest, the
government must be guided solely by the national interest and
the attitude of the other non-belligerents.[23]

Visconti-Venosta replied at once. Two questions, he said,
were being asked. What had Italy done? What did she intend
to do? In answer to the first, he could only repeat what he had
said before. The Italian government had not been idle. Heed-
ful of the nation's wishes, it had joined other powers in attempting to ward off the war. To further this endeavor, it had
exchanged communications with Prussia and France. Throughout, it had displayed complete impartiality, animated as it was
by friendship and respect for both sides. Now that the war had
come, the various non-belligerents desired to localize the conflict and escape involvement. Italy shared this wish, and in

[22] *Rendiconti del parlamento italiano. Sessione del 1869–70 (seconda
della legislatura X): discussioni della camera dei deputati,* IV: dal 13
luglio al 25 agosto 1870, p. 3420.

[23] *Ibid.,* pp. 3420–21.

co-operation with other countries had adopted a policy of observation.[24]

These remarks were received with many signs of approval, but La Porta and his comrades on the Left were not satisfied. La Porta had been promised time for a short reply, and he utilized it to insist that the only correct course was to serve the country's "highest interests." It was not enough to say that Italy, together with the other non-belligerents, was pursuing a policy of observation. Was Visconti-Venosta actually doing everything in his power to localize the war? The Italian government must take the lead. The foreign minister had not indicated that it was doing so. He must rectify the omission.[25]

This time it was Lanza who replied. He admitted that Italy might not escape the repercussions of the present crisis. It was as yet impossible to be sure, for changes in the international situation could affect the government's position. The premier thus appeared to leave the way open for ultimate intervention, but the impression was somewhat attenuated by his defense of the foreign minister's statement. Although necessarily cautious, Lanza said, that statement was quite unambiguous. Discussing the recent past, Visconti-Venosta had mentioned Italy's efforts on behalf of peace. Alluding to the present, he had indicated the government's intention of collaborating with others in an attempt to keep the war from becoming general.[26]

The remarks of the two ministers had a tranquilizing effect on public opinion, although the fear did persist that the king might decide to oust the cabinet and conclude an alliance with Napoleon. This, it was generally agreed, would provoke the extremists in the "revolutionary party" to carry out their threat of an insurrection.[27] Kübeck, who was in the chamber when both men spoke, was naturally anxious to hear more. Shortly after parliament adjourned for the day, he hurried to the foreign office, where Visconti-Venosta assured him that the government continued to possess complete freedom of action.[28]

[24] *Ibid.*, p. 3421.   [25] *Ibid.*, pp. 3421–22.   [26] *Ibid.*, p. 3423.

[27] *Le carte di Giovanni Lanza*, V, No. 1694, p. 205.

[28] Kübeck to Beust, July 18, 1870, No. 3721/809, HHSA, PA, Italien, Berichte 1870, Karton XI/77.

But the foreign minister was equally emphatic about his desire to see the war localized. After all, as he was at pains to point out, his remarks on the subject merely expressed what most Italians thought and felt. For the first time he disclosed to Kübeck that he knew about the negotiations for a triple alliance. His own views, as he stated them now, were explicit enough. While reaffirming his friendliness toward France, he criticized the proposed arrangements on the grounds that they would involve Italy in war "prematurely and contrary to public opinion." However, he did stress the need for an understanding with Austria.[29]

A short while later, Kübeck talked with Victor Emmanuel, and it became apparent that the sovereign, who often described Visconti-Venosta as completely subservient to the royal will, did not expect any insurmountable resistance. The king indicated that he was supporting a plan which had been worked out in Paris by Napoleon with the concurrence of Vimercati and Vitzthum. It called for the offer of "neutral" mediation to the two belligerents. But Austria and Italy alone were to be the mediators, and the terms of the proposed settlement were such that Prussia was bound to say no. Of course, Victor Emmanuel knew this. He told Kübeck that as soon as the offer was rejected, the triple alliance could be put into effect. Reiterating his readiness "to go all the way" with Francis Joseph, he said he planned to send Vimercati to Vienna with urgent instructions.[30] As for Rome, it was already settled that it would be evacuated immediately after he had notified Napoleon of his willingness to respect the September Convention.[31] Kübeck naturally wondered how Visconti-Venosta was taking all this, and he could hardly have been surprised by what he discovered. The foreign minister, it seemed, had "some doubts" about the proposed Austro-Italian mediation. He felt that Great Britain should have been invited to participate, which of course would have completely altered the character of the

[29] *Ibid.*

[30] Kübeck to Beust, July 19, 1870, No. 4427/35, *ibid.*

[31] *Ibid.*

move; in any case, he did not relish its "excessively transparent goal."[32] He conveyed his misgivings to Vienna and renewed his plea for a frank exchange between the two governments.[33]

3

Sella, who continued to lead the neutralists in the cabinet, was firm, but so was the king. As Paget had pointed out in his letter to Hammond, Victor Emmanuel was "no joke under these circumstances." Doggedly determined to have his way, and seconded by Vimercati, who stayed on in Florence for the cabinet discussions, he succeeded in rallying some of the ministers to his side. But the majority grouped around Sella and fortified by him could not bring themselves to sanction an alliance with France. Having anticipated a much easier time, the king was chagrined. "I am obliged," he explained in a telegram to Napoleon, "to indulge the susceptibilities of a ministry formed with a pacific purpose." He also blamed the "rapidity of events," which "has prevented me from carrying our old plans into effect as promptly as I would have liked."[34] Visconti-Venosta, unable as usual to take a strong line in face-to-face encounters with Victor Emmanuel, resorted to the columns of the *Opinione*. That paper not only insisted that the government must co-operate with the other non-belligerents in all efforts to circumscribe the war; it also proclaimed with unwonted baldness that neutrality was the only policy to which Italy could advantageously adhere. This of course did not mean that the issue was settled definitively. Russia might not remain passive, and Austria, whose hostility to Prussia was well known, could be expected to become restive. So long as the danger existed that the war might spread, it was impossible for the government to commit itself unalterably to anything. But in the present circumstances, the national interest demanded a policy of non-intervention.[35]

Invaluable assistance for Visconti-Venosta came from the

[32] *Ibid.*   [33] Artom, pp. 45, 48.

[34] Halperin, *Italy and the Vatican at War*, p. 10.

[35] *L'Opinione*, July 19, 1870.

Austrian cabinet. Curtopassi's allusion to the start of a pro-French trend in the Magyar press proved a false portent. Throughout the Hapsburg monarchy, and especially in Hungary, public opinion showed itself to be strongly in favor of neutrality—so long as Russia stayed out of the war. The attitude of the Italian cabinet represented another important datum in the eyes of Francis Joseph, who refused to take too seriously the personal preferences and machinations of Victor Emmanuel. Fear of Russia overshadowed all else. On July 14, Andrássy, probably the most powerful politician in the Dual Monarchy, had emphasized in the Hungarian chamber of deputies the necessity of pursuing a policy of strict neutrality. He knew, of course, that Russia would not brook Austrian intervention on the side of France, and this, together with his indifference to Austrian ambitions in Germany, continued to determine his position on the all-important question now confronting the empire's policy-makers. But Beust, although resigned to nonintervention as unavoidable for the time being (the attitude of the Magyars and of the strong German elements in Austria dimmed the prospects of any other policy), nevertheless still hoped to effect a change of course and frowned on the issuance of a formal declaration of neutrality. He put the matter thus to the Marquis de Cazaux, the French chargé d'affaires: "Everyone knows that we cannot be Prussia's ally; therefore such a declaration would mean that we are no longer neutral." He went on to imply that he, unlike Francis Joseph and most of the ministers, would not be averse to provoking Russian—and hence Austrian—intervention at some future date. Speaking "very vaguely," he alluded to a plan that included among other things the reconstitution of Poland.[36]

The conflict of views in Vienna's highest circles had a full airing at the crown council in the Hofburg on July 18. After Beust, Andrássy, and other ministers had had their say, Francis Joseph decided in favor of a declaration of neutrality that was to be accompanied by military preparations on a limited scale; these were designed to put the empire in a state of readiness

---

[36] Telegram from Cazaux to Gramont, July 15, 1870, AMAE, Autriche, mai–juillet 1870, tome 502 (OD, XXVIII, No. 8548, p. 403).

for all eventualities in the east.[37] The outcome represented an unmistakable triumph for Andrássy and the party that insisted on making everything contingent on what Russia might do. Andrássy did not question the necessity of a restricted increase in armaments and even coupled it with his plea for non-involvement in any conflict to which Russia was not a party. Beust, however, chose to place a very different interpretation on the emperor's decision, although he must have known that his words would give rise to false hopes at the Tuileries. On the twentieth, he wrote to Metternich: "We consider the cause of France as our own, and we will contribute to the success of her arms within the limits of the possible." He described Austria's declaration as a means of "completing our armaments without exposing ourselves to a sudden attack by Prussia or Russia."[38]

Nonetheless, it seemed plain that for the moment at least Beust's policy of revenge had been suspended if not abandoned, and this was confirmed by Artom's report of a conversation with the Austrian chancellor.[39] The triple alliance favored by Victor Emmanuel was suddenly knocked into pieces. Now that the Austrian government had spoken, the cabinet majority, still led by Sella, saw little danger in humoring the king. On July 21 it authorized Vimercati, who was about to leave for Vienna, to say that Italy was ready to conclude an alliance with France and Austria. But the treaty would first have to be signed by France and Austria; only then would Italy adhere to it.[40] The reference to a tripartite alliance was of course dwarfed by the stipulation, on which Sella had insisted,[41] that Austria must commit herself before Italy did; in view of the unwillingness of Andrássy and the Hungarians to

---

[37] Friedrich Engel-Janosi, "Austria in the Summer of 1870," *Journal of Central European Affairs*, V (1945–46), 347–51; W. E. Mosse, *The European Powers and the German Question 1848–1871* (Cambridge, 1958), pp. 306–8; Nola, pp. 424–25.

[38] Halperin, *Italy and the Vatican at War*, p. 3.

[39] Artom, p. 49.

[40] Halperin, *Italy and the Vatican at War*, p. 10.

[41] See Oncken, III, No. 918, p. 474.

sanction any military action against Prussia, the continuation of Austrian neutrality seemed assured so long as Russia made no move. As a further condition (Visconti-Venosta had already alerted Artom to this),[42] the cabinet majority stipulated that the king must enlist Austria's aid in seeking a solution to the Roman question which would clearly prefigure the annexation of the Eternal City.[43] What the ministers had in mind was most emphatically not a mere renewal of the September Convention, with which Victor Emmanuel had hitherto declared himself satisfied, but something they knew Napoleon could not possibly agree to: recognition of Italy's right to occupy strategic points in the papal territory.[44] After the close of the cabinet meeting, Visconti-Venosta telegraphed Artom: "I herewith . . . confirm what I have written you concerning the insufficiency of a return to the September Convention as the condition of an alliance."[45] This, for all practical purposes, doomed the negotiations. Although anxious to secure Italy's help, Napoleon was unable, for reasons of internal politics, to assent to anything more than the renewal of the pact of 1864.

4

For some unaccountable reason, Victor Emmanuel remained confident that the alliance would still materialize.[46] Meanwhile, Visconti-Venosta pushed ahead with his plan for a

[42] Artom, p. 46.

[43] Oncken, III, No. 930, p. 484.

[44] *Ibid.*, pp. 485–86; Halperin, *Italy and the Vatican at War*, p. 12.

[45] Artom, p. 62. Simultaneously, the Belgian minister in Florence reported: "Il [Artom] est chargé, assure-t-on, de sonder les dispositions du cabinet autrichien quant au maintien d'une neutralité absolue, et surtout de s'enquérir dans quelles éventualités l'Autriche croirait devoir modifier son attitude. M. Artom aurait en outre pour mission de faire connaître les vues du gouvernement italien sur les moyens de préparer la solution de la question Romaine. Il s'agirait de substituer, à Civita Vecchia et sur d'autres points de l'État pontifical, des troupes Italiennes aux troupes Françaises" (Solvyns to d'Anethan, July 21, 1870, No. 95, Belgium, Archives du ministère des affaires étrangères, Correspondance politique, Légations: Italie, IV, 1868–1870).

[46] See Kübeck to Beust, July 20, 1870, No. 398, HHSA, PA, Italien, Berichte 1870, Karton XI/77.

league of neutrals that would keep the war circumscribed and also enhance the possibility of shortening it by diplomatic means. On the twenty-second he again took the matter up with Paget. He expressed the hope that England would sponsor a combined, multilateral treaty of neutrality. The first to sign must of course be Austria; Italy and the other non-belligerent powers would follow.[47] Russia lent a helping hand. Although she did not formally proclaim her neutrality until the twenty-fourth, her decision was known in diplomatic circles a few days before. This virtually eliminated the chances of Austrian intervention. The position of the non-interventionists in the Italian cabinet was correspondingly strengthened. On the twenty-fifth Visconti-Venosta was able to announce in the chamber of deputies that the government was maintaining a strictly neutral attitude.[48]

The French, however, refused to give up, and their desperate efforts to bring Italy into the war despite her insistence on a condition they could not accept—the scrapping of the September Convention—were abetted anew by Victor Emmanuel. Misled by Visconti-Venosta's pliability when in the royal presence, the king boasted that the foreign minister would yet do everything he wanted;[49] and some Sinistra circles continued to harbor the suspicion that Visconti-Venosta was secretly working for an alliance with France.[50] In the country generally, it was believed that the battle between Victor Emmanuel and the

[47] Visconti-Venosta to Cadorna, July 22, 1870, No. 56, MAE, AS, Divisione politica, 1867–1888, registri copia-lettere in partenza, Inghilterra, busta 1167: 22 maggio 1869–29 luglio 1872. Alluding to the "very lively satisfaction" with which the Austrian declaration of neutrality had been received in Florence, Solvyns emphasized the following point in a dispatch of July 23, 1870, to the Belgian foreign minister, Baron d'Anethan: "Appuyer de ses efforts tout ce qui tend à circonscrire les hostilités, telle est, pour le moment, l'unique politique et le véritable intérêt de l'Italie" (No. 101, Belgium, Archives du ministère des affaires étrangères, Correspondance politique, Légations: Italie, IV, 1868–1870).

[48] *Rendiconti del parlamento italiano. Sessione del 1869–70 (seconda della legislatura X): discussioni della camera dei deputati*, IV: dal 13 luglio al 25 agosto 1870, p. 3673.

[49] See Oncken, III, No. 939, p. 495.

[50] *Le carte di Giovanni Lanza*, V, No. 1699, p. 212.

cabinet was not over and that the sovereign would eventually manage to take Italy into the French camp. There were even rumors that he had already concluded a pact with Napoleon. Since public opinion remained strenuously opposed to intervention, it reacted to all this with consternation and anger against the king.[51]

Visconti-Venosta himself, intent on his own plans, grew restive. The British, although sympathetic and anxious to help, disliked his idea of a formal multilateral treaty. They much preferred separate, informal understandings with each of the non-belligerent powers and insisted that the object which Visconti-Venosta had in mind could be achieved quite satisfactorily that way. He concurred, thus setting the stage for what was to prove the first of a series of agreements. Meanwhile, Napoleon behaved according to expectations: pronouncing what seemed to be his last word on the subject, he forbade Victor Emmanuel to occupy even a single point in the papal territory.[52] Visconti-Venosta was acutely mindful of this when he saw Vitzthum, who was in Florence with the draft of a still-born Austro-Italian treaty prepared by Beust and Vimercati. The document envisaged a possible shift from armed neutrality to intervention by the two powers. Visconti-Venosta told Vitzthum on July 31 that in view of the attitude of the French government, Italy would await developments[53]—a polite way of saying that no progress was to be expected.

Seven days later Florence learned of the Prussian victory at Wörth. Victor Emmanuel, who all along had been sure the French would win,[54] continued doggedly to favor intervention despite France's darkening military prospects and Napoleon's position on the Roman question. Lanza, reflecting increasing

---

[51] *Ibid.*, Nos. 1696 and 1713, pp. 209, 229. The suspicion that a secret military convention already bound Italy to France was noted some days before by Solvyns (Dispatch of July 20, 1870 to d'Anethan, No. 91, Belgium, Archives du ministère des affaires étrangères, Correspondance politique, Légations: Italie, IV, 1868–1870).

[52] For Napoleon's intransigent position on the September Convention, see Oncken, III, Nos. 925 and 926, pp. 478, 479.

[53] *Ibid.*, No. 939, p. 500.

[54] Chabod, p. 655.

concern over the balance of power,[55] executed a *volte-face* and sided with the sovereign.[56] The two men were overruled by the cabinet, which held an emergency meeting to consider the imperial government's request for an army corps of 60,000 men to be dispatched to France via the Mont Cenis. Sella, prophesying that France would surely lose the war, again led the neutralists. The upshot of the tense deliberations was a decision to suspend all action on the question of a Franco-Italian alliance.[57] Less than a fortnight later, in the wake of further French reverses, the king finally threw in the sponge and pronounced the alliance a lost cause.[58]

5

Russia, acting independently of Italy, gave wholehearted support to the idea of a league of neutrals. The cabinet of St. Petersburg stressed not only the need to localize the war[59] but also the urgency of ending it as soon as possible.[60] The tsar himself pressed for action,[61] and his move coincided with the achievement of a preliminary agreement between England and Italy. On August 10 Granville talked to Bernstorff, who had inquired about various rumors. The foreign secretary was unusually expansive. He said among other things:[62]

[T]he Italian Government . . . represented to that of Her Majesty that it had been much pressed by France, and desired the assistance of Her Majesty's Government to resist such pressure. . . . The cabinet of Florence was told that, although it was not the present policy of England to enter into any positive engagement for combined neutrality, yet that Her Majesty's Government would be ready, if by

[55] For expressions of this concern, see *ibid.,* pp. 116, 121.

[56] *Ibid.,* p. 567.

[57] Stefano Castagnola, *Da Firenze a Roma: diario storico-politico del 1870–71* (Turin, 1896), pp. 4–7.

[58] *Ibid.,* p. 3.

[59] Buchanan to Granville, August 1, 1870, No. 286, PRO, FO 65/803.

[60] Buchanan to Granville, August 3, 1870, No. 292, *ibid.*

[61] Buchanan to Granville, August 5, 1870, No. 294, *ibid.*

[62] Granville to Lyons, August 10, 1870, *British and Foreign State Papers 1869–1870,* LX, 996.

so doing they could assist Italy to resist external pressure, to agree with Italy that neither power should depart from its neutrality without an interchange of ideas, and an announcement to one another of any change of policy. The Italian Government warmly assented to such an arrangement.

Granville waited another week, during which the fortunes of war continued to go steadily against France. Then, on August 17, he addressed the following note to Cadorna in accordance with a prearranged procedure:[63]

Her Majesty's Government have received at different times, with great satisfaction, through Her Majesty's Minister at Florence, the assurances of the Government of the King of Italy of their desire to maintain strict neutrality in the war that unhappily prevails between France and Prussia, and of their readiness to enter into engagements with this country for the maintenance of the common neutrality of both.

Those assurances . . . have been repeated by you in conversations that I have had the honour to hold with you.

Her Majesty's Government are of opinion that it would not be expedient, at all events at the present moment, to enter into any formal and combined engagement for the maintenance of neutrality. They are, however, prepared, and indeed would think it very desirable to do so, to agree with other neutral Powers, and specifically with Italy, that neither party to such arrangement should depart from its neutrality without a previous communication of ideas and an announcement to one another of any change of policy as regards their neutrality.

I have therefore to request that you will make this known to your Government, whose acceptance of the proposal through you, in the same form as it is made, will constitute the agreement between the two countries without the necessity of any more formal Act in which it should be recorded.

Two days later Granville received the answering communication from Cadorna. It ran in part:[64]

[63] Granville to Cadorna, August 17, 1870, *British and Foreign State Papers 1870–1871* (London, 1877), LXI, 682–83.

[64] Cadorna to Granville, August 19, 1870, *ibid.*, pp. 687–88.

In execution of the orders which I have received from his Excellency le Chevalier Visconti-Venosta, I have the honour to inform your Lordship that the Government of His Majesty the King congratulate themselves on the notification of the proposition [of August 17] . . . which meets the aim they have had in view since the commencement of the war. They accept it consequently with much satisfaction, and consider as understood and agreed that neither of the Contracting Parties in the present engagement can depart from her neutrality without a previous interchange of ideas, and without informing each other reciprocally of every change of policy with reference to their neutrality.

Thus Italy's neutrality was firmly tethered to England's, and Visconti-Venosta could feel more secure about the future. However, the paramount object was still to make sure of Austria. With this in mind, Granville proceeded to carry out Visconti-Venosta's original suggestion. When he drafted his note to Cadorna, he also dispatched an identical invitation to Austria and other non-belligerents. He restated Great Britain's objection to a "formal or combined engagement" for the maintenance of neutrality. There was no need to have "a solemn Treaty, or even . . . a Protocol." It would be quite enough to incorporate the agreement in "letters to be interchanged between the several Parties."[65]

Russia, approached in advance,[66] had as expected responded enthusiastically.[67] In the meantime, Beust heard about the Italian initiative for a combined treaty of neutrality and alluded to it when he saw the British ambassador, Lord Bloomfield, on August 17. Bloomfield explained the British approach. Beust seemed to approve and "to be quite willing to come to an understanding with other Powers."[68] At a crown council held on August 22, he recommended acceptance of Granville's invitation.[69] France's military reverses had dismayed the chan-

65 For the text of this communication, see *ibid.*, pp. 684–85.

66 Buchanan to Granville, August 11, 1870, No. 307, PRO, FO 65/803.

67 Buchanan to Granville, August 16, 1870, No. 314, *ibid.*

68 Bloomfield to Granville, August 18, 1870, *British and Foreign State Papers 1870–1871*, p. 689.

69 Mosse, p. 325; Engel-Janosi, "Austria in the Summer of 1870," pp. 352, 353.

cellor. His interventionist velleities had dwindled almost to the vanishing point; soon they disappeared altogether. For catastrophe overtook France on September 2, when her finest army surrendered at Sedan. Napoleon himself was among the prisoners. Two days later, the Second Empire fell. When Victor Emmanuel received the news of Sedan, he could only say: "Nous l'avons échappé belle."[70] The tripartite alliance so often discussed in the past few years now belonged to history's scrap heap, and Beust merely registered this fact when he notified Granville that Austria accepted the British proposal.[71] The exchange of letters occurred on September 10.[72]

Visconti-Venosta's ordeal was finally over: the neutrality of Italy was safe for the remainder of the war. Already the prewar days seemed remote. The July crisis, it was now apparent, marked the end of one era and the beginning of another. Throughout this interlude, Visconti-Venosta served his country well. To be sure, irresolution and procrastination are anything but commendable. But on the other hand, prudence, *sangfroid*, and unfailing realism were the very qualities Italy, weakest among the great powers, needed most in a foreign minister. She was therefore fortunate to have had Visconti-Venosta as her guide in the summer of 1870.

The Franco-Prussian crisis thrust upon him a role he could not have relished. Like Victor Emmanuel, he was deeply attached to France and reluctant to separate himself from her. Yet, in the summer of 1870, he had no choice. The primary consideration was of course Italy's well-being. Involvement in a Franco-Prussian war, whatever the justification in terms of territorial or diplomatic advantages, was bound to hurt far more than it could profit because of a vulnerability that was uniquely Italian. The nation was psychologically unready; the armed forces were unprepared and inadequate; the economy was weak and disordered. If the country had gone to war, the

[70] Chabod, p. 655.

[71] Apponyi to Granville, September 10, 1870, *British and Foreign State Papers 1870–1871*, p. 739.

[72] Granville to Apponyi, September 10, 1870, *ibid.*, pp. 739–40; Apponyi to Granville, September 10, 1870, *ibid.*, p. 740.

monarchical regime with the House of Savoy at its head would have been exposed to the danger of republican disturbances at home. And of what avail even the great prize, Rome, if in the process Italy jeopardized her very existence as a kingdom? Thus, until the French declaration of July 15, Visconti-Venosta could have but one goal: a peaceful settlement of the Franco-Prussian dispute.

As a Francophile, he could justify this position by arguing that a war with Prussia over the Hohenzollern candidature would bring France no commensurate gain. He considered Napoleon ill-advised to think of French security in outmoded dynastic terms. In Spain, as elsewhere, there were forces at work that counted for a good deal more than family ties in determining the course of international relations. To be sure, Visconti-Venosta had no doubt that if France decided to fight, she would win; like so many others, he took her military superiority for granted. But after such a struggle she would be no better off than before; and in the meanwhile all Europe would have been subjected to an inordinate strain. A product of the idealism of the *risorgimento* and for a while an ardent Mazzinian, Visconti-Venosta was a good European; although necessarily giving priority to the national interest, he rarely lost sight of what was best for the Continent as a whole.

The localization of the war, for which he strove so persistently, not only saved Italy from involvement; it also contributed significantly to the defeat of France. The leaders of the Second Empire blamed Great Britain; it was she who took the lead in promoting the so-called League of Neutrals in August, 1870. Granville had to listen to some bitter remarks on the subject from the French ambassador. Although Granville did explain that Great Britain had acted at the urgent request of Italy, French resentment continued to be directed against the English rather than the Italians. Here too the role Visconti-Venosta played was not one he would have chosen. Yet after July 15, as before, he could not envisage any irreparable harm befalling France as a consequence of his endeavors; he continued to believe that even without allies, she would emerge triumphant and maintain the existing (and in his estimation salutary) distribution of strength on the Continent. The cata-strophic outcome of the war for France shocked and distressed him. Plainly, he did not wish to see Germany supplant France as Europe's predominant power. To prevent this there was little he could do after the battle of Sedan save co-operate with others in mediatory efforts to attenuate the harshness of the peace terms. In any case, he had his hands full because of new and spectacular developments in the Roman question.

Many years later, during the twilight of his career, Visconti-Venosta worked to recement the ties between Italy and France; and in 1915, after his death, Italy did enter the lists on the side of France. The two Latin nations thus renewed the armed comradeship of 1859. But now the giant that bestrode Central Europe was not the Hapsburg empire but the Germanic power that had attained its first great apogee in the war of 1870.

INDEX

Alexander II, Tsar of Russia, 7, 186
Amadeus, Duke of Aosta, 13, 21–22, 41–51, 58, 85, 89–91, 95, 98, 121–23, 126, 143
Andrássy, Count Gyula, 7, 174–76, 181–83
Aosta candidature, 21–22, 41–42, 44, 47–52, 86–87, 90–91, 122–23, 127, 130–31, 143–44
Artom, Isacco, 144–45, 173–76, 182–83
Asturias, Prince of, 80
Ausgleich of 1867, 129

Barral, Count Camillo de, 53
Benedetti, Count Vincent, 53, 88, 98, 137, 139–41, 160
Bernstorff, Count Albrecht von, 138, 186
Bertani, Agostino, 100
Beust, Count Friedrich von, 7–8, 33, 65, 67, 71–73, 79–80, 127–29, 135–37, 146, 148–49, 172, 174–76, 181–82, 185, 188–89
Biancheri, Giovanni, 109, 111–18
Bismarck, Count Otto von, 1, 7, 16–17, 36, 39, 60–61, 69, 74–75, 80, 87, 96–97, 103, 106, 126, 130, 137, 141–42, 149, 150–51, 153, 155, 167
Blanc, Alberto, 36, 143–44
Bloomfield, Lord, 188
Bonghi, Ruggero, 149, 167
Brassier de Saint Simon, Count, 36
Bray, Count Otto von, 96, 157
Bülow, Prince Bernhard von, 3

Cadorna, Carlo, 11, 35, 50, 81–85, 122, 138, 142–43, 172, 187–88

Cairoli, Benedetto, 100
Caracciolo, Marquis, 16, 51–52, 87
Cavour, Count Camillo di, 59, 144
Cazaux, Marquis de, 181
Cerruti, Marcello, 15–16, 19, 34–35, 38–39, 44, 50, 52–53, 89–90, 98, 121, 123–24
Charles, Prince of Hohenzollern-Sigmaringen, 13
Charles V, 9
Chigi, Msgr. Flavio, 68–69
Clarendon, Lord, 35
Corps législatif, 9–10, 18, 20, 24–25, 27–28, 34, 38, 42, 46, 63, 67, 82, 84, 87, 96, 106, 127, 143, 146
Corte, Clemente, 109, 117–18
Cortes, 19, 36, 38, 40–41, 43, 45, 47, 52–53, 58, 74, 76, 106, 120, 124, 143
Crispi, Francesco, 100–101
Crown council in Hofburg: July 18, 181–82; August 22, 188
Curtopassi, Count Francesco, 11, 79–80, 87, 129, 135–36, 144, 174–76, 181

Damiani, Abele, 109, 115
D'Anethan, Baron, 184 n.
Danubian Principalities, 13, 129, 176
Depretis, Agostino, 106
Destra, 3, 5, 63, 105, 109, 113, 149, 165, 167
Dina, Giacomo, 12 n.
Diritto, 100–101, 106–9

France, 132–34
Francis Joseph, Emperor of Austria,

7–8, 23, 70, 72, 161, 179, 181–82
Frederick William, Crown Prince
    of Prussia, 60, 153

Garibaldi, Giuseppe, 25, 60, 62–64,
    69, 148
Genoa, Duke of, 13, 22, 42, 44, 48–
    49, 73
Gladstone, William E., 91
Gorchakov, Prince Aleksandr, 51,
    87, 141
Govone, General Giuseppe, 4, 87,
    88–90, 98–99, 121–23, 126, 131,
    145
Gramont, Duke of, 9–13, 15–20,
    26–28, 30–32, 38–39, 42, 46–47,
    54–55, 57, 68–69, 76, 81, 84, 87,
    96, 103, 106, 110, 113, 117–18,
    127, 134, 140, 142–46, 162
Granville, Lord, 35, 42–44, 46, 49–
    50, 81–85, 90–91, 97, 122–25,
    138, 142–43, 17, 171, 175, 186–
    90
Greppi, Count Giuseppe, 96, 158

Hammond, Edmund, 147, 158–59,
    180
Havas news agency, 27
Hohenzollern candidature, 1, 9, 11,
    16, 18, 20–22, 36, 40, 46–48, 53,
    55–58, 74, 76, 80–82, 84–85, 88–
    89, 91–93, 95, 98–99, 103–4,
    110–11, 121–22, 130, 132, 135,
    137, 139–40, 143, 146, 177, 190

Iberian union, 22
Isonzo, 66, 173
Italian chamber of deputies, 100,
    106, 109–18, 125, 163–64
Italie, 105

Karl Anton, Prince of Hohenzollern-
    Sigmaringen, 14, 130–31, 140
Kübeck, Baron, 32–34, 70–74, 80,
    87, 94, 128, 132, 146–47, 159–60,
    178–79
Kühnenfeld, Baron Franz Kuhn
    von, 8

Lanza, Giovanni, 3–4, 69–70, 73,
    75, 111, 117, 130, 160–61, 167–
    68, 178, 185–86
La Porta, Luigi, 177–78
Launay, Count Edoardo de, 15–18,
    35–36, 38–39, 56, 88, 97–99, 121,
    123, 125–27, 137, 139, 141–42,
    149–58
Layard, Austen Henry, 42–47, 90–
Lazzaro, Giuseppe, 101
League of neutrals, 8, 175, 184–90
Leopold, Prince of Hohenzollern-
    Sigmaringen, 1, 8–17, 19–20, 22,
    34–36, 38, 40–48, 52–55, 57–58,
    74, 76, 80, 82, 84, 88–89, 93,
    98–99, 108, 119–23, 127, 130–32,
    134–38, 140, 144, 146, 150, 160
Lissa, 60
Loftus, Lord Augustus, 88, 96–97,
    123, 153
Lyons, Lord, 16, 31–32, 98

Malaret, Baron, 19–23, 28–34, 40,
    48, 52–53, 81, 83, 92, 128, 131,
    151, 162
Mazzini, Giuseppe, 69, 148
Menabrea, General Luigi, 65–67,
    69, 73, 116, 159–60
Mentana, 6, 25, 29, 62–63, 148, 164
Mercier de Lostende, Baron, 38,
    43–44
Metternich, Prince Richard von, 80,
    133 n., 182
Miceli, Luigi, 101, 109, 111–15,
    118–19
Migliorati, Marquis Giovanni An-
    tonio, 96, 157
Monde, 24 n.
Montemar, Marquis Francisco de,
    10–11, 40, 89–90
Moret y Prendergast, 45–46

Napoleon III, 1, 5–7, 12–13, 19–20,
    23, 31–32, 34, 39, 44, 54, 57,
    61–72, 75–77, 80, 91–93, 95,
    100–102, 125, 133, 135, 139–40,
    142, 146, 148–49, 154–55, 160–
    67, 173–76, 178–80, 185, 188,
    190
Nice, 63, 66, 71, 154
Nicholas I, Tsar of Russia, 156

Nicotera, Giovanni, 109, 116–19, 163

Nigra, Costantino, 8–10, 15–16, 18, 26–28, 32, 34–35, 38–39, 48, 50, 53–56, 64–65, 75, 77, 92–94, 98–99, 121, 124, 127, 130, 132–34, 139–41, 44

Nikolsburg, 65

Norddeutsche Allgemeine Zeitung, 108

Nuovo antologia, 149

Oliva, Antonio, 101, 109, 115–16, 119

Ollivier, Émile, 24–26, 28, 39, 55, 67–68, 70, 100, 102–4, 110, 112–13, 117, 140, 145–46

Olózaga, Salustiano de, 46–47

Opinione, 12–14, 37, 57–58, 118–20, 131, 134, 146, 163–64, 166, 168, 175, 180

Paget, Sir Augustus, 40–41, 47–49, 51, 90–91, 122–26, 130, 138, 143–44, 147, 158–59, 170–72, 180, 184

Papacy, 6, 63, 68–69, 77

Pepoli, Count Gioacchino, 11

Perseveranza, 149

Prim, Marshal Juan, 9–10, 14–17, 20–22, 38–47, 52–53, 81, 83, 91, 102, 130

Rascón, Juan Antonio, 36

Rattazzi, Urbano, 29, 62, 114

Riforma, 100–105

Roman question, 5, 20, 27, 31, 54, 64–65, 75, 77, 86, 94, 101, 105, 109–10, 114–16, 118–19, 129, 162, 174–75, 183, 185, 191

Rouher, Eugène, 63–65

Russell, Lord, 159

Sadowa, 6–7, 12, 60, 103–4

Sagasta, Práxedes M., 43, 45, 121, 124

Savoy, 63, 71, 154

Savoy, House of, 22, 42, 44, 47, 51, 155, 190

Schweinitz, General Hans von, 136

Sedan, 189, 191

Sella, Quintino, 4, 69–70, 73, 75, 86, 160–61, 167–69, 180, 182, 186

September Convention, 5–6, 20, 24–25, 28–30, 33–34, 62–63, 67, 69, 75, 77, 94–95, 100–102, 161–62, 166, 168, 174–75, 179, 183–84

Serrano, Marshal Francisco, 10, 15–16, 19–20, 42, 45, 47, 121

Sinistra, 5, 61, 63, 69, 100–109, 111, 113–16, 118, 148–49, 163–66, 168, 176–78, 184

Solms, Count Eberhard von, 39, 54–55

Solvyns, 145, 184 n.

Stefani news agency, 24–25, 132

Thiers, Adolphe, 63

Thile, Karl von, 17, 88, 97–98, 125–27, 142

Ticino, 66

Trentino, 31, 60–61, 66, 71, 129

Tripartite alliance negotiations, 6–8, 18, 23, 31, 64–66, 70–72, 161, 173, 179

Tunis, 66, 173

Union, 24 n., 26

Univers, 24 n., 26

Venetia, 59–61, 69

Veuillot, Louis, 24 n.

Victor Emmanuel II, King of Italy, 5, 7, 20–23, 32, 42, 50–51, 59–67, 69–78, 85–86, 90–95, 122–23, 127, 130, 148, 152, 156, 159–62, 165–69, 179–86, 189

Victoria, Queen of Great Britain, 36, 122

Vimercati, Count Ottaviano, 67, 69, 76–77, 91–93, 95, 139, 160–63, 166–68, 179–80, 182, 185

Visconti-Venosta, Emilio, 2–8, 10–12, 14–28, 30, 32–36, 38–41, 44, 47–58, 69–81, 83–101, 109–15, 117–19, 121–33, 135, 137–39,

143–47, 150–52, 154, 157–61, 165–80, 183–85, 188–91

Vitzthum, Count, 161, 167–68, 179, 185

War of 1866, 3–4, 6, 31, 60, 65

Werther, Baron Karl von, 15, 54, 142

Wesdehlen, Count Georg von, 36, 143–44

William, King of Prussia, 1, 15–17, 35–36, 38–39, 45, 47, 53, 55, 70, 74, 82, 87–88, 93, 96, 98–99, 121–23, 126–28, 132, 134, 137–39, 141–42, 160

Wörth, 185